EDL WORD CLUES™

G

Senior Author

Helen Frackenpohl Morris
Educational Developmental Laboratories

Consultant

Arthur S. McDonald
Nova Scotia Department of Education

Lesson Authors

Nancy Joline
Alan Petraske

Test Author

Marie H. Hughes
Rumson-Fair Haven (N.J.) Regional High School

INTRODUCTION

What do you do when you encounter a word that is not familiar? Do you stop to look it up, do you try to analyze its parts, or do you look for clues in the way the word is used in its setting or surroundings?

There are several methods that may be used in unlocking the meaning of unfamiliar words. But the quickest and most practical approach is knowing how to use the context, or the words around the unknown word, to unlock its meaning. This method is called using context clues or "word clues."

You may say, "Why not look up all unknown words in a dictionary?" The dictionary is, of course, one of our most valuable tools in meeting and dealing with new words. You can't get by without it. But there are many times a dictionary will not be available. Even if you're reading with a dictionary near at hand, you don't want to stop every few minutes to look up a word. The chain of thought would be interrupted so often that you would lose much of the pleasure and profit in your reading.

Let's look at some of the ways we can get the meaning of a word from context without looking it up in the dictionary.

1. One way to use context clues is to look for a *synonym*, or a word that has the same meaning. Sometimes a writer or a speaker will give a synonym for an unfamiliar word just to make sure that we understand it. For example, look at this sentence:

    "The horse evolved, or changed, into its present form over millions of years."

    In this case, the author thought that you might not know the meaning of *evolved*, so he or she provided a synonym—*changed*.

2. Another context clue is a definition or explanation that precedes or follows a difficult word. For example, you might not know what the word *evaporation* means, but by studying its use in the context of this sentence, you could find its meaning:

    "When a liquid or solid changes into a gas or vapor, we say it evaporates."

    This sentence makes it very clear that *evaporation* means the changing of a liquid or solid into a gas or vapor.

3. At other times, the context may give us a fairly good meaning of a word by telling what it is like or even what it is not like. We might call these clues of similarities or differences. Do you know what *aquatic* means? See if you can figure out its meaning from these two sentences:

    "Not all mammals live on land. There are many aquatic mammals, such as the otter, polar bear, and whale."

    Now you know that *aquatic* refers to something that does not live on land. You also know that the animals referred to are at home in the water. Therefore, you can reason that *aquatic*, in this instance, means "living in or near water."

4. Another way to use context clues is to notice the circumstances in which the word appears. When you are aware of information given in connection with a word, you can "put two and two together" and guess its meaning. Read this sentence in which the word *erosion* is used:

    "A great deal of damage is done to our farmland each year by erosion. Rain falls and runs down the hillsides with great force, carrying valuable topsoil along with it and cutting gullies through the land."

    It is not difficult to see that erosion is something that has to do with moving soil and dirt and has the effect of leaving gullies behind. *Erosion*, therefore, must mean "the wearing away of soil."

There will be times when none of these four approaches will work. When you cannot use context clues, you must use the dictionary. But even then, you will need to use context clues in order to select the appropriate dictionary definition. The dictionary might give you the generally accepted meaning or perhaps a number of different meanings. It is up to you to choose the correct meaning and adapt it to the context with which you are working.

The WORD CLUES series will help you use context clues to discover the meanings of unfamiliar words. This series consists of seven books on a variety of reading levels. One way to find your starting level is to use the *EDL Word Clues Self-Placement Guide*.* It will help you find the WORD CLUES book with which you should start.

EDL Word Clues Self-Placement Guide. Copyright© 1975 Educational Developmental Laboratories, Inc.

EDL Division
Steck-Vaughn Company

ISBN 1-55855-803-9

Dictionary entries for Books, G, H, and I are taken from SCOTT, FORESMAN INTERMEDIATE DICTIONARY by E. L. Thorndike and Clarence L. Barnhart. Copyright © 1979, 1974 by Scott, Foresman and Company. Reprinted by permission.

2 3 4 5 6 PO 04 03 02 01 00

HOW TO USE THIS BOOK

WORD CLUES is a programmed book. It teaches you in a step-by-step fashion and tells you immediately whether you are right or wrong.

You don't read the pages in this book in the usual way. You have probably noticed that the pages are divided into bands of white and gray. Each of these bands is called a frame, and all of the frames are numbered. You work through the book "by the numbers," turning the page for each new frame, and **working only on the right-hand pages**. After starting with frame 1, you go on to 1a, 1b, 1c, 2a, 2b, 2c, etc.

Each of the 30 lessons in the book starts with the beginning of a story. You then complete 30 frames to help you master ten words. The three frames for each word are labeled *a*, *b*, and *c*.

The *a* frame Here the word is introduced. It is divided into syllables and its pronunciation is given. Say the word to yourself. This may help you think of its meaning. If you are not sure of the pronunciation, refer to the pronunciation key on the inside back cover. Then read the sentence or sentences in which the word is used. Looking at the way the word is used, write a definition or synonym in the space provided. If you are not sure, guess. This is not a test but rather a way to help you find out how well you know the word's meaning.

The *b* frame The word is used again. This time, the setting contains more clues to the meaning of the word. Find these clues and use them to complete the meaning, or synonym, exercise in this frame. Then check to see if you were correct by turning the page and looking at the extreme left of the *c* frame. If you were wrong, circle the correct meaning, and then read the sentences again with this meaning in mind.

The *c* frame The dictionary entry* appears at the left. When a word has multiple meanings, study all of them. Also notice if the word can be used as several parts of speech. If other forms of the word are given, study these too. Notice any pronunciation changes.

The right side of the *c* frame gives you a chance to see if you understand how the word can be used. You will find two kinds of exercises: usage exercises and analogies. For some of the usage exercises you will need to refer to the dictionary entry. Other times, you will have to rely on your experience.

The analogy exercises deal with relationships between pairs of words. A definition of analogy is "likeness in some ways between things that are otherwise different."

To complete an analogy exercise, you need to figure out how two words are related, and then apply this knowledge to another pair of words.

Here is one type of analogy:

Winter is to **summer** as **day** is to
- a. light
- b. night
- c. cold
- d. warm

Winter and summer are opposites. To complete the analogy, you select the word that is the opposite of day. The answer is, of course, choice c—night.

Sometimes analogies deal with synonyms, as in this example:

Rough is to **crude** as
- a. coarse is to smooth
- b. bark is to tree
- c. tender is to gentle
- d. cruel is to kind

Here you look for a choice in which the words are synonyms. The answer is choice c, because tender and gentle are synonyms.

Notice the difference between the two examples given so far. In the first, you looked for *one word* to complete the analogy. In the second, you looked for a *pair of words* that are related in the same way as the words in the first pair.

Here are some additional kinds of analogies:
PART-WHOLE: **Leaf** is to **plant** as **page** is to **book**.
FUNCTION: **Write** is to **pencil** as **paint** is to **brush**.
QUALITY: **Smooth** is to **satin** as **coarse** is to **burlap**.
You will encounter other kinds of analogies as you work through the lessons in this book.

A special kind of punctuation is used to express analogies. It looks like this:
Smile : cheer :: frown : worry
This would be read as:
Smile *is to* cheer *as* frown *is to* worry. This special punctuation is used in all of the analogy exercises in this book.

When you have finished the *c* exercise, check your answers by turning the page and looking to the left of the next frame. If you were wrong, circle the correct meaning and then reread the exercise to see why you were wrong. You are then ready to proceed to the next *a* frame.

Whenever you use WORD CLUES, be ready to give it your complete attention. Never leave a word until you are sure you understand its meaning or meanings.

Now you are ready to start on frame 1.

---

*Dictionary entries are taken from SCOTT, FORESMAN INTERMEDIATE DICTIONARY by E. L. Thorndike and Clarence L. Barnhart. Copyright© 1979, 1974 by Scott, Foresman and Company.

BOOK G
ANSWER KEY FOR MASTERY TESTS

Lesson 1	Lesson 6	Lesson 11	Lesson 16	Lesson 21	Lesson 26
1. a	51. a	101. e	151. c	201. c	251. d
2. d	52. e	102. c	152. c	202. b	252. e
3. b	53. d	103. e	153. d	203. d	253. e
4. c	54. e	104. b	154. a	204. e	254. b
5. a	55. c	105. b	155. d	205. b	255. c
6. d	56. b	106. b	156. c	206. c	256. a
7. a	57. e	107. e	157. b	207. a	257. d
8. e	58. a	108. c	158. e	208. d	258. d
9. c	59. d	109. a	159. e	209. c	259. c
10. a	60. e	110. b	160. d	210. a	260. c
Lesson 2	**Lesson 7**	**Lesson 12**	**Lesson 17**	**Lesson 22**	**Lesson 27**
11. d	61. a	111. b	161. c	211. b	261. c
12. a	62. b	112. e	162. e	212. a	262. d
13. c	63. e	113. a	163. e	213. a	263. a
14. e	64. b	114. b	164. a	214. e	264. e
15. b	65. c	115. e	165. d	215. c	265. c
16. c	66. d	116. c	166. c	216. e	266. b
17. e	67. e	117. d	167. e	217. d	267. d
18. d	68. d	118. e	168. b	218. c	268. a
19. c	69. c	119. c	169. b	219. a	269. c
20. c	70. a	120. a	170. e	220. e	270. b
Lesson 3	**Lesson 8**	**Lesson 13**	**Lesson 18**	**Lesson 23**	**Lesson 28**
21. a	71. a	121. d	171. e	221. a	271. d
22. b	72. e	122. a	172. c	222. d	272. e
23. c	73. d	123. e	173. a	223. b	273. c
24. e	74. c	124. d	174. b	224. d	274. e
25. a	75. b	125. c	175. c	225. e	275. a
26. c	76. c	126. b	176. d	226. e	276. b
27. b	77. b	127. c	177. e	227. c	277. e
28. e	78. c	128. d	178. b	228. a	278. b
29. d	79. a	129. c	179. e	229. d	279. c
30. e	80. e	130. b	180. d	230. e	280. a
Lesson 4	**Lesson 9**	**Lesson 14**	**Lesson 19**	**Lesson 24**	**Lesson 29**
31. d	81. c	131. a	181. e	231. e	281. a
32. b	82. e	132. b	182. d	232. b	282. b
33. a	83. a	133. c	183. a	233. c	283. b
34. e	84. b	134. b	184. c	234. d	284. e
35. c	85. a	135. c	185. d	235. d	285. e
36. b	86. b	136. d	186. a	236. b	286. a
37. e	87. c	137. a	187. e	237. e	287. b
38. c	88. e	138. e	188. d	238. c	288. d
39. e	89. c	139. c	189. a	239. e	289. d
40. a	90. b	140. b	190. b	240. b	290. c
Lesson 5	**Lesson 10**	**Lesson 15**	**Lesson 20**	**Lesson 25**	**Lesson 30**
41. d	91. b	141. b	191. e	241. a	291. c
42. b	92. e	142. c	192. d	242. b	292. a
43. e	93. d	143. e	193. e	243. b	293. d
44. b	94. a	144. d	194. d	244. c	294. c
45. e	95. b	145. c	195. a	245. a	295. e
46. c	96. d	146. e	196. e	246. c	296. b
47. c	97. a	147. a	197. c	247. d	297. d
48. d	98. e	148. b	198. d	248. e	298. b
49. a	99. b	149. a	199. b	249. d	299. e
50. e	100. d	150. e	200. e	250. b	300. c

ANSWER KEY FOR BOOK G POSTTEST

1. b 2. c 3. d 4. c 5. b 6. c 7. b 8. b 9. b 10. c 11. d 12. a 13. d 14. c 15. b 16. c 17. d 18. b 19. d 20. d 21. d 22. b 23. b 24. c 25. b

LESSON

1

The Space Shuttle vs. the Beach

Ted Silverman is an engineer who designs parts for the Space Shuttle program. He took his daughter Marsha with him when he went to the John F. Kennedy Space Center to see a space shot. Ted hoped his daughter would apply for a job in the Space Program when she finished school. Although Marsha did very well in her science and math courses, she was more interested in sight-seeing than in the work of engineers and scientists.

26a

a cute (ə kyüt′)

Suddenly he seemed to have an **acute** pain.

Write a definition or synonym:

51a

in ci dent (in′ sə dənt)

Amanda was told to bring Ranger from his stall to meet the man who might buy him. That was bad enough, but it led to an even worse **incident**.

Write a definition or synonym:

76b

Everyone stopped and looked up, squinting because of the sun, to see what was **overhead**.

Overhead means:
__a. on the head
__b. making a noise
__c. high in the sky
__d. around your head

101b

It was impossible for the bank to give **satisfactory** service if the safe remained locked. Many customers would start to complain if the bank couldn't take care of their banking needs.

Satisfactory means:
__a. friendly
__b. satisfied
__c. pleasing
__d. honest

126c

spec i men (spes′ə mən), one of a group or class taken to show what the others are like; sample: *He collects specimens of all kinds of rocks and minerals. The statue was a fine specimen of Greek sculpture. n.*

1. Which of the following might be **specimens**?
   __a. a mushroom __d. a duck's egg
   __b. piles of hay __e. flocks of geese
   __c. a dozen matches __f. fleas
2. Can a **specimen** be an example of something bad?
   __ Yes __ No

176b

Linda looked just wonderful when the tryouts began. In fact, the casting director said he had only one **complaint**: Linda couldn't act! "What's wrong with that?" Linda demanded. "I can always learn to act!"

Complaint means:
___**a.** a suggestion
___**b.** a comparison
___**c.** an urging
___**d.** a finding of fault

Go back to page 154 and continue on frame 176c.

201a

cor re spond ent (kôr′ ə spon′ dənt)

I wrote to Anouk right away and filled my first letter with questions. Anouk turned out to be a good **correspondent**.

Write a definition or synonym:

Go back to page 154 and continue on frame 201b.

226a

b

au thor i ty (ə thôr′ ə tē)
Dirty John Hatfield went to the phone booth and called Clean Gene to demand the blackmail money. In the meantime, the moving company stopped at the Hatfield house. They had been told to load the furniture and take it to Alaska. Finding no one in **authority** to stop them, they went on with their work.

Write a definition or synonym:

Go back to page 154 and continue on frame 226b.

a, c, d

LESSON  The First American Frontier

Last spring, our project in American Studies was to write a paper on the American frontier. When people think of the frontier, they think of the Great Plains and the pioneers in the Far West. But the first frontier was much further to the East, in the hills and forests of Kentucky. The first great frontiersman, and my personal favorite, was Daniel Boone, the pioneer of the Wilderness Trail.

Go back to page 154 and continue on frame 251a.

275c

d

cor dial (kôr′jəl), **1** warm and friendly in manner; hearty: *Her friends gave her a cordial welcome.* **2** liqueur. 1 *adj.*, 2 *n.* —**cor′dial ly,** *adv.* —**cor′dial ness,** *n.*

1. In some jobs, being **cordial** is of more importance than in others. Check those jobs in which being **cordial** is important.
   ___**a.** salesperson   ___**d.** minister
   ___**b.** bookkeeper   ___**e.** beekeeper
   ___**c.** airline attendant ___**f.** house painter
2. Would you be likely to find a **cordial** in a glass? Yes___   No___

Go back to page 154 and continue on frame 276a.

300c

d

be calmed (bi kämd′ *or* bi kälmd′), kept from moving because there is no wind: *The sailboat lay becalmed on the lake.* adj.

ANALOGY becalmed : in motion :: soothed :
___**a.** denied
___**b.** angered
___**c.** prohibited
___**d.** postponed
___**e.** argued

The End

1a

ex cur sion (ek skėr′ zhən)

On their first day at the Kennedy Space Center, Marsha teased her father until he agreed to take her on an **excursion**.

Write a definition or synonym:

26b

Shep suddenly yelped and began to whine. It must have been an **acute** pain to make him do that. Fortunately we soon arrived at the hospital.

Acute means:
___**a.** unusual
___**b.** sharp
___**c.** sudden
___**d.** frightening

51b

The **incident** would never have taken place if Amanda had been in a better frame of mind. Looking back, she decided that what happened was entirely her own fault.

A synonym for **incident** is:
___**a.** time
___**b.** event
___**c.** accident
___**d.** trouble

76c

c

o ver head (ō′vər hed′ *for 1*; ō′vər hed′ *for 2,3*), **1** over the head; on high; above: *the stars overhead.* **2** placed above; placed high up: *overhead wires.* **3** general expenses of running a business, such as rent, lighting, heating, taxes, repairs. 1 *adv.,* 2 *adj.,* 3 *n.*

1. Which items would probably *not* be found **overhead**?
   ___**a.** space shuttle   ___**d.** ceiling
   ___**b.** stone foundation   ___**e.** ground
   ___**c.** bird   ___**f.** power line
2. Which of the following would be the **overhead** of a store?
   ___**a.** the things sold in the store
   ___**b.** the cost of running the store

101c

c

sat is fac tor y (sat′i sfak′tər ē), satisfying; good enough to satisfy; pleasing or adequate. *adj.* —sat′is-fac′tor i ness, *n.*

Check the sentence(s) in which **satisfactory** is used correctly.
___**a.** I am satisfactory that it is necessary.
___**b.** Although the road was bumpy, it was satisfactory.
___**c.** When the sun came up it was satisfactory.
___**d.** He works in the satisfactory.

127a

1. a, d
2. Yes

se lec tion (si lek′ shən)

Sally soon learned that there was a wide **selection** of plants in the cactus family.

Write a definition or synonym:

176a

a, e

com plaint (kəm plānt′)

After Linda paid for the new dress and shoes, she had only a few dollars left. But she made no **complaint**.

Write a definition or synonym:

LESSON

21

a, b, d

A Message from Egypt

Our class started corresponding with pen pals from different countries a few weeks ago. My pen pal, who is named Anouk, lives in a village in Egypt. I chose to write to Anouk because I thought Anouk was a boy's name. Well, it wasn't. Anouk turned out to be a girl. What's more, she thought my name, which is Carmen, belonged to a boy. Things got pretty confusing there for a while.

225c

d

kid nap (kid′nap), steal (a child); carry off (a person) by force. *v.*, **kid naped, kid nap ing** or **kid napped, kid-nap ping.** —**kid′nap er, kid′nap per,** *n.*

Which of the following would be **kidnaping**?
__a. taking a colt away from a mother horse
__b. holding someone for ransom
__c. stealing money from someone

250c

a

er a (ir′ə), **1** an age in history; historical period: *The years from 1817 to 1824 in United States history are often called the Era of Good Feelings.* **2** period of time starting from an important or significant happening, date, etc.: *We live in the 20th century of the Christian era.* **3** one of the five very large divisions of time in geological history. *n., pl.* **er as.**

Which of the following can correctly be described as an **era**?
__a. the Age of Discovery
__b. the death of Napoleon
__c. the term of office of a President
__d. the period of time the United States was a colony of England
__e. the day the Declaration of Independence was signed

275b

The doctor was tired after spending all night and most of the morning at the hospital on an emergency case. Even so, she managed a **cordial** greeting. She gave me a hearty handshake as she entered the examination room.

A synonym for **cordial** is:
__a. businesslike
__b. usual
__c. brief
__d. friendly

300b

Sure enough, as Stephanie and Bill continued to tell each other how scenic they were, the breeze died and the boat slowed down. Then the wind disappeared, and the boat stopped moving and lay there, **becalmed**. Uncle Robert had the good sense to keep reading a book which he kept handy for such occasions.

Becalmed means:
__a. lost at sea
__b. bored or disinterested
__c. worried
__d. prevented from moving by lack of wind

1b

Ted agreed to go on the **excursion**, but only because they would have to wait several days for the next rocket launching. Little trips to see the sights were not his idea of a good time.

A synonym for **excursion** is:
___a. bus ride
___b. trip
___c. walk
___d. visit

---

b

26c

a cute (ə kyüt′), **1** sharp and severe: *A toothache can cause acute pain.* **2** brief and severe: *An acute disease like pneumonia reaches a crisis within a short time.* **3** threatening; critical: *The long drought caused an acute shortage of water in the city.* **4** quick in perceiving and responding to impressions; keen: *Dogs have an acute sense of smell.* **5** having a sharp point. *adj.* —**a cute′ly**, *adv.* —**a cute′ness**, *n.*

Which of the following can be **acute**?
___a. one's hearing ___d. a circle
___b. a scholar ___e. an illness
___c. an angle ___f. a hum

---

b

51c

in ci dent (in′sə dənt), **1** happening; event: *an exciting incident.* **2** a less important happening: *She told us all of the main facts of her trip and a few of the amusing incidents.* **3** liable to happen; belonging: *Hardships were incident to the lives of the pioneers.* **1,2** *n.*, **3** *adj.* [*Incident* is from Latin *incidentem*, meaning "happening, befalling," which comes from *in-*, meaning "on," and *cadere*, meaning "to fall."]

Check the sentence(s) in which **incident** is used correctly.
___a. I shall always remember that frightening incident.
___b. I had an incident and cut my finger.
___c. We made the trip without incident.
___d. The incident has come when we must make a move.
___e. Falls are incident to a beginning rider.

---

1. b, e
2. b

77a

hel i cop ter (hel′ ə kop′ tər)

The Coast Guard had sent a **helicopter** just in time to rescue Manny and his band.

Write a definition or synonym:

---

b

102a

cus tom ar y (kus′ tə mer′ ē)

It was **customary** to open the safe at nine o'clock.

Write a definition or synonym:

127b

There were so many kinds of cactus that Sally wouldn't be able to photograph all of them. She narrowed her **selection** to concentrate on barrel-shaped cacti.

A synonym for **selection** is:
___a. tasting
___b. handling
___c. choice
___d. sampling

175c

b

al ter a tion (ôl/tə rā/shən), **1** change in the appearance or form of anything; altered or changed condition: *My coat fit better after the alterations were made.* **2** an altering: *The alteration of our house took three months. n.*

Alterations may be likely in which of the following?
___**a.** plans   ___**d.** sky
___**b.** flower   ___**e.** suit
___**c.** oatmeal   ___**f.** moon

200c

b

cem e ter y (sem/ə ter/ē), place for burying the dead; graveyard. *n., pl.* **cem e ter ies.**

Which of the following words would *not* describe a **cemetery**?
___**a.** noisy   ___**d.** lively
___**b.** enjoyable   ___**e.** quiet
___**c.** calm

225b

Dirty John wasn't keen on **kidnaping** the McCoys. They weren't worth much. Clean Gene would not pay more than a few hundred dollars to get Clean Irene back unharmed. In the meantime, the Hatfields would have to feed her and look at her while they kept her prisoner.

Kidnap means:
___**a.** put under lock and key
___**b.** beat with the fists
___**c.** leave without permission
___**d.** carry off by force

250b

The carved statue belonged to a different **era**, like the old mansion itself. They came from a time when our grandparents were young. Bette Lou and I thanked the old woman. We were sure we would be the only ones who actually brought a white elephant to the "white elephant" sale!

Era means:
___**a.** a historical period
___**b.** a geographical section
___**c.** a beginning
___**d.** an ancient time

275a

c, d,
e, f

cor dial (kôr/ jəl)

The doctor was very **cordial** and very polite. She also had a pleasant smile.

Write a definition or synonym:

300a

b, c, d

be calmed (bi kämd/ *or* bi kälmd)
"You're more scenic than a rugged shoreline!" Stephanie whispered back.
"What's that?" called Uncle Robert. Then he stopped paying attention to the young couple. To his experienced eye, it seemed very much like they were going to be **becalmed.**

Write a definition or synonym:

6

1c

b

ex cur sion (ek skėr′zhən), **1** a short trip taken for interest or pleasure, often by a number of people together: *Our club went on an excursion to the mountains.* **2** trip on a train, ship, or aircraft, at fares lower than those usually charged. *n.*

Check the place(s) to which an **excursion** might be made.
___**a.** a shopping mall
___**b.** the basement
___**c.** the seashore
___**d.** an art museum

27a

a, b,
c, e

lob by (lob′ ē)

I had to wait in the **lobby** with Shep.

Write a definition or synonym:

52a

a, c, e

sen si ble (sen′ sə bəl)

What probably saved Amanda's life was the **sensible** cold-weather clothing she was wearing.

Write a definition or synonym:

77b

Many aircraft resemble giant birds, but this **helicopter** looked more like a huge insect with a propeller on its head. It stayed in the air without moving while Manny and his band climbed the ladder to safety. It made even more noise than the rock concert.

A **helicopter** is:
___**a.** a spaceship
___**b.** a bird that lives near water
___**c.** a kind of balloon
___**d.** a flying machine without wings

102b

If the bank did not open its safe at the **customary** time, people would be annoyed. They would arrive at the normal opening time and have to wait because the bank wasn't open for business.

A synonym for **customary** is:
___**a.** ordinary
___**b.** necessary
___**c.** usual
___**d.** required

127c

c

se lec tion (si lek′shən), **1** act of selecting; choice: *His selection of a hat took a long time. The shop offered a very good selection of hats.* **2** person, thing, or group chosen: *The plain blue hat was her selection. n.*

Check the sentence(s) in which **selection** is used correctly.
___**a.** I made my selection of books in the library.
___**b.** He offered us a selection of cookies.
___**c.** The dog is a selection.
___**d.** Be careful in your selection of matching colors.

175b

Linda's dress needed a number of **alterations**: the waist had to be taken in, the sleeves shortened a little, and the neck remade. Linda fussed while they worked on the dress. She just had to have it for the big tryout that would occur the next day.

Alteration means:
- __a. discussion
- __b. change
- __c. argument
- __d. hesitation

200b

In the **cemetery** we saw the graves of many mountain climbers. Their gravestones indicated the mountain on which they had died. Some had their axes and climbing ropes resting on their graves. It was a very sad spot.

A **cemetery** is:
- __a. a monument
- __b. a graveyard
- __c. a field
- __d. a town

225a

b, d

kid nap (kid′ nap)

As soon as the trucks with the alligators and the cement had driven off, Plain Jane and her children made a raid on the McCoy's kitchen. They intended to **kidnap** Clean Irene and anyone else they could find.

Write a definition or synonym:

250a

c

e ra (ir′ ə)

The old woman smiled sweetly and asked us to follow. Then we saw it, neatly boxed on a long table. It was a white elephant, carved out of stone, standing almost three feet high! Whatever else it was, it was a product of a bygone **era**. Bette Lou and I had never seen anything like it before.

Write a definition or synonym:

274c

c

clad (klad), clothed; a past tense and a past participle of **clothe**. *v.*

Who would be especially concerned about how he or she was **clad**?
- __a. baby
- __b. beggar
- __c. bride
- __d. student
- __e. doctor operating
- __f. movie star

299c

d

scen ic (sē′nik *or* sen′ik), **1** of natural scenery: *The scenic splendors of Yellowstone Park are famous.* **2** having much fine scenery: *a scenic highway.* **3** of stage scenery or stage effects: *The production of the musical comedy was a scenic triumph. adj.* —**scen′i cal ly,** *adv.*

Which of the following can correctly be described as **scenic**?
- __a. a photograph of a person
- __b. a painting of the first Thanksgiving
- __c. backdrop of a play
- __d. Yosemite National Park
- __e. a football game

2a

a, c, d

pam phlet (pam′ flit)

Marsha had a **pamphlet** on each of the excursions she wanted to take.

Write a definition or synonym:

27b

Other people were sitting in the **lobby**, waiting with their pets. Every now and then the receptionist would call out someone's name.

Lobby means:
__**a.** elevator
__**b.** cafeteria
__**c.** large room
__**d.** entrance hall

52b

Because of the freezing cold, it seemed **sensible** to wear two pairs of wool socks, two pairs of long pants, and two sweaters under her winter jacket. It was too bad Amanda didn't use the same good judgment in choosing a path to follow.

A synonym for **sensible** is:
__**a.** warm
__**b.** wise
__**c.** thoughtful
__**d.** proper

77c

d

hel i cop ter (hel′ə kop′tər), aircraft without wings that is lifted from the ground and kept in the air by horizontal propellers. *n.* [*Helicopter* is from French *hélicoptère*, which came from Greek *helikos*, meaning "a spiral," and *pteron*, meaning "wing."]

Which of the following would be helpful if you were to pilot a **helicopter**?
__**a.** good vision   __**d.** training
__**b.** ability to swim __**e.** hot air
__**c.** intelligence

102c

c

cus tom ar y (kus′tə mer′ē), according to custom; usual: *Ten o'clock is her customary bedtime. adj.* —**cus′tom-ar′i ness**, *n.*

Which of the following might be **customary** events?
__**a.** eating dinner __**d.** eating caviar
__**b.** a surprise party __**e.** talking with a friend
__**c.** Thanksgiving __**f.** skydiving

128a

a, b, d

var y (ver′ ē *or* var′ ē)

Members of the cactus family have one feature in common: their ability to store moisture. This storage is necessary because the amount of rain **varies** widely from month to month.

Write a definition or synonym:

175a

b, c, e

al ter a tion (ôl′ tə rā′ shən)

Linda explained to the salesperson why the **alterations** in her dress must be made that very afternoon.

Write a definition or synonym:

200a

1. a
2. b

cem e ter y (sem′ ə ter′ ē)

We took a walk through the little Zermatt **cemetery**.

Write a definition or synonym:

224c

b

be tray (bi trā′), **1** hand over or expose to the power of an enemy by being disloyal: *The traitor betrayed his country.* **2** be unfaithful to: *She betrayed her promise.* **3** mislead; deceive: *He was betrayed by his own enthusiasm.* **4** show signs of; reveal: *The girl's wet shoes betrayed the fact that she had walked through puddles.* v. —**be tray′er**, *n.*

Check the sentence(s) in which **betrayed** can correctly be used in place of the word(s) in italics.

__a. The woman *gave away* her old clothes.
__b. His shifty eyes *showed* his guilt.
__c. She *showed* them the pictures.
__d. He was *deceived* by the man he thought was his friend.

249c

b

prom i nent (prom′ə nənt), **1** well-known or important; distinguished: *a prominent citizen.* **2** easy to see: *I hung the picture in a prominent place in the living room.* **3** standing out; projecting: *Some insects have prominent eyes.* *adj.* —**prom′i nent ly**, *adv.*

ANALOGY **prominent : outstanding ::**
__a. adorable : melancholy
__b. absurd : commercial
__c. colossal : gigantic
__d. solitary : typical
__e. satisfactory : vivid

274b

The nurse was **clad** in white from head to toe. Her cap and uniform were stiffly starched, and her shoes were white and clean. She looked as though she could take care of any problem. I wondered what the doctor would be like.

A synonym for **clad** is:
__a. completely
__b. appearing
__c. dressed
__d. working

299b

Since Uncle Robert was sailing the boat, Stephanie and Bill had time to admire the green water, the fluffy clouds and the rugged shoreline.

"One of the pleasures of sailing is the enjoyment of such **scenic** beauty," Uncle Robert said.

"I think you're more **scenic** than a fluffy cloud!" Bill whispered to Stephanie.

Scenic means having to do with:
__a. water
__b. navigation
__c. sailing
__d. scenery

10

2b

A man at the travel bureau had given Marsha the **pamphlets** before they left home. While her father fussed, Marsha turned the pages eagerly, trying to decide what she wanted to see first.

Another word for **pamphlet** is:
- __a. ticket
- __b. booklet
- __c. map
- __d. card

27c

d

lob by (lob′ē), **1** entrance hall; passageway: *the lobby of a theater. A hotel lobby usually has chairs and couches to sit on.* **2** person or persons that try to influence members of a lawmaking body. **3** try to influence the members of a lawmaking body: *The conservation group lobbied to outlaw the use of certain traps by hunters.* 1,2 *n., pl.* **lob bies;** 3 *v.,* **lob bied, lob by ing.** —**lob′by er,** *n.*

1. In which of the following places might one find a **lobby?**
   - __a. a park   __c. a drugstore
   - __b. a theater   __d. a hotel
2. **Lobbying** goes on in which of the following places?
   - __a. the North Pole   __c. desert regions
   - __b. Washington, D.C.   __d. doctors' offices

52c

b

sen si ble (sen′sə bəl), **1** having or showing good sense or judgment; wise: *She is too sensible to do anything foolish.* **2** aware; conscious: *I am sensible of your kindness.* **3** that can be noticed: *There is a sensible difference between yellow and orange.* **4** able to be perceived by the senses. **5** sensitive. *adj.* —**sen′si ble ness,** *n.*
sen si bly (sen′sə blē), **1** in a sensible manner; with good sense. **2** so as to be felt. *adv.*

1. Check the phrase(s) in which **sensible** is used correctly.
   - __a. sensible ice cream   __d. sensible thought
   - __b. sensible fright   __e. sensible plan
   - __c. sensible arrangement
2. Which of the following can you be **sensible** of?
   - __a. something you can hear
   - __b. something that has not happened yet
   - __c. how you look when you are asleep

78a

a, c, d

con ceal (kən sēl′)

Looking up at the rocks, we could see the drums and one guitar almost **concealed** by the rising waters.

Write a definition or synonym:

103a

a, c, e

an nounce ment (ə nouns′ mənt)

The manager made an **announcement**.

Write a definition or synonym:

128b

Desert plants and animals have learned to live without depending on a regular supply of water. The rain that falls may **vary** from a few drops on one occasion to a cloudburst that drenches the ground.

A synonym for **vary** is:
- __a. shrink
- __b. increase
- __c. grow
- __d. change

174c

d

pref er a ble (pref′ər ə bəl), to be preferred; more desirable. *adj.* —**pref′er a ble ness**, *n.*

Which phrases include one thing **preferable** to another?
___**a.** black and white ___**d.** sun and moon
___**b.** good and bad ___**e.** sickness and health
___**c.** work and play ___**f.** off and on

199c

b

ut most (ut′mōst), **1** greatest possible; greatest; highest: *A balanced diet is of the utmost importance to health.* **2** most distant; farthest; extreme: *She walked to the utmost edge of the cliff.* **3** the most that is possible; extreme limit: *He enjoyed himself to the utmost at the circus.* 1,2 *adj.*, 3 *n.*

1. Something of the **utmost** importance *cannot* be described as:
___**a.** a trifle
___**b.** necessary
___**c.** valuable
2. The *opposite* of the **utmost** edge would be:
___**a.** the farthest edge
___**b.** the closest edge
___**c.** the most distant edge

224b

Plain Jane Hatfield stepped outside to refuse to accept the alligators and cement. It was all a practical joke, she told the men. Their neighbors, the McCoys, had played it many times before. The chief delivery man was annoyed, and the deep frown on his face **betrayed** his feelings.

Betray means:
___**a.** hit
___**b.** give away
___**c.** punish
___**d.** reward

249b

Bette Lou thought it was fine that the woman's family was so **prominent**. The more wealthy and famous her family had been, the better the object she could contribute.

A synonym for **prominent** is:
___**a.** well-liked
___**b.** well-known
___**c.** useful
___**d.** rich

274a

a, d, f

clad (klad)

The neatly **clad** nurse asked me to sit down and wait.

Write a definition or synonym:

299a

b, c

sce nic (sē′ nik *or* sen′ ik)

Instead of tying up at one of the smaller wharves, Uncle Robert decided to sail along the coast before heading back home. Stephanie and Bill relaxed and enjoyed the **scenic** beauty all around them.

Write a definition or synonym:

2c

b

pam phlet (pam′flit), booklet in paper covers. It often deals with a question of current interest. *n.*

Check the places where a **pamphlet** is likely to be found.
___a. in a library
___b. at a carnival
___c. in a restaurant
___d. in a travel agency

28a

1. b, d
2. b

pro hib it (prō hib′ it)

Letting pets loose in the lobby was **prohibited**.

Write a definition or synonym:

53a

1. c, d, e
2. a

ex treme (ek strēm′)

Ranger seemed as unhappy as Amanda was when she led him from his stall. The horse was restless and he was **extremely** cold.

Write a definition or synonym:

78b

Finally, the water **concealed** all but the top of the drums. It took hours before the water went down and you could see what was left of the group's instruments: not much.

A synonym for **conceal** is:
___a. show
___b. hide
___c. damage
___d. wet

103b

In her **announcement** she told the customers that the safe was locked and that the bank would open it when the safecracker arrived. Some of the customers felt better when they knew what was going on.

An **announcement** is:
___a. a warning
___b. something made known
___c. an appearance
___d. making an apology

128c

d

var y (ver′ē *or* var′ē), **1** make or become different; change: *The driver can vary the speed of an automobile.* **2** be different; differ: *Stars vary in brightness. v.,* **var ied, var y ing. —var′y ing ly,** *adv.*

Which of the following might be likely to **vary**?
___a. sky   ___d. horse
___b. typewriter   ___e. groundhog
___c. weather   ___f. scissors

13

298c

a

wharf (hwôrf), platform built on the shore or out from the shore, beside which ships can load and unload. n.
pl. wharves or wharfs.
wharves (hwôrvz), a plural of wharf. n.

Check the sentence(s) in which **wharves** is used correctly.
___**a.** The wharves moved slowly through the water, pulled by the tugs.
___**b.** There was little activity on the wharves while the dock workers were on strike.
___**c.** The wharves were crowded with cargo.

273c

c

punc tu al (pungk'chü al), on time; prompt: *She is punctual to the minute.* *adj.* —**punc'tu al ly,** *adv.* —**punc'tu-al ness,** *n.*

For which of the following would it be most important to be **punctual**?
___**a.** an appointment   ___**d.** a class
___**b.** brushing one's teeth   ___**e.** watering flowers
___**c.** washing dishes   ___**f.** concert

249a

b, d, f

prom i nent (prom'a nant)

Bette Lou and I both listened politely while the old woman talked about our town as it had been fifty or sixty years ago. It seemed that her family had been very **prominent.**

Write a definition or synonym:

224a

c, d, e

be tray (bi trā')

Just before the blackmail was to begin, the Hatfields found three trucks of cement and a shipment of alligators being unloaded in front of their house. Clean Gene and the McCoys had struck again! The Hatfields were furious, of course; but their faces did not **betray** their feelings.

Write a definition or synonym:

199b

It is of the **utmost** importance to go with a guide if you are inexperienced. Every year a few people are killed because they did not follow this essential advice.

Utmost means:
___**a.** usual
___**b.** greatest possible
___**c.** advisable
___**d.** proven

174b

Linda knew this dress was **preferable** to the others she had tried on. It looked better than the others and she liked the colors more.

Preferable means:
___**a.** costlier
___**b.** of higher quality
___**c.** prettier
___**d.** more desirable

3a

a, d

ma rine (mə rēn′)

Marsha decided to begin with a trip to the exhibit of **marine** life.

Write a definition or synonym:

28b

There was a sign on the wall which said that letting pets loose was **prohibited**. Fights among the animals might result if they were allowed to run about.

Prohibit means:
__**a.** permit
__**b.** dislike
__**c.** forbid
__**d.** arrange

53b

The wind was strong and the snow was blowing into Amanda's face. Her cheeks and nose grew **extremely** cold—cold enough to hurt.

A synonym for **extremely** is:
__**a.** very
__**b.** somewhat
__**c.** slightly
__**d.** uncomfortably

78c

b

con ceal (kən sēl′), **1** put out of sight; hide: *He concealed the surprise gift in the closet.* **2** keep secret: *They concealed their identities by wearing masks.* v. —**con ceal′a ble**, *adj.*

ANALOGY **conceal : reveal ::**
__**a.** hide : discuss
__**b.** show : decide
__**c.** lose : find
__**d.** explain : forget
__**e.** allow : permit

103c

b

an nounce ment (ə nouns′mənt), **1** an announcing; making known. We speak of the announcement of a speaker, a meeting, a wedding, a concert, etc. **2** what is announced or made known: *The principal made two announcements. The announcement was published in the newspapers.* n.

ANALOGY **announcement : notify ::**
__**a.** bed : dress
__**b.** soap : laundry
__**c.** tools : buy
__**d.** speech : work
__**e.** party : celebrate

129a

a, c

oc ca sion al (ə kā′ zhə nəl)

An **occasional** cloud is seen.

Write a definition or synonym:

174a

a, c, e

pref er a ble (pref′ ər ə bəl)

This one was **preferable** to any of the others.

Write a definition or synonym:

199a

a, c, d

ut most (ut′ mōst)

It is of the **utmost** importance not to be reckless in climbing a mountain.

Write a definition or synonym:

223c

c

bail[1] (bāl), **1** guarantee of money necessary to release a person under arrest from jail or prison until a trial is held: *They put up bail for their friend who was arrested for speeding.* **2** amount of money guaranteed. **3** obtain the release of (a person under arrest) by supplying bail: *They bailed out their friend.* 1,2 *n.,* 3 *v.* —**bail′a ble,** *adj.*
go bail for, supply bail for.
bail[2] (bāl), the curved handle of a kettle or pail. *n.*
bail[3] (bāl), throw (water) out of a boat with a bucket, pail, or any other container: *She bailed water from the sinking boat. v.*

Check the sentence(s) in which a form of **bail** is used correctly.
__a. He pitched a bail of hay.
__b. After the trial the bail was paid.
__c. Kim Jones' bail was set at $500.
__d. His friend bailed him out.
__e. We had to bail steadily so that the boat would not sink.

248c

c

or na men tal (ôr′nə men′tl), **1** of or for ornament; used as an ornament: *ornamental plants.* **2** decorative: *ornamental designs in wallpaper. adj.* —**or′na men′tal ly,** *adv.*

Something **ornamental** can be described as:
__a. necessary   __d. added
__b. extra   __e. required
__c. rare   __f. beautifying

273b

Although I was **punctual,** the doctor was not. I had to wait thirty minutes before I was called into the examination room.

A synonym for **punctual** is:
__a. ready
__b. early
__c. prompt
__d. correct

298b

Several fishing boats were unloading on each side of the long **wharves.** Bill knew they were lobster boats because he could make out the piles of lobster pots stacked up on the top of the **wharves.**

Wharves are:
__a. loading platforms for ships
__b. large buildings for storage
__c. flat-bottom boats for transporting goods
__d. natural harbors for ships

3b

Ted waited impatiently while Marsha stared at the huge glass tank filled with saltwater. Marsha seemed fascinated with the porpoises, the sea horses, and the other **marine** creatures.

Marine means:
__a. rare
__b. able to swim
__c. captured
__d. of the sea

28c

c

pro hib it (prō hib′it), **1** forbid by law or authority: *Picking flowers in this park is prohibited.* **2** prevent: *Rainy weather and fog prohibited flying. v.* —**pro hib′it er, pro-hib′i tor,** *n.*

ANALOGY prohibit : allow ::
__a. learn : discover
__b. pick : destroy
__c. leave : go
__d. refuse : accept
__e. smoke : litter

53c

a

ex treme (ek strēm′), **1** much more than usual; very great; very strong: *She drove with extreme caution during the snowstorm.* **2** at the very end; farthest possible; last: *the extreme north.* **3** something extreme; one of two things as far or as different as possible from each other: *Love and hate are two extremes of feeling.* **4** the highest degree: *Joy is happiness in the extreme.* 1,2 *adj.,* **ex trem-er, ex trem est;** 3,4 *n.* —**ex treme′ly,** *adv.* —**ex-treme′ness,** *n.*

Check the sentence(s) in which **extremely** is used correctly.
__a. There was extremely time for everything.
__b. I was extremely careful with my drawing.
__c. I was extremely interested in her plan.
__d. He was extremely hurt.

79a

c

mas sive (mas′ iv)

We climbed the same **massive** rocks that Manny must have climbed to reach the top of the cliff. We hoped we would find a broken guitar or something by which to remember Manny.

Write a definition or synonym:

104a

e

satch el (sach′ əl)

Lucas Sandoz arrived within the hour, carrying a heavy **satchel**.

Write a definition or synonym:

129b

For the most part, the sky is a clear blue. An **occasional** cloud may drift across the sky, but this is not a common sight on the desert.

Occasional means happening:
__a. once in a while
__b. frequently
__c. briefly
__d. regularly

173c

c

styl ish (stī′lish), having style; fashionable: *He wears stylish clothes. adj.* —**styl′ish ly,** *adv.* —**styl′ish ness,** *n.*

Which of the following can be used to describe something that is **stylish**?
___a. up-to-date
___b. just like grandmother wore
___c. in fashion
___d. everyday
___e. like all my friends wear

198c

d

com mu ni ca tion (kə myü′nə kā′shən), 1 a giving or exchanging information or news by speaking, writing, etc.; communicating. 2 information or news given; letter, message, etc., which gives information or news. 3 means of going from one place to another; passage; connection. 4 act or fact of passing along; transfer. 5 **communications,** *pl.* a system of communicating by telephone, telegraph, radio, television, etc. b system of routes or facilities for transporting military supplies, vehicles, and troops. *n.* **(Definition adapted)**

Check the sentence(s) in which a form of **communication** is used correctly.
___a. She received a communication from the President.
___b. He spoke with a strange communication.
___c. The storm knocked out all of their communications.
___d. There was no communication between the enemy tribes.

223b

Both families knew that sooner or later one of them would be arrested for the terrible tricks they were playing. They would need **bail** money to get the prankster released from jail until his or her trial.

Bail is money paid:
___a. to replace money that has been stolen
___b. to cover the cost of food in prison
___c. to free a person until her trial
___d. to keep someone from getting out of jail

248b

At the time the house was built, people felt that simple designs were not attractive. Only objects covered with **ornamental** designs were thought to be worth owning. Today, these objects are quite rare. I was sure we could sell whatever the old woman decided to give us.

Ornamental means:
___a. very beautiful
___b. made of stone
___c. for decoration
___d. unusual

273a

b, c, e

punc tu al (pungk′ chü əl)

When I called the doctor's office, the nurse gave me an appointment and reminded me to be **punctual**.

Write a definition or synonym:

298a

a, c, d

wharves (hwôrvz)

As the boat sailed back into the bay, Uncle Robert identified the boats they could see at the **wharves**.

Write a definition or synonym:

3c

d

ma rine (mə rēn′), **1** of the sea; found in the sea; produced by the sea: *Seals and whales are marine animals.* **2** of shipping; of the navy; for use at sea: *marine law, marine power, marine supplies.* **3** shipping; fleet: *our merchant marine.* **4** soldier formerly serving only at sea, now also serving on land and in the air. **5** Also, **Marine.** person serving in the Marine Corps. **6 marines,** *pl.* Marine Corps. 1,2 *adj.,* 3-6 *n.*

Which of the following could be described as **marine**?
__a. a bear   __d. a lion
__b. a dolphin __e. transportation
__c. a painting

29a

d

punc ture (pungk′ chər)

It turned out that Shep had a small **puncture**.

Write a definition or synonym:

54a

b, c

ap par ent (ə par′ ənt)

Apparently, Ranger felt that something was wrong.

Write a definition or synonym:

79b

It was hard to get to the top of one rock. It was even harder to stretch to reach the one above it. Seldom have I seen such **massive** rocks.

Massive means:
__a. slippery
__b. sharp
__c. big
__d. hard

104b

The **satchel** contained some small explosives and some tools for opening safes. It was surprising how much he took out of it.

Satchel means:
__a. luggage
__b. jacket
__c. small bag
__d. suitcase

129c

a

oc ca sion al (ə kā′zhə nəl), **1** happening or coming now and then, or once in a while: *We had fine weather all through July except for an occasional thunderstorm.* **2** caused by or used for some special time or event: *A piece of occasional music was played at the inauguration.* **3** for use once in a while: *occasional chairs. adj.*

Check the sentence(s) in which **occasional** is used correctly.
__a. We saw an occasional sparrow that winter.
__b. The occasional boat sailed every hour.
__c. This certainly is an occasional!
__d. Who is acting occasional now?

297c

d

throb (thrōb), **1** beat rapidly or strongly: *The long climb up the hill made my heart throb. My injured foot throbbed with pain.* **2** a rapid or strong beat: *A throb of pain shot through his head.* **3** beat steadily. **4** a steady beat; *the throb of a pulse.* 1, 3 *v.*, throbbed, throb bing; 2, 4 *n.*

Throbbing can be correctly used to describe which of the following?
_a. machines running in a factory
_b. a scream
_c. drums in the jungle
_d. a frightened bird
_e. an elephant walking through the jungle

272c

d

ne ces si ty (nə ses/ə tē), **1** fact of being necessary; extreme need: *the necessity of eating.* **2** that which cannot be done without; a necessary thing: *Water is a necessity.* **3** that which forces one to act in a certain way: *Necessity often drives people to do disagreeable things.* **4** need; poverty: *a family in great necessity. n., pl.* ne ces si ties.

Which of the following are **necessities**?
_a. good looks
_b. food
_c. sleep
_d. college education
_e. air
_f. sports

248a

**1, a, c, e
2. No**

or na men tal (ôr/nə men/tl)

Everything in the room seemed old and expensive. Even the walls were covered with **ornamental** carvings.

Write a definition or synonym:

223a

a, c, d

bail (bāl)

Just before Dirty John Hatfield began his blackmail scheme, his wife and children chipped in to raise enough money for **bail**, just in case something went wrong once again.

Write a definition or synonym:

198b

A party of mountain climbers is completely out of touch with the rest of the world. If a member of such a party should be injured, however, it becomes necessary to send a message for help. Flares that send out a bright light are taken along for **communication** purposes.

Communication means:
_a. a giving of treatment
_b. making light
_c. emergency measure
_d. a giving of information

173b

The colors and lines were tasteful. The dress looked as **stylish** as one that had been made in Paris for a real movie star. And the shoes fit, too!

A synonym for **stylish** is:
_a. inexpensive
_b. colorful
_c. fashionable
_d. common

4a

b, c, e

la bel (lā′ bəl)

All the exhibits had **labels** on them.

Write a definition or synonym:

29b

Something sharp on the automobile had made a **puncture** in Shep's side. Although the opening was small, the **puncture** was quite deep. The doctor cleaned it and sewed it up. She said that Shep would be fine in a few days.

Puncture means:
___**a.** sharp pain
___**b.** slight injury
___**c.** hole made by something pointed
___**d.** long cut made by a sharp edge

54b

Each time Amanda took a step forward, Ranger began to neigh and paw the ground. These actions were usually signs of fear or distress. **Apparently**, Ranger knew that something dangerous was taking place.

Apparently means:
___**a.** curiously
___**b.** seemingly
___**c.** noisily
___**d.** naturally

79c

c

mas sive (mas′iv), **1** big and heavy; large and solid; bulky. **2** giving the impression of being large and broad: *a massive forehead. adj.* —**mas′sive ly,** *adv.* —**mas′sive-ness,** *n.*

Which of the following are *not* **massive**?
___**a.** a Siamese cat ___**d.** an aircraft carrier
___**b.** a mouse ___**e.** a clam
___**c.** a volcano ___**f.** a needle

104c

c

satch el (sach′əl), a small bag for carrying clothes, books, etc.; handbag. *n.*

ANALOGY **satchel : trunk :: cottage :**
___**a.** cave
___**b.** mansion
___**c.** tail
___**d.** hole
___**e.** wall

130a

a

a bun dant (ə bun′ dənt)

When she went shopping, Sally learned that dates were **abundant**.

Write a definition or synonym:

21

297b

Suddenly, a large motorboat crossed in front of them. The heavy **throb** of the motorboat's engines was so loud, they could hear nothing else. As the boat passed, the engine's noise softened to a faint hum.

Throb means:
___a. push
___b. move faster
___c. stop beating
___d. beat strongly

272b

When the cut became very red and painful, I realized that seeing a doctor was a **necessity**. It wasn't going to heal by itself.

A **necessity** is something that:
___a. happens at regular intervals
___b. is unpleasant to experience
___c. is helpful
___d. cannot be done without

247c

d

tap es try (tap'ə strē) **1** fabric with pictures or designs woven in it, used to hang on walls, cover furniture, etc. **2** cover with tapestry; cover with a pattern like that of tapestry. **1** *n., pl.* **tap es tries; 2** *v.,* **tap es tried, tap es tried, tap es try ing.** —**tap'es try like'**, *adj.*

1. Which of the following might be needed in making a **tapestry**?
___a. thread   ___d. glue
___b. paint brush   ___e. a theme
___c. loom

2. Would you be likely to find **tapestries** made in many homes today?
Yes___ No___

222c

d

a li as (ā'lē əs), **1** name other than a person's real name used to hide who he or she is; assumed name: *The spy's real name was Harrison, but he sometimes went by the alias of Johnson.* **2** otherwise called: *The thief's name was Jones, alias Williams.* **1** *n., pl.* **a li as es; 2** *adv.*

Who might be likely to use an **alias**?
___a. a writer   ___d. a secret agent
___b. a housewife   ___e. a doctor
___c. a criminal   ___f. a politician

198a

b, c, d

com mu ni ca tion (kə myü' nə kā' shən)

Flares are usually taken along for purposes of communication.

Write a definition or synonym:

173a

1. a
2. b

styl ish (stī' lish)

At last, Linda found an outfit she liked. Both the dress and the shoes were tasteful and stylish.

Write a definition or synonym:

4b

There were many unusual animals which neither Ted nor Marsha could recognize easily. By reading each **label**, Marsha was able to learn each animal's name. Ted thought that kind of learning was a waste of time.

Another word for **label** is:
_a. writing
_b. tag
_c. design
_d. picture

29c

c

punc ture (pungk′chər), **1** hole made by something pointed. **2** make such a hole in. **3** have or get a puncture. **4** act or process of puncturing. **5** reduce, spoil, or destroy as if by a puncture. 1,4 *n.*, 2,3,5 *v.*, **punc tured, punc tur ing. —punc′tur a ble,** *adj.* **—punc′ture less,** *adj.* **—punc′tur er,** *n.*

Check the sentence(s) in which a form of **puncture** is used correctly.
_a. Do not puncture that sentence.
_b. The balloon was punctured.
_c. She punctured the skin with a needle.
_d. He punctured the alfalfa with a bag.

54c

b

ap par ent (ə par′ənt), **1** plain to see or understand; so plain that one cannot help seeing or understanding it: *The stain is apparent from across the room. It is apparent that she enjoys her work.* **2** appearing to be; seeming: *The apparent truth was really a lie. adj.* **—ap par′ent ly,** *adv.* **—ap par′ent ness,** *n.*

Check the sentence(s) in which **apparently** is used correctly.
_a. Apparently there is green cheese on the moon.
_b. Apparently this rug has been washed recently.
_c. She rode apparently down the street.
_d. Apparently it is not the custom to wear shorts in St. Peter's in Rome.

80a

a, b, e, f

prob a ble (prob′ ə bəl)

We **probably** will visit the beach again next week. By that time many more people will have heard of Manny Spellbinder.

Write a definition or synonym:

105a

b

clue (klü) .

Then he started looking for a **clue** to the problem.

Write a definition or synonym:

130b

Growing conditions had been very good, so the dates were **abundant**. Sally saw so many dates for sale in the market that she decided to send each of her friends a year's supply of dates.

Abundant means:
_a. ordinary
_b. frequent
_c. very plentiful
_d. favorable

172c

a

ex treme (ek strēm′), **1** much more than usual; very great; very strong: *She drove with extreme caution during the snowstorm.* **2** at the very end; farthest possible; last: *the extreme north.* **3** something extreme; one of two things as far or as different as possible from each other: *Love and hate are two extremes of feeling.* **4** the highest degree: *Joy is happiness in the extreme.* 1,2 *adj.,* **ex trem-er, ex trem est;** 3,4 *n.* —**ex treme′ly,** *adv.* —**ex-treme′ness,** *n.*

1. Which of the following are **extremes**?
   __**a.** freezing and boiling   __**c.** fall and winter
   __**b.** snow and sleet
2. Check the phrase(s) in which **extreme** is used correctly.
   __**a.** extreme money   __**c.** extreme food
   __**b.** extreme poverty

197c

d

crev ice (krev′is), a narrow split or crack; fissure: *Tiny ferns grew in crevices in the stone wall.* *n.*

Which of the following might have **a crevice**?
__**a.** clouds   __**d.** a sidewalk
__**b.** a rock   __**e.** a pool of water
__**c.** a piece of wood   __**f.** a flower

222b

Dirty John could not use his real name while he blackmailed Clean Gene McCoy. If Gene knew Dirty John's true identity, he would never pay the blackmail money. John opened the phone book and picked out a name to use as an **alias**.

Alias means:
__**a.** real name
__**b.** funny name
__**c.** nickname
__**d.** other name

247b

Bette Lou and I stared at the beautiful **tapestries** that hung on the walls. We saw one **tapestry** that showed a knight killing a dragon. Some of the threads seemed to be made of gold and silver.

Tapestry means:
__**a.** picture of historical events
__**b.** oil painting
__**c.** long drapes or curtains
__**d.** fabric with woven pictures

272a

a, c, d

ne ces si ty (nə ses′ ə tē)

Then I realized that seeing a doctor was a **necessity**.

Write a definition or synonym:

297a

a, c, d

throb (throb)

Soon they heard the **throb** of a motorboat's engine.

Write a definition or synonym:

4c

b

la bel (lā′bəl), **1** slip of paper or other material attached to anything and marked to show what or whose it is, or where it is to go: *Can you read the label on the bottle?* **2** put or write a label on: *The bottle is labeled "Poison."* **3** a word or phrase used to describe some person, thing, or idea: *In winter, Chicago deserves its label of "the Windy City."* **4** describe as; call; name: *label someone a liar.* 1,3 *n.*, 2,4 *v.*, **la beled, la bel ing** or **la belled, la bel ling.** —**la′bel er, la′bel ler,** *n.*

1. On which items might a **label** be found?
   __**a.** a box for shipment   __**c.** a cup of coffee
   __**b.** a bottle of medicine __**d.** a thumb tack
2. If you **label** something you:
   __**a.** notice it   __**c.** recognize it
   __**b.** name it   __**d.** store it

30a

b, c

phy si cian (fə zish′ ən)

Then and there I decided to become a **physician**.

Write a definition or synonym:

55a

b, d

tread (tred)

Amanda was so upset that she ignored Ranger's warning. She put Ranger's halter on. Together, the girl and her horse began to **tread** through the deep snow.

Write a definition or synonym:

80b

If the weather stays warm, we will **probably** return to Foster's Beach, but of course we can't be sure. Manny will **probably** become a big star soon. In fact, it's almost one hundred percent sure. I can still hear his music breaking like big waves inside my poor head!

Probably means:
__**a.** more likely than not
__**b.** not at all likely
__**c.** all together
__**d.** certainly

105b

All Lucas needed was a **clue** as to what was causing the trouble. Then he would know what to do. After all, there are over a hundred parts in a safe that could be causing the trouble. After a few minutes he found what he wanted. A tiny insect had crawled into the delicate clock that controlled the lock.

A synonym for **clue** is:
__**a.** reminder
__**b.** suggestion
__**c.** thought
__**d.** guide

130c

c

a bun dant (ə bun′dənt), **1** more than enough; very plentiful: *an abundant supply of food.* **2** having more than enough; abounding: *a river abundant in salmon. adj.* —**a bun′dant ly,** *adv.*

Check the phrase(s) in which **abundant** is used correctly.
__**a.** abundant book   __**d.** abundant supplies
__**b.** abundant weather   __**e.** abundant dog
__**c.** abundant rainfall __**f.** abundant clock

d	**296c** **gauge** (gāj), 1 a standard measure; scale of standard measurements; measure. There are gauges of the capacity of a barrel, the thickness of sheet iron, the diameter of a shotgun bore or of a wire, etc. 2 instrument for measuring. A steam gauge measures the pressure of steam. 3 measure accurately; find out the exact measurement of with a gauge. 4 estimate; judge: *It's difficult to gauge the educational value of television.* 5 distance between the rails of a railroad. Standard gauge between rails is 56½ inches (1.44 meters). 1, 2, 5 *n.*, 3, 4 *v.*, gauged, gaug·ing. Also, gage, gage. —gauge/a·ble, *adj.*

In which of the following is something being **gauged?**

—a. An employer judges the value of her employee.
—b. A man knows how much money he has in the bank.
—c. An electrician measures wire to see if it will fit tightly in an opening.
—d. An engineer uses a slide rule.

---

b	**271c** **nui·sance** (nü/sns or nyü/sns), thing or person that annoys, troubles, offends, or is disagreeable; annoyance: *Flies are a nuisance. n.*

Which of the following might likely be a **nuisance?**

—a. smell from a swamp
—b. a world war
—c. mud on the sidewalk
—d. mosquitoes
—e. a forest fire
—f. fishing

---

b, d	**247a** **tap·es·try** (tap/ ə strē) We talked for a while about this and that. Then I mentioned the sale again. "I know, dear," she smiled. "I have just the thing for you." For a minute, I thought she was talking about one of her tapestries.

Write a definition or synonym:

---

a, e, f	**222a** **a·li·as** (ā/lē əs) Dirty John Hatfield called up his victim, using an alias, of course.

Write a definition or synonym:

	197b It is sometimes necessary to cross deep crevices in the ice. If one falls into a crevice, there is small hope of being brought up alive. A crevice in a glacier is usually called a "crevasse" (krə vas/).

A crevice is:

—a. a pool
—b. a hole
—c. a space
—d. a crack

	172b After all, Linda thought, red, green, and purple stripes were a little loud. The colors were pretty, but taken together, they made the dress rather **extreme.**

Extreme means:

—a. very strong
—b. unusual
—c. amazing
—d. unaccustomed

5a

1. a, b
2. b

dis please (dis plēz′)

On the return to their motel, Marsha was aware that her father was **displeased**.

Write a definition or synonym:

30b

Being able to take care of injured people or animals must be a wonderful way to spend one's life. I decided then and there that I would study hard and become a **physician**.

Physician means:
__a. kind person
__b. rescuer
__c. doctor of medicine
__d. animal doctor

55b

Amanda and Ranger tried to **tread** lightly as they walked across the surface of the snowdrifts. At every moment, Amanda expected to plunge up to her hips in the snow.

A synonym for **tread** is:
__a. stamp
__b. slide
__c. step
__d. run

80c

a

prob a bly (prob′ə blē), more likely than not. *adv.*

Check the sentence(s) in which **probably** is used correctly.
__a. My mother probably will come tomorrow.
__b. It is never probably to be expected.
__c. He failed to solve that arithmetic probably.
__d. She goes to a probably school.

105c

d

clue (klü), **1** fact or object which aids in solving a mystery or problem: *The police could find no fingerprints or other clues to help them solve the robbery.* **2** show (something) by means of a clue. **3** INFORMAL. give a clue to: *The note clued us to what was going on.* **1** *n.*, 2,3 *v.*, **clued**, **clu ing** or **clue ing**.

1. Who would be most interested in **clues**?
__a. a pilot
__b. a detective
__c. a swimmer
2. Which of the following would be a **clue** to the solving of a mystery?
__a. a confession by the criminal
__b. a fingerprint
__c. a police officer

LESSON 14 | Sunday Driving

I think it's a mistake to own a car when you live in a city like New York. Public transportation will take you anywhere you want to go. But my father disagrees. He keeps a car so that we can drive to Long Island every Sunday to visit relatives. The trip last Sunday was typical.

296b

When another sailboat approaches, the person at the tiller must **gauge** the speed and direction of both boats, to avoid a collision. Stephanie said she had trouble judging distance, so she was relieved when Uncle Robert offered to take control of the tiller again.

Gauge means:

___ **a.** remove
___ **b.** see ahead
___ **c.** record
___ **d.** judge

271b

I had cut my thumb while playing football. The cut was a **nuisance** because I kept bumping it against things and it didn't seem to heal.

Nuisance means:

___ **a.** punishment
___ **b.** annoyance
___ **c.** unnecessary thing
___ **d.** harmful experience

246c

c

ma hog a ny (mə hog'ə nē), 1 any of several large tropical American trees which yield a hard, reddish-brown wood. 2 its wood, used in making furniture. 3 made of mahogany; *a mahogany chest of drawers.* 4 a dark reddish-brown. 5 a dark reddish brown. 1,2,5 *n., pl.* ma hog a-nies; 3,4 *adj.*

In which of the following would **mahogany** be most likely to be used?

___ **a.** kitchen sink
___ **b.** dining table
___ **c.** garage
___ **d.** chair
___ **e.** lawn furniture
___ **f.** automobile

221c

c

black mail (blak'māl'), 1 money gotten from a person by threatening to tell or reveal something bad about him or her. 2 get or try to get blackmail from. 3 an attempt to get money by threats. 1,3 *n.,* 2 *v.* —**black'mail'er,** *n.*

Which of the following would describe someone who was being **blackmailed**?

___ **a.** worried
___ **b.** joyful
___ **c.** relieved
___ **d.** excited
___ **e.** afraid
___ **f.** guilty

197a

a, b

crev ice (krev'is)

One of the dangers of mountain climbing is the presence of crevices in the glaciers.

Write a definition or synonym:

172a

a, c

ex treme (ek strēm')

Linda did find one outfit that made her look absolutely beautiful. However, she rejected it because she felt the colors were too **extreme** for the role of a wealthy young lady.

Write a definition or synonym:

5b

The weather report said that the cloudy weather would continue for another day or two. When you are waiting for a space shot, it is difficult not to become impatient. Marsha hoped that was the only reason her father was **displeased**.

Displease means:
___**a.** annoy
___**b.** make sad
___**c.** become ill
___**d.** become tired

30c

c

phy si cian (fə zish′ən), doctor of medicine. *n.*

A **physician** would be most likely to do which of the following?
___**a.** fit shoes ___**d.** sell drugs
___**b.** set bones ___**e.** remove tonsils
___**c.** type letters ___**f.** teach football

55c

c

tread (tred), **1** set the foot down; walk; step: *Don't tread on the flower beds. They trod through the meadow.* **2** set the feet on; walk on or through; step on: *tread the streets.* **3** press under the feet; trample on; crush: *tread grapes.* **4** make, form, or do by walking: *Cattle had trodden a path to the pond.* **5** act or sound of treading: *We heard the tread of marching feet.* **6** way of walking: *He walks with a heavy tread.* **7** the part of stairs or a ladder that a person steps on: *The stair treads were covered with rubber to prevent slipping.* **8** the part of a wheel or tire that presses against the ground, rail, etc. 1-4 *v.*, **trod, trod den** or **trod, tread ing;** 5-8 *n.* —**tread′er,** *n.* **(Definition adapted)**

1. On which of the following would one be likely to **tread**?
___**a.** grass ___**d.** piano
___**b.** chair ___**e.** swing
___**c.** rug ___**f.** slide
2. The **treads** of an automobile tire are likely:
___**a.** to be painted white
___**b.** to wear out
___**c.** to be on the side of the tire

LESSON ⑨ Linda Superstar Becomes an Actress

a

When Linda Superstar was still in high school, she did take part in the junior class play, just as it says in the fan magazines. But Linda's career on the stage began much differently than she likes to admit. Linda wasn't an actress at all when she started out. She was a director—the very worst director our school had ever seen. When she finally decided to get up on stage and act, it was because there was no place else she could go!

106a

1. b
2. b

in jec tion (in jek′ shən)

Lucas decided to use an **injection** of a mild explosive.

Write a definition or synonym:

131a

se dan (si dan′)

It took us twenty minutes to get our **sedan** out of the garage.

Write a definition or synonym:

171c

d

pos i tive (poz′ə tiv), 1 permitting no question; without doubt; sure. 2 too sure; too confident. 3 definite; emphatic. 4 showing agreement or approval. 5 the simple form of an adjective or adverb, as distinct from the comparative and superlative. 6 of the simple form of an adjective or adverb. 7 showing that a particular disease, condition, germ, etc., is present. 8 able definitely to do or add something; practical. 9 of the kind of electrical charge produced by rubbing glass with silk. 10 greater than zero; plus. 11 a positive degree or quantity. 12 (in photography) having the lines and shadows in the same position as in the original subject. 13 print made from a photographic film or plate. 1-4,6-10,12 *adj.*, 5,11,13 *n.* **(Definition adapted)**

Check the sentence(s) in which **positive** is used correctly.

___**a.** Heat is a positive thing; cold is the absence of heat.

___**b.** His test was positive, showing that he did not have the disease.

___**c.** She gave a positive answer to my question.

196c

b

ven ture (ven′chər), 1 a risky or daring undertaking: *Our courage was equal to any venture. A lucky venture in oil stock made him rich.* 2 expose to risk or danger: *She ventured her life to rescue me.* 3 dare: *No one ventured to interrupt the speaker.* 4 dare to come or go: *We ventured out on the thin ice and fell through.* 5 dare to say or make: *He ventured an objection.* 1 *n.*, 2-5 *v.*, **ven tured, ven tur- ing.**

Venture can correctly be used to describe which of the following?

___**a.** buying stock in a new company

___**b.** swimming across a rough channel

___**c.** reading an exciting story

___**d.** taking a hike in the woods

221b

Dirty John knew that Clean Gene had once robbed a bank. To raise some money, John decided to **blackmail** his neighbor. Gene was willing to pay because he wanted to keep that part of his past a secret.

To **blackmail** means:

___**a.** to report something to the police

___**b.** to try to get a share of another's belongings

___**c.** to get money by threatening to tell something

___**d.** to try to find out someone's secrets

246b

The dark brown **mahogany** walls were carved with strange designs. We knocked on them, wondering whether there were secret passages behind them. We sat down quickly when the old woman returned with our tea.

Mahogany is a kind of:

___**a.** fabric

___**b.** stone

___**c.** wood

___**d.** decoration

271a

nui sance (nü′ sns *or* nyü′ sns)

At first I thought of the cut on my hand as just a **nuisance.**

Write a definition or synonym:

296a

a, b

gauge (gāj)

Stephanie took a turn at the tiller. As Bill looked on, Uncle Robert tried to teach Stephanie how to **gauge** speed and distance.

Write a definition or synonym:

5c

a

dis please (dis plēz′), not please; annoy; offend: *You displease your parents when you disobey them.* *v.,* **displeased, dis pleas ing.** —**dis pleas′ing ly,** *adv.* —**dis pleas′ing ness,** *n.*

Who would be most likely to **displease** people?
__a. a laughing baby __d. a good student
__b. a bully __e. a show-off
__c. a bike rider

---

b, e

LESSON 4 | What Makes a Newspaper Run

Last fall, when Mr. Sandoval started teaching at our school, he decided we had to have a school newspaper. He started talking about it, trying to build up some interest. That didn't work at all. None of us really knew the different jobs that had to be done to put out a paper. Mr. Sandoval decided the best way to find out was to go and take a close look. He arranged for the whole class to visit the office and printing plant of the *Daily Observer.*

56a

1. a, c
2. b

bound ar y (boun′ dər ē)

The **boundary** of the pond behind the barn was covered by the deep snow.

Write a definition or synonym:

81a

as sem bly (ə sem′ blē)

Every year the junior class presents a play at our school **assembly.**

Write a definition or synonym:

106b

He made the **injection** of the explosive into the lock's timer. He had a special needlelike tool for this task.

Injection means:
__a. act of forcing liquid in
__b. act of exploding
__c. a cure or remedy
__d. a means of accomplishing something

131b

My mother got in the back, and my brother and I argued about who was going to ride in the front seat. My father told us to stop fighting. "With a big car like this **sedan**," he said, "there's room for everybody."

Sedan means:
__a. an auto having no back seat
__b. a closed auto seating four or more
__c. a small truck
__d. an open car seating two people

31

171b

Each time Linda looked through another rack of dresses, she was **positive** that she would find the perfect dress. But the longer she looked, the less certain she became.

A synonym for **positive** is:
__a. unsure
__b. glad
__c. insisting
__d. sure

196b

He and the other members of the expedition had to sleep in an upright position one night, roped against the side of a mountain. They also had to cross a great glacier. I did not think I would have the courage for such a **venture**.

A **venture** is:
__a. an emergency
__b. a risky undertaking
__c. a long journey
__d. an impossible task

221a

black mail (blak′ māl′)

In the first show, Dirty John Hatfield dreamed up a crazy scheme to **blackmail** Clean Gene McCoy.

Write a definition or synonym:

a, c, f

246a

ma hog a ny (mə hog′ ə nē)

Bette Lou said she thought the walls and ceiling were made of **mahogany**.

Write a definition or synonym:

a, b, c, e

LESSON 28 | The Boy Who Hated Doctors

When I was a kid, I fell and broke my arm. It didn't hurt much until the doctor started fixing it. Ever since then, I've thought of all doctors as mean people who do terrible things to you while they pretend to cure you. Doctors would tell you anything, I felt, just to get their hands on you again. They would even tell you that simple cuts and scratches can become seriously infected if not treated properly. Well, they're right. But I had to learn that for myself, the hard way.

d

295c

slack (slak), **1** not tight or firm; loose: *a slack rope.* **2** part that hangs loose: *Pull in the slack of the rope.* **3** careless: *a slack worker.* **4** slow: *The horse was moving at a slack pace.* **5** not active; not brisk; dull: *Business is slack at this season.* **6** a dull season; quiet period. **7** make or become slack; let up: *He slacked his pace so we could catch up. The breeze slacked.* 1,3-5 *adj.*, 2,6 *n.*, 7 *v.* —**slack′ly**, *adv.* —**slack′ness**, *n.*

Check the sentence(s) in which a form of **slack** is used correctly.
__a. Banks cannot afford to have slack employees.
__b. Summer is a slack time in the television industry.
__c. They raced along at a slack pace.
__d. He thought he had slacked his money.

32

6a

b, e

can cel (kan′ səl)

The next day's shot had been **canceled**. Ted took Marsha to the beach, to the zoo, and then to the biggest hamburger shop they had ever seen.

Write a definition or synonym:

31a

pub lish er (pub′ li shər)

We were taken first to the office of the **publisher** of the newspaper.

Write a definition or synonym:

56b

Amanda had to take Ranger past the pond to get to the front of the house where the buyer was waiting. The snow made it impossible to see the **boundary** of the pond. Without realizing it, Amanda had crossed over from the frozen ground to the frozen water.

Boundary means:
__a. bottom
__b. border
__c. side
__d. cement

81b

The junior class play is always given twice. The first time is at the school **assembly**, so that all of the students see the play at the same time. The second time is an evening performance for parents.

A synonym for **assembly** is:
__a. school
__b. class
__c. meeting
__d. holiday

106c

a

in ject (in jekt′), **1** force (liquid, medicine, etc.) into a passage, cavity, or tissue: *inject penicillin into a muscle, inject fuel into an engine.* **2** throw in; insert: *While she and I were talking he injected a remark into the conversation. v.* —**in jec′tor,** *n.*
in jec tion (in jek′shən), **1** act or process of injecting: *The medicine was given by injection rather than by mouth.* **2** liquid injected: *A nurse prepared the injection. n.*

1. An **injection** might be given for which of the following?
   __a. pain   __d. quickness
   __b. illness   __e. intelligence
   __c. prevention of disease   __f. football
2. Which of the following is an example of an **injection**?
   __a. A man puts laundry into a washing machine.
   __b. A speaker throws a few funny remarks into her talk.

131c

b

se dan (si dan′), **1** a closed automobile with a front and back seat, seating four or more persons. **2** sedan chair. *n.*

Who would be most likely to use a **sedan** for work?
__a. messenger   __d. farmer
__b. cowboy   __e. driving instructor
__c. traveling salesperson __f. peddler

LESSON 23 "Fighting Families"

There's a new show on TV called "Fighting Families." It's about two neighboring families with typically average grown-ups and normal kids. But there's an importance difference: The two families can't stand each other, and they're not afraid to show how they feel. One family is named Hatfield, the other is named McCoy. Each show has a new trick or prank that one family plays on the other. Nobody gets hurt and the audience laughs a lot. But it makes you wonder sometimes.

245c

co los sal (kə los′əl), of huge size; gigantic; vast: *Sky-scrapers are colossal structures.* adj. —co los′sal ly, adv.

Which of the following would be least likely to be colossal?

__a. closet   __d. ocean
__b. football stadium   __e. auditorium
__c. thimble   __f. shrimp

270c

a dapt (ə dapt′), 1 make fit or suitable; adjust: *Can you adapt your way of working to the new job?* 2 change so as to make suitable for a different use: *The story was adapt-ed for the movies from a novel by Jane Austen.* v. —a dapt′er, a dap′tor, n.

Who of the following had to adapt to a new way of life?

__a. Elsa of *Born Free*
__b. Swiss Family Robinson
__c. the Pilgrims
__d. the Eskimos
__e. Robinson Crusoe

295b

The slack line meant the sail was loose and the boat was losing speed. Uncle Robert turned the boat so that the sail filled with wind and pulled the loose line taut. Immediately the boat picked up speed.

Slack means:

__a. broken
__b. knotted
__c. cut
__d. loose

171a

pos i tive (poz′ə tiv)   Write a definition or synonym:

When Linda set out on her shopping trip, she was positive she would find the right outfit to wear for the part of Melissa.

196a

ven ture (ven′chər)   Write a definition or synonym:

Hal told us about his last venture.

6b

There was no use hoping the weather would be clear by the next day. The men in charge **canceled** the arrangements that had been made. The shot would be scheduled again when the weather improved.

Cancel means:
___**a.** delay
___**b.** change
___**c.** do away with
___**d.** be finished with

31b

She told us she had become interested in newspapers by selling them as a girl. Her interest grew when she later wrote newspaper articles. Then for ten years she had served as editor of the *Daily Observer*. At last, she became **publisher** of the newspaper.

A **publisher** is one who:
___**a.** holds a public office
___**b.** produces a newspaper
___**c.** operates a printing press
___**d.** sells a newspaper

56c

b

bound ar y (boun′dər ē), a limiting line or thing; limit; border: *Lake Superior forms part of the boundary between Canada and the United States. n., pl.* **bound ar ies.**

ANALOGY boundary : center ::
___**a.** state : city
___**b.** suburb : downtown
___**c.** forest : road
___**d.** limit : freedom
___**e.** edge : middle

81c

c

as sem bly (ə sem′blē), **1** a gathering of people for some purpose; meeting: *The principal addressed the school assembly.* **2** a meeting of lawmakers. **3 Assembly,** the lower branch of the state legislature of some states of the United States. **4** a coming together; an assembling: *unlawful assembly.* **5** a putting together; fitting together: *the assembly of parts to make an automobile.* **6** the complete group of parts required to put something together: *the tail assembly of an airplane. n., pl.* **as sem blies.**

1. The **assembly** of an airplane would take place:
___**a.** on a landing strip
___**b.** in flight
___**c.** in the factory
2. When **assembly** sounds at an army camp, the soldiers will:
___**a.** walk off the field
___**b.** line up in rows
___**c.** go in to eat

107a

1. a, b, c
2. b

as sist ance (ə sis′ təns)

After the lock timer was blown off, Lucas asked for some **assistance.**

Write a definition or synonym:

132a

c, e

turn pike (térn′ pīk′)

We drove off and headed for the **turnpike.**

Write a definition or synonym:

LESSON

18

Linda Superstar Starts Her Climb to the Top

Becoming a world-famous actress isn't easy—not even for Linda Superstar. Linda had a chance to try out for the lead role in a movie. Her first concern was making sure the casting director would notice her. After she had planned all the bright, witty things she would say, Linda took almost all of the money she had saved and went shopping for the clothing she thought would win her the part.

195c

b

tro phy (trō′fē), **1** any prize, cup, etc., awarded to a victorious person or team: *The champion kept her tennis trophies on the mantelpiece.* **2** a spoil or prize of war, hunting, etc.: *The hunter kept the lion's skin and head as trophies.* **3** anything serving as a remembrance. *n., pl.* **tro phies.** —**tro′phy less,** *adj.*

Which of the following are likely to have **trophies**?
__a. a conquered army __d. a farmer
__b. an Oscar winner __e. a victorious general
__c. a racehorse owner __f. a famous golfer

220c

a

fresh man (fresh′mən), student in the first year of high school or college. *n., pl.* **fresh men.**

ANALOGY **freshman : newcomer :: beginner :**
__a. veteran
__b. teacher
__c. senior
__d. junior
__e. greenhorn

245b

The high hanging lamps and the dark corners of the **colossal** living room made it look like a witches' ballroom. It was larger than our basketball court at school.

A synonym for **colossal** is:
__a. comfortable
__b. huge
__c. tall
__d. pretty

270b

The wild dingo of Australia can **adapt** itself to life as a tame animal or can remain in a wild state. It can learn to be happy in either condition.

Adapt means:
__a. grow to like
__b. adopt
__c. adjust
__d. recognize

295a

b

slack (slak)

Stephanie and Bill were busy comparing their experiences over the winter when Uncle Robert called their attention to a **slack** line.

Write a definition or synonym:

6c

can cel (kan′səl), **1** put an end to, set aside, or withdraw; do away with; stop. **2** make up for; compensate for; balance. **3** cross out; mark, stamp, or punch so that it cannot be used again. **4** in mathematics: **a** reduce (a fraction) by dividing both the numerator and the denominator by the same quantity. **b** reduce (an equation) by dividing both members by a common factor. *v.,* **can celed, can cel ing** or **can celled, can cel-ling. —can′cel a ble, can′cel la ble,** *adj.* **—can′cel er, can′cel ler,** *n.* **(Definition adapted)**

c

Which of the following can be described as **canceled**?
__**a.** a new show just seen on TV
__**b.** a stamp on a letter just received
__**c.** a picnic called off because of rain
__**d.** an important date circled on the calendar

31c

b

pub lish er (pub′li shər), person or company whose business is to publish books, newspapers, magazines, etc.: *Look at the bottom of the title page of this book for the publisher's name.* n.

Which of the following would be important to a **publisher** of books?
__**a.** the weather
__**b.** the price of paper
__**c.** the latest fashions
__**d.** a popular author

57a

e

dis o bey (dis′ ə bā′)

"Come on, Ranger," Amanda commanded. But for the first time, the horse **disobeyed**.

Write a definition or synonym:

82a

1. c
2. b

e lab or ate (*adj.* i lab′ ər it; *v.* i lab′ ə rāt′)

At first, Linda planned to have a very **elaborate** stage set.

Write a definition or synonym:

107b

With four men giving him **assistance**, Lucas pried and pulled open the locked safe door.

A synonym for **assistance** is:
__**a.** help
__**b.** relief
__**c.** strength
__**d.** observation

132b

At the first toll station on the **turnpike**, my father gave the man a dime. The man in the booth told us to be sure to observe the speed limit, which was 55 miles per hour.

A **turnpike** is:
__**a.** a highway through the country
__**b.** a place where several roads meet
__**c.** a road on which toll is paid
__**d.** a road on which there is no speed limit

170c

d

ac tu al ly (ak′chü ə lē), really; in fact: *Are you actually going to camp this summer or just wishing to go? adv.*

Check the phrase(s) in which **actually** is used correctly.

___**a.** actually hot   ___**d.** actually movie
___**b.** actually frozen   ___**e.** actually alive
___**c.** actually picture   ___**f.** more actually

195b

Mountain climbers are not likely to have a shelf full of silver cups. Their satisfaction is in knowing what they have accomplished, rather than in winning any real **trophies**.

A **trophy** is:
___**a.** a victory
___**b.** a prize
___**c.** a contest
___**d.** a battle

220b

Often, I thought, the upperclassmen will ignore or look down upon a lowly **freshman**. After her first year was over, Arlene would probably feel much more at home.

Freshman means:
___**a.** first-year student
___**b.** young person
___**c.** person who misbehaves
___**d.** part-time student

245a

1. b, e
2. Yes

co los sal (kə los′ əl)

I told the old woman about the white elephant sale and she invited us to sit in her living room while she made us some tea. Bette Lou looked around in amazement. The living room was **colossal**!

Write a definition or synonym:

270a

a dapt (ə dapt′)

Some wild dogs can **adapt** themselves to many conditions.

Write a definition or synonym:

294c

c

jet ty (jet′ē), **1** structure of stones or wooden piles projecting out from the shore to break the force of a current or waves; breakwater. **2** a landing place; pier. *n., pl.* **jet ties.**

ANALOGY jetty : harbor ::
___**a.** tower : steeple
___**b.** fence : yard
___**c.** corner : street
___**d.** car : highway
___**e.** waves : beach

7a

b, c

site (sīt)

Finally the launching time was announced. On the drive to the **site**, Ted tried to get Marsha interested in what they would see.

Write a definition or synonym:

32a

b, d

su per vise (sü′ pər vīz)

We were next taken to meet the editor who **supervised** the newsroom.

Write a definition or synonym:

57b

Instead of going with Amanda, Ranger broke and ran away from her. It must have been fear of the deep snow that made him **disobey**.

Disobey means:
__a. turn and run
__b. refuse to obey
__c. escape
__d. avoid

82b

However, the students who were going to design and build the stage set couldn't stand taking orders from Linda. They all quit. That's when Linda decided she was against having an **elaborate** set. "All we need is a table and a few chairs," Linda said. "A simple set will be more effective than one that is too complicated."

Elaborate means:
__a. difficult
__b. specially made
__c. of many colors
__d. having many details

107c

a

as sist ance (ə sis′təns), an assisting; aid; help: *I need your assistance. n.*

People in certain jobs are more likely to give **assistance** than those in other jobs. Check the people who would be most likely to give **assistance**.
__a. teacher   __d. salesperson
__b. nurse   __e. gardener
__c. football player __f. explorer

132c

c

turn pike (tėrn′pīk′), **1** toll road. **2** road that has, or used to have, a gate where toll is paid. *n.*

Who would be most likely to use a **turnpike**?
__a. a horseback rider   __d. a traveler
__b. a racing car driver __e. a duck hunter
__c. a pilot   __f. a tourist

294b

Out beyond the **jetty** was the open sea. Bill and Stephanie had been content to stay in the harbor where the wind was not too strong. As the boat left the bay, they saw workmen replacing the rocks that had been torn from the **jetty** in a recent storm.

A **jetty** is:

—**a.** an island
—**b.** a lightship
—**c.** a breakwater
—**d.** a canal

40

269c

a

awe (ô), **1** great fear and wonder; fear and reverence: *The sight of the great waterfall filled us with awe.* **2** cause to feel awe; fill with awe: *The majesty of the mountains awed us.* **1** *n.,* **2** *v.,* **awed, aw·ing.**

Which of the following might be likely to cause a person to feel **awe**?

—**a.** a giant bear   —**d.** a hornet
—**b.** an enjoyable book   —**e.** a great cathedral
—**c.** the Grand Canyon   —**f.** a bush

244c

c

pil·lar (pil'ər), **1** a slender, upright structure; column. Pillars are usually made of stone, wood, or metal and used as supports or ornaments for a building. Sometimes a pillar stands alone as a monument. **2** anything slender and upright like a pillar. **3** an important support or supporter; *a pillar of society, a pillar of the church. n.*
from pillar to post, from one thing or place to another without any definite purpose.

1. Where would you be most likely to find a **pillar**?
—**a.** on a cottage
—**b.** on a state capitol
—**c.** on a farm
—**d.** on a bed
—**e.** on a Southern plantation
2. If someone were called a **pillar** of society, would this be a compliment?
Yes—   No—

220a

a, c, d

fresh·man (fresh' mən)

Poor Arlene! All of a sudden, I felt older and wiser than she was. Maybe things would seem better after a while. After all, Arlene was only a **freshman.**

Write a definition or synonym:

195a

b

tro·phy (trō' fē)

A mountain climber does not seek **trophies.**

Write a definition or synonym:

170b

It was no longer a dream. The railroad was **actually** there, ready to speed the growth of the United States.

A synonym for **actually** is:

—**a.** finally
—**b.** safely
—**c.** actively
—**d.** really

7b

Ted explained that the Kennedy Space Center had been chosen as the **site** for the launching because of its good climate and its location near the ocean.

Another word for **site** is:
___**a.** hill
___**b.** scene
___**c.** place
___**d.** land

32b

Many people were busy writing news articles which were then given to the editor. Others were on the phone taking down important facts being given to them by a reporter. It was the editor's job to **supervise** all their activity.

Another word for **supervise** is:
___**a.** teach
___**b.** direct
___**c.** study
___**d.** correct

57c

b

dis o bey (dis/ə bā/), refuse to obey; fail to obey: *The student who disobeyed the teacher was punished. v.*

Check the sentence(s) in which a form of **disobey** is used correctly.
___**a.** He will not disobey your order.
___**b.** It disobeyed my plans.
___**c.** You must not disobey your parents.
___**d.** She disobeyed the lessons I had taught her.

82c

d

e lab or ate (i lab/ər it *for 1;* i lab/ə rāt/ *for 2,3*), **1** worked out with great care; having many details: *The scientists made elaborate plans for launching a new satellite.* **2** work out with great care; add details to: *The author spent months elaborating plans for a new book.* **3** talk or write in great detail; give added details: *The witness was asked to elaborate on one of his statements.* 1 *adj.,* 2,3 *v.,* **e lab o rat ed, e lab o rat ing.** —**e lab/or ate ly,** *adv.* —**e lab/or ate ness,** *n.* —**e lab/o ra/tor,** *n.*

1. Which of the following could be **elaborate**?
   ___**a.** a pencil
   ___**b.** an astronaut's space suit
   ___**c.** a city dump
   ___**d.** planning a surprise party
2. If you were asked to **elaborate** on an answer, which of the following would you do?
   ___**a.** give more information
   ___**b.** give a different answer

108a

a, b, d

a jar (ə jär/)

Soon the heavy safe door was **ajar.**

Write a definition or synonym:

133a

d, f

ex ceed (ek sēd/)

We passed a sign that warned us not to **exceed** the speed limit.

Write a definition or synonym:

170a

b, e, f

ac tu al ly (ak′ chü ə lē)

The Union Pacific Railroad was **actually** finished.

Write a definition or synonym:

194c

d

con quest (kon′kwest *or* kong′kwest), **1** act of conquering: *the conquest of a country, the conquest of disease.* **2** thing conquered; land, people, etc., conquered: *The city was an easy conquest for the invaders. n.*

ANALOGY conquest : defeat :: entrance :
___a. recess
___b. exit
___c. door
___d. decide
___e. attitude

219c

d

coun sel (koun′səl), **1** act of exchanging ideas; talking things over; consultation: *We benefited from our frequent counsel.* **2** advice: *A wise person gives good counsel.* **3** lawyer or group of lawyers: *Each side of a case in a court of law has its own counsel.* **4** give advice to; advise: *She counsels sophomores to help them choose their courses.* **5** recommend: *The doctor counseled operating at once.* 1-3 *n.,* 4,5 *v.,* **coun seled, coun sel ing** or **coun selled, coun sel ling. (Definition adapted)**

Counsel might be important to which of the following?
___a. parent and child
___b. dog and cat
___c. criminal and lawyer
___d. teacher and student
___e. milkman and truck
___f. rider and horse

244b

The stone **pillars** at the entrance were very tall. They looked like huge guards on each side of the door. The old woman between them looked very dainty and delicate. Right away, I decided I liked her.

A synonym for **pillar** is:
___a. step
___b. fence
___c. column
___d. gate

269b

Some people feel a sense of **awe** for the power and the bravery of the wolf. This feeling of amazement is experienced by most humans who have come to know the wolf.

Awe means:
___a. wonder
___b. pleasure
___c. silence
___d. terror

294a

a, b, c, e

jet ty (jet′ ē)

Soon Uncle Robert's boat was sailing out past the **jetty.**

Write a definition or synonym:

7c

c

site (sīt), position or place (of anything); location: *The site for the new school has not yet been chosen. n.*

Check the sentence(s) in which **site** is used correctly.
___a. The site for the new school is a pretty one.
___b. That is the site of the new homes.
___c. When the sun went down, the site was gone.
___d. In his dirty clothes, he was quite a site.

32c

b

su per vise (sü′pər vīz), look after and direct (work or workers, a process, etc.); oversee; superintend; manage: *Study halls are supervised by teachers. v.,* **su per vised, su per vis ing.**

Which of the following people would be likely to **supervise**?
___a. a waiter ___d. a painter
___b. a teacher ___e. a general
___c. a truck driver ___f. a supervisor

58a

a, c

com mo tion (kə mō′ shən)

Amanda's father said that he and the buyer were just going inside when they heard the **commotion**.

Write a definition or synonym:

83a

1. b, d
2. a

mem o rize (mem′ ə rīz′)

Linda worked very carefully with the actors and actresses. She made sure they **memorized** their parts in the play.

Write a definition or synonym:

108b

When the door of the safe was **ajar** Pauline looked inside to see if everything was all right. Then she opened the bank door wide and announced that the day's business would begin.

Ajar means:
___a. wide open
___b. unlocked
___c. slightly open
___d. knocked down

133b

We all laughed. With the traffic as heavy as it was, we were lucky if we could **exceed** 25 miles per hour.

Exceed means:
___a. ignore
___b. go beyond
___c. break
___d. equal

b

169c

cli max (klī′maks), **1** the highest point of interest; most exciting part: *A visit to the Grand Canyon was the climax of our vacation.* **2** bring or come to a climax: *Her election to the Senate climaxed a long career in politics.* **3** series of ideas arranged so that there is a steady rise of force and interest. 1,3 *n., pl.* cli max es; 2 *v.*

What might be a **climax** to a person's day?
___**a.** a visit to the city dump
___**b.** a visit to the zoo
___**c.** doing homework
___**d.** eating breakfast
___**e.** a birthday dinner
___**f.** leaving for vacation

194b

Those who do not climb mountains cannot understand how climbers feel about their sport. Many climbers think of the mountain as a foe offering a challenge. The **conquest** of a mountain like the Matterhorn gives one a tremendous sense of success.

Conquest means:
___**a.** threat
___**b.** danger
___**c.** presence
___**d.** victory

219b

Arlene felt she had picked the wrong college. That's why she was putting on weight and didn't even know her school colors. She needed someone older and wiser to **counsel** her. She was telling me to talk things over so I wouldn't make the same mistake she did!

Counsel means:
___**a.** inform
___**b.** praise
___**c.** criticize
___**d.** advise

c

244a

pil lar (pil′ ər)

Between the huge **pillars** at the entrance to the mansion stood an old woman. She had neat white hair and was dressed in a faded gown that hung down to her ankles.

Write a definition or synonym:

d

269a

awe (ô)

The wolf arouses **awe** in some people.

Write a definition or synonym:

b

293c

nav i ga tion (nav′ə gā′shən), **1** act or process of navigating. **2** art or science of finding a ship's or an aircraft's position and course. *n.*

Which of the following might be connected with **navigation**?
___**a.** a knowledge of the stars
___**b.** airplane instruments
___**c.** a lighthouse
___**d.** automobile tires
___**e.** a computer

8a

a, b

gi gan tic (jī gan′ tik)

The sight of the **gigantic** spacecraft filled Ted with excitement, but it left Marsha cold.

Write a definition or synonym:

33a

b, e, f

pol i cy (pol′ ə sē)

We learned that each newspaper has a **policy**.

Write a definition or synonym:

58b

Amanda had stepped onto the frozen pond and fallen through into deep water. The noise produced by the cracking ice, Ranger's neigh, and Amanda's screams was just terrible. When her father heard the **commotion**, he came running.

Another word for **commotion** is:
__a. splash
__b. cries
__c. cracking
__d. disturbance

83b

The cast worked until they knew their lines word for word. Linda wanted to make sure every part had been **memorized**. "Think how bad you would feel," Linda said, "if you forgot what to say when the curtain went up!"

Memorize means:
__a. remember well
__b. study very hard
__c. learn by heart
__d. look at carefully

108c

c

a jar (ə jär′), slightly open: *Please leave the door ajar. adj.*

Which of the following could be **ajar**?
__a. a book
__b. a gate
__c. a face
__d. a window
__e. a pencil

133c

b

ex ceed (ek sēd′), **1** be more or greater than: *The sum of 5 and 7 exceeds 10. Lifting that heavy trunk exceeds my strength.* **2** do more than; go beyond: *Drivers are not supposed to exceed the speed limit. v.*

Check the sentence(s) in which a form of **exceed** is used correctly.
__a. I exceeded on my test.
__b. You have exceeded the limits of my patience.
__c. If you do not first exceed, try again.
__d. He exceeded down the road.

293b

After Bill and Stephanie were settled down in the bow of the sailboat, Uncle Robert gave them a lesson in **navigation**. He let them each steer the boat, using the tiller. He showed them how to use special charts to fix the boat's position and plan their course.

Navigation is:
—**a.** knowledge of the parts of a boat
—**b.** the steering of a boat
—**c.** becoming a sailor
—**d.** following orders or directions

268c

d

fe·ro·cious (fə rō'shəs), **1** very cruel; savage; fierce: *The bear's ferocious growl terrified the hunter.* **2** INFORMAL. intense: *a ferocious headache. adj.* —**fe·ro'cious·ly,** *adv.* —**fe·ro'cious·ness,** *n.*

ANALOGY ferocious : kind :: shy :
—**a.** critical
—**b.** fierce
—**c.** quiet
—**d.** bossy
—**e.** savage

243c

c

typ·i·cal (tip'ə kəl), **1** being a type; representative: *The typical Thanksgiving dinner consists of turkey, cranberry sauce, several vegetables, and mince or pumpkin pie.* **2** of a type; characteristic: *the hospitality typical of frontier people. adj.*

ANALOGY typical : unusual :: valuable :
—**a.** regular
—**b.** ordinary
—**c.** worthless
—**d.** important
—**e.** costly

219a

c, d, e

coun·sel (koun'səl)

Finally, after the game, Arlene told me to be sure to have someone **counsel** me when I chose a college. That's when I understood what was bothering Arlene.

Write a definition or synonym:

194a

b, e

con·quest (kon' kwest or kong' kwest)

The **conquest** of the Matterhorn is something every mountain climber dreams of.

Write a definition or synonym:

169b

Cheers grew louder and the excitement grew. Then came the **climax** of the occasion. A message was telegraphed to the world: "The last rail is laid ... the last spike is driven ... the Pacific Railroad is completed!"

Climax means:
—**a.** last part
—**b.** most exciting part
—**c.** result
—**d.** necessary part

8b

The part where the passengers would ride was large enough by itself. But with the attached rockets beneath it, the craft seemed **gigantic**. Ted said he always felt very small when he looked up at it. Marsha said nothing at all.

A synonym for **gigantic** is:
__a. large
__b. tall
__c. huge
__d. long

33b

The **policy** of the *Daily Observer* was to mix local, regional, and national news in a fixed proportion. The paper stuck to this way of covering the news even though some readers preferred a different system.

Policy means:
__a. plan of action
__b. feeling
__c. idea
__d. important decision

58c

d

com mo tion (kə mō′shən), violent movement; confusion; disturbance; tumult: *Their fight caused quite a commotion in the hall. n.*

ANALOGY **commotion : storm :: destruction :**
__a. hurricane
__b. confusion
__c. intersection
__d. thunder
__e. calm

83c

c

mem o rize (mem′ə rīz′), commit to memory; learn by heart: *memorize the alphabet. v.,* **mem o rized, mem o riz ing.** —**mem′o riz′er,** *n.*

ANALOGY **memorize : repeat :: learn :**
__a. walk
__b. study
__c. practice
__d. master
__e. wonder

109a

b, d

con grat u late (kən grach′ ə lāt)

The manager **congratulated** Lucas.

Write a definition or synonym:

134a

b

speed om e ter (spē dom′ ə tər)

We really didn't need to watch the **speedometer**.

Write a definition or synonym:

293a

b, c

nav i ga tion (nav' ə gā' shən)

Stephanie was eager to learn something about the **navigation** of a sailboat.

Write a definition or synonym:

268b

It is true that no single animal can survive when cornered by a pack of hungry wolves. Sooner or later the **ferocious** wolves can bring any prey to the ground.

Ferocious means:
__a. unfriendly
__b. noisy
__c. angry
__d. fierce

243b

Even the front door of this house was different. It was made of a heavy, dark wood and had mysterious carvings all over it. The **typical** modern door is quite plain.

"Let's leave now and talk about the door later," said Bette Lou. But it was too late. Slowly, the heavy door opened.

Typical means:
__a. an outward expression
__b. similar to
__c. being a type
__d. identical to

218c

d

at ti tude (at'ə tüd or at'ə tyüd), **1** way of thinking, acting, or feeling: *As the family next door got to know us better, their attitude changed from formality to friendliness.* **2** position of the body suggesting an action, purpose, emotion, etc.: *He raised his fists in the attitude of a boxer ready to fight.* *n.*

In which of the following phrases is **attitude** used correctly?
__a. proper attitude __d. brown attitude
__b. high attitude __e. stubborn attitude
__c. good attitude __f. long attitude

193c

b

lei sure (lē'zhər), **1** time free from required work in which you may rest, amuse yourself, and do the things you like to do: *She's been too busy to have much leisure.* **2** free; not busy: *leisure hours.* **1** *n.*, **2** *adj.* —**lei'sure less,** *adj.*

Which of the following are likely to have the most **leisure**?
__a. mother with seven children
__b. five-year-old child
__c. man with two jobs
__d. doctor
__e. wealthy person
__f. newspaper boy

169a

b

cli max (klī' maks)

Then came the **climax** of the ceremony.

Write a definition or synonym:

8c

c

gi gan tic (jī gan′tik), big like a giant; huge: *An elephant is a gigantic animal. adj.* —**gi gan′ti cal ly,** *adv.*

    __a. pagan : nymph
    __b. small : large
    __c. special : ordinary
    __d. strange : unusual
    __e. high : new

33c

a

pol i cy[1] (pol′ə sē), **1** plan of action; way of management: *It is a poor policy to promise more than you can do. The candidates explained their policies.* **2** practical wisdom; prudence. *n., pl.* **pol i cies.** [*Policy*[1] came into English about 600 years ago from French *policie,* and can be traced back to Greek *polis,* meaning "city."]
pol i cy[2] (pol′ə sē), a written agreement about insurance: *My fire insurance policy states that I shall receive $40,000 if my house burns down. n., pl.* **pol i cies.**

Check the sentence(s) in which **policy** is used correctly.
    __a. My policy is to do my homework right after school.
    __b. It is good policy to think before you act.
    __c. I went to the library to get a policy.
    __d. The policy of keeping a horse is very high.
    __e. Her insurance agent sent her a policy.

59a

a

hoist (hoist)

With Ranger's help, Amanda's father was able to **hoist** his daughter from the icy water.

Write a definition or synonym:

84a

b

al le giance (ə lē′ jəns)

Finally, everything was ready and the assembly began. First, there was the Pledge of **Allegiance**.

Write a definition or synonym:

109b

Pauline **congratulated** Lucas for his quick, clean work. She had been afraid that the explosion would damage the inside of the safe.

Congratulate means:
    __a. shake hands with
    __b. give a reward to
    __c. express pleasure at success
    __d. have a short talk with

134b

The **speedometer** stayed at 20 miles per hour most of the time. What a slow trip!

A **speedometer** is:
    __a. a road sign
    __b. a gas tank
    __c. an instrument to test temperature
    __d. an instrument to indicate speed

168c

d

dis tin guished (dis ting′gwisht), **1** famous; well-known: *a distinguished American poet.* **2** looking important or superior: *Your new suit gives you a distinguished look. adj.*

ANALOGY **distinguished : unknown ::**

—**a.** plumber : mail carrier
—**b.** skillful : awkward
—**c.** farm : building
—**d.** worker : important
—**e.** beach : road

193b

He was the president of a large company and therefore did not have much **leisure** time. Whenever he could take a vacation, however, he went mountain climbing.

Leisure means:
—**a.** pleasure
—**b.** free
—**c.** lazy
—**d.** unemployed

218b

Arlene kept acting like a grown woman and treating me like a child. Her **attitude** was annoying. She never behaved that way before. I started wondering why.

Attitude means:
—**a.** appearance
—**b.** conversation
—**c.** way of dressing
—**d.** way of acting

243a

b, c,

typ i cal (tip′ ə kəl)

I was sure of one thing, and I told Bette Lou: whatever we found inside would not be **typical!**

Write a definition or synonym:

268a

a, c,
d, e

fe ro cious (fə rō′ shəs)

The wolf is commonly regarded as a **ferocious** animal.

Write a definition or synonym:

292c

a

keel (kēl), **1** the main timber or steel piece that extends the whole length of the bottom of a ship or boat. The whole ship is built up on the keel. **2** OLD USE. ship. **3** part in an aircraft resembling a ship's keel. *n.*
keel over, 1 turn upside down; upset: *The sailboat keeled over in the storm.* **2** fall over suddenly: *keel over in a faint.*
on an even keel, horizontal: *The boat sailed on an even keel in good weather.*

Check the sentence(s) in which a form of **keel** is used correctly.
—**a.** The white keels of the ships stood out against the blue sky.
—**b.** The mast suddenly keeled over during the storm.
—**c.** The boat keeled over, dumping the passengers into the water.

9a

d

post pone (pōst pōn′)

Then the Silvermans learned that the launching time had been **postponed** again.

Write a definition or synonym:

34a

a, b, e

ac cur a cy (ak′ yər ə sē)

A reporter must write with **accuracy**.

Write a definition or synonym:

59b

There was a rope fastened to the end of Ranger's halter. Amanda's father tossed the free end of the rope to his daughter. Then he and Ranger pulled and pulled until they **hoisted** Amanda up from the icy water.

Hoist means:
___**a.** drag
___**b.** lift up
___**c.** push out
___**d.** carry

84b

The Pledge of **Allegiance**, in which we promise to be faithful to our country, is always said at the beginning of our assembly program.

A synonym for **allegiance** is:
___**a.** honor
___**b.** praise
___**c.** joining
___**d.** loyalty

109c

c

con grat u late (kən grach′ə lāt), express one s pleasure at the happiness or good fortune of: *The judge congratulated the winner of the race. v.,* **con grat u lat ed, con grat u lat ing.**

Which of the following would a person be most likely to **congratulate**?
___**a.** a horse   ___**d.** a policeman
___**b.** a college graduate   ___**e.** a singer
___**c.** a bride and bridegroom ___**f.** a bank teller

134c

d

speed om e ter (spē dom′ə tər), instrument to indicate the speed of an automobile or other vehicle, and often the distance traveled. *n.*

Which of the following would be most likely to have a **speedometer**?
___**a.** a lawn mower   ___**d.** a sedan
___**b.** a hay rake   ___**e.** a motorcycle
___**c.** a racing car   ___**f.** a cart

168b

It was appropriate that the last spike be driven in by a **distinguished** person. Governor Leland Stanford of California was chosen for the honor.

A synonym for **distinguished** is:
___a. political
___b. intelligent
___c. rich
___d. famous

193a

a

lei sure (lē′ zhər)

Hal's **leisure** time was spent mountain climbing.

Write a definition or synonym:

218a

a, c

at ti tude (at′ ə tüd *or* at′ ə tyüd)

Arlene's **attitude** bothered me.

Write a definition or synonym:

242c

d

anx i e ty (ang zī′ə tē), **1** uneasy thoughts or fears about what may happen; troubled, worried, or uneasy feeling: *We all felt anxiety when the airplane was caught in the storm.* **2** eager desire: *Her anxiety to succeed led her to work hard. n., pl.* **anx i e ties.**

Check the sentence(s) in which **anxiety** is used correctly.
___a. She had a feeling of great calmness and anxiety.
___b. The mother felt some anxiety for her children.
___c. When prices fell suddenly, anxiety was felt by the store owners.
___d. He had a great anxiety about spiders.
___e. The anxiety of the Indians was due to their good training.

267c

b

pref er ence (pref′ər əns), **1** act or attitude of preferring; liking better: *My preference is for beef rather than lamb.* **2** thing preferred; first choice: *My preference in reading is a mystery story.* **3** the favoring of one above another: *A teacher should not show preference for any student. n.*

You cannot show a **preference** for a thing if you:
___a. are undecided about it
___b. like it better than anything else
___c. like something else better
___d. have no feeling about it
___e. like something equally well

292b

Without a **keel** in the water, the boat would slip sideways. It would not be able to hold its course.

A **keel** is:
___a. a board extending the length of a ship's bottom
___b. the wheel by which a boat is steered
___c. the upper surface, or deck, of a boat
___d. the mainsail of a boat

9b

There was a breathtaking wait while the equipment was checked. This final check **postponed** the takeoff for an hour. Finally there was a great roaring sound, and then the rocket lifted into the air!

Another word for **postpone** is:
__a. cancel
__b. continue
__c. arrange
__d. delay

34b

First, one must get the exact facts and then use those facts with **accuracy** in the story. A newspaper cannot afford to make mistakes.

A synonym for **accuracy** is:
__a. skill
__b. cleverness
__c. speed
__d. correctness

59c

b

hoist (hoist), **1** raise on high; lift up, often with ropes and pulleys: *hoist a flag, hoist sails.* **2** a hoisting; lift; boost: *She gave me a hoist up the wall.* **3** elevator or other apparatus for hoisting heavy loads. 1 *v.*, 2,3 *n.* —**hoist′-er,** *n.*

Which of the following would be likely to **hoist** something?
__a. a farmer __d. an artist
__b. a dockworker __e. a banker
__c. an actress __f. an elevator

84c

d

al le giance (ə lē′jəns), **1** the loyalty owed to one's country or government: *I pledge allegiance to the flag.* **2** loyalty to any person or thing: *We owe allegiance to our friends.* *n.*

To which of the following might one give **allegiance**?
__a. one's country __d. one's family
__b. a friend __e. a president or king
__c. one's house __f. a foreign ruler

110a

b, c, e

re main der (ri mān′ dər)

For the **remainder** of the morning, Pauline mopped her brow and tried to relax.

Write a definition or synonym:

135a

c, d, e

land scape (land′ skāp)

At least I could enjoy looking at the **landscape**.

Write a definition or synonym:

292a

keel (kēl)

Uncle Robert was determined not to be left out of the conversation. He showed Bill and Stephanie the different parts of the boat and explained the particular importance of the keel.

Write a definition or synonym:

1, a, c, e   2, a

267b

Jackals will eat decayed meat. However, they do not necessarily have a **preference** for this kind of food. Often, it is easier for them to eat what other animals have killed and left behind.

Preference is the act of:
—a. liking least
—b. liking better
—c. taking notice
—d. forming an opinion

242b

Our **anxiety** grew greater as we waited for someone to come to the door. It was natural for us to worry. After all, no one we knew had ever been to the place. What would the owner be like? What would we find if we did go inside?

Anxiety means:
—a. a fear of a particular thing
—b. a feeling of excitement
—c. a sense of weakness
—d. a general feeling of fear

217c

b

re fer (ri fer/), **1** send or direct for information, help, or action: *Our teacher refers us to many good books.* **2** hand over; submit: *Let's refer the dispute to the umpire.* **3** turn for information or help: *A person refers to a dictionary to find the meaning of words.* **4** direct attention to or speak about: *The speaker referred to the Bible.* **5** assign to or think of as caused by: *They referred their failure to bad luck.* **6** relate; apply: *The rule refers only to special cases.* *v.,* re ferred, re fer ring. **—re fer/rer,** *n.*

Check the sentence(s) in which a form of **refer** is used correctly.
—a. His teacher referred him to a good doctor.
—b. She referred carefully through the book.
—c. If you refer your problem to your mother, she will help you.
—d. I always refer with my friends when I don't know something.

192c

a

fa vor a ble (fā/vər ə bəl), **1** favoring; approving: *"Yes" is a favorable answer to a request.* **2** being to one's advantage; helping; promising: *A favorable wind made the boat go faster.* *adj.* **—fa/vor a ble ness,** *n.*

ANALOGY **favorable** : **threatening** ::
—a. sunshine : clouds
—b. dangerous : gun
—c. necessary : desirable
—d. boring : cabbage
—e. useful : tools

168a

a, d

dis tin guished (dis ting/gwisht)

Several **distinguished** people attended the ceremony.

Write a definition or synonym:

9c

d

post pone (pōst pōn′), put off till later; put off to a later time; delay: *The picnic was postponed because of rain.* v., post poned, post pon ing. —post pon′er, n.

Check the sentence(s) in which a form of **postpone** is used correctly.
__**a.** We will postpone our move until next year.
__**b.** The bell has postponed the class.
__**c.** He postponed his sandwiches for lunch.
__**d.** The race was postponed because of rain.

34c

d

ac cur a cy (ak′yər ə sē), a being without errors or mistakes; correctness; exactness: *I question the accuracy of that report.* n.

Accuracy would be important in which of the following?
__**a.** measuring   __**d.** shooting
__**b.** sleeping   __**e.** walking
__**c.** smiling

60a

a, b, f

ad mi ra tion (ad′ mə rā′ shən)

Amanda's father said he had heard Ranger snorting and neighing. Amanda's screams had not been loud enough to be heard. Everyone was filled with **admiration** for the way Ranger had behaved.

Write a definition or synonym:

85a

a, b, d, e

com e dy (kom′ ə dē)

Then our play began. From the way the audience behaved, it seemed as if we were presenting a **comedy**.

Write a definition or synonym:

110b

The bank was open for business. But it would take time to repair the broken timing gears in the safe door. The repair crew from the safe company worked that day and the next. However, it took the **remainder** of the week to complete all the repairs.

Remainder means:
__**a.** part
__**b.** rest
__**c.** majority
__**d.** end

135b

The country **landscape** is always a pleasant change from what we see in the city. We enjoy the green grass, trees, and houses that we see along the way.

A **landscape** is:
__**a.** a view from a car
__**b.** a route taken by travelers
__**c.** a view of scenery on land
__**d.** land with buildings on it

291c

pic·tur·esque (pik/chə resk/), 1 quaint or interesting enough to be used as the subject of a picture. 2 making a picture for the mind; vivid; *picturesque language. adj.* —pic/tur·esque/ly, *adv.* —pic/tur·esque/ness, *n.*

c

1. **Picturesque** can be used correctly to describe which of the following?
__ a. a colorful description
__ b. shelves of library books
__ c. a skiing village
__ d. a flagpole
__ e. an old castle
2. If a scene is picturesque, it is:
__ a. attractive
__ b. unattractive

267a

pref·er·ence (pref'ar ans)

Jackals have a **preference** for meat.

Write a definition or synonym:

a, b, c, d

242a

anx·i·e·ty (ang zī' a tē)

As we waited for the front door to open, Bette Lou and I felt some **anxiety.**

Write a definition or synonym:

a, c, d

217b

At first I thought Arlene was trying to identify the players when she **referred** to the program that gave their names and numbers. Then I realized she was trying to figure out which team she should root for.

Refer means:
__ a. make a note of
__ b. turn for information
__ c. read carefully
__ d. take out

192b

If there is any sign of approaching bad weather, an expedition will be postponed. The weather reports for the next three days, however, were **favorable.** Hal was prepared to leave early in the morning.

Favorable means:
__ a. promising
__ b. doubtful
__ c. happy
__ d. lucky

167c

ap·pro·pri·ate (ə prō'prē it for 1; ə prō'prē āt for 2,3), 1 right for the occasion; suitable; proper: *Plain, simple clothes are appropriate for school wear.* 2 set apart for some special use: *The state government appropriated money for a new road into our town.* 3 take for oneself; use as one's own: *You should not appropriate other people's belongings without their permission.* 1 *adj.,* 2,3 *v.* —ap·pro'pri·ate·ly, *adv.* —ap·pro'pri·ate·ness, *n.*

c

Check the sentence(s) in which a form of **appropriate** is used correctly.
__ a. The town appropriated money for the park.
__ b. Many people from Boston are appropriate.
__ c. She is a very appropriate person.
__ d. The cat appropriated the dog's bed.

10a

a, d

a muse ment (ə myüz′ mənt)

When the launch was complete, Marsha saw that her father was watching her with **amusement**.

Write a definition or synonym:

35a

a, d

gos sip (gos′ ip)

The editor told us that the *Daily Observer* had no **gossip** column.

Write a definition or synonym:

60b

Then Amanda's father said that selling Ranger was out of the question. Somehow, they would find enough money to keep Ranger in the family. Amanda's **admiration** for her father had never been greater than it was that day.

Admiration is a feeling of:
__**a.** sadness and regret
__**b.** delight and approval
__**c.** amazement and disbelief
__**d.** fear and horror

85b

The longer the play went on, the louder the audience laughed. It was the best **comedy** the school had seen in years.

Comedy means:
__**a.** serious play
__**b.** amusing play
__**c.** well-written play
__**d.** musical show

110c

b

re main der (ri mān′dər), **1** the part left over; the rest: *After studying an hour, she spent the remainder of the afternoon playing.* **2** in arithmetic: **a** number left over after subtracting one number from another. In 9 − 2, the remainder is 7. **b** number left over after dividing one number by another. In 14 ÷ 3, the quotient is 4 with a remainder of 2. *n.*

Check the phrase(s) in which **remainder** is used correctly.
__**a.** the remainder of the pie
__**b.** the remainder of the year
__**c.** the remainder of the broom
__**d.** the remainder of the dog
__**e.** the remainder of me
__**f.** the remainder house

135c

c

land scape (land′skāp), **1** view of scenery on land that can be taken in at a glance from one point of view: *From the church tower the two hills with the valley formed a beautiful landscape.* **2** painting, etching, etc., showing such a view. **3** make (land) more pleasant to look at by arranging trees, shrubs, flowers, etc.: *This park is landscaped.* 1,2 *n.,* 3 *v.,* **land scaped, land scap ing.**

1. If you wanted your property **landscaped**, you would need a:
  __**a.** gardener __**b.** builder __**c.** painter
2. A **landscape** by an artist would be likely to include:
  __**a.** waves __**b.** trees __**c.** furniture

291b

Stephanie quickly commented that the neat white buildings, colorful boats, and bright blue water did make a **picturesque** scene. In fact, all during the summer, artists came there to make paintings of it.

Picturesque means:

___**a.** like nature
___**b.** realistic
___**c.** like a picture
___**d.** unusual

266c

mod er ate (mod'ər it *for 1-4;* mod'ə rāt' *for 5,6),* **1** kept or keeping within proper bounds; not extreme: *moderate expenses, moderate styles.* **2** not violent; calm: *moderate in opinion.* **3** not very large or good; fair; medium: *make a moderate profit.* **4** person who holds opinions that are not extreme: *a political moderate.* **5** make or become less extreme or violent: *The wind is moderating.* **6** act as moderator; preside (over). **1-3** *adj.,* **4** *n.,* **5,6** *v.,* **mod er at ed, mod er at ing. —mod/er ate ly,** *adv.* **—mod/er ate- ness,** *n.*

d

Check the sentence(s) in which a form of **moderate** is used correctly.

___**a.** New York has a moderate climate.
___**b.** Both candidates are moderates.
___**c.** Music gives me a moderate amount of pleasure.
___**d.** The sheriff came to moderate the mood of the mob.

241c

cir cu lar (sėr'kyə lər) **1** round like a circle: *The full moon has a circular shape.* **2** moving in a circle; going around a circle: *A merry-go-round makes a circular trip.* **3** of a circle. **4** letter, notice, or advertisement sent to each of a number of people. **1-3** *adj.,* **4** *n.* —**cir/cu lar ly,** *adv.*

c

Which of the following could be described as **circular?**

___**a.** a saucer   ___**d.** a dime
___**b.** a crescent moon   ___**e.** a football
___**c.** a doughnut   ___**f.** a piece of pie

217a

re fer (ri fėr')

Arlene had to **refer** to her program several times during the first few minutes of the game.

b, d,
e, f

Write a definition or synonym:

192a

fa vor a ble (fā' vər ə bəl)

At our hotel we met a mountain climber named Hal Hansen. He planned to start up the mountain on the following day, if the weather was **favorable**.

a, d

Write a definition or synonym:

167b

A special ceremony on May 10, 1869, marked the completion of the first railroad that stretched across the continent. An **appropriate** symbol was the gold spike that was driven into the last tie.

A synonym for **appropriate** is:

___**a.** necessary
___**b.** interesting
___**c.** suitable
___**d.** attractive

10b

"I thought you couldn't care less about seeing a space shot," said Ted, smiling with **amusement**. "You sure looked funny with your eyes the size of saucers and your mouth wide open!"

Amusement means:
___a. causing amazement
___b. being made to admire
___c. being made to laugh
___d. making fun of someone

35b

"One of our policies is to print only facts," said the editor. "That's why we won't print a **gossip** column based on idle talk about people and speculation about their affairs."

Gossip means:
___a. current events
___b. advice to people
___c. talk about people
___d. comics and cartoons

60c

b

ad mi ra tion (ad/mə rā/shən), **1** a feeling of wonder, pleasure, and approval: *The beauty of the performance excited admiration.* **2** person or thing that is admired: *a spectacular painting that was the admiration of all who viewed it. n.*

For which of the following things might one show **admiration**?
___a. a forest fire ___d. mud pies
___b. a daring rescue ___e. homework
___c. beautiful music ___f. a new suit

85c

b

com e dy (kom/ə dē), **1** an amusing play or show having a happy ending. **2** an amusing happening. *n., pl.* **com e-dies.**

ANALOGY comedy : laughter :: onions :
___a. fruit
___b. knife
___c. garden
___d. dinner
___e. tears

a, b

LESSON 12

Human Beings vs. the Sea

People who know how to sail often feel superior to people who can only run a motorboat. Driving a motorboat takes skill, of course. But it takes a different kind of skill to handle a sailboat. When you sail, you challenge the forces of nature, such as the wind and the waves, and you use these forces to overcome nature itself. When you operate a motorboat, or "stinkpotter" as sailing people call them, you let a piece of machinery do all the work. Or so the sailors say.

136a

1. a
2. b

hearse (hėrs)

A **hearse** slowed us down.

Write a definition or synonym:

167a

ap pro pri ate (*adj.* ə prō′ prē it; *v.* ə prō′ prē āt)

It was thought that a ceremony would be **appropriate** when the two lines were joined.

Write a definition or synonym:

a, d

191c

viv id (viv′id), **1** strikingly bright; strong and clear; brilliant: *Dandelions are a vivid yellow.* **2** full of life; lively: *a vivid description of an experience.* **3** strong and distinct: *I have a vivid memory of the fire.* **4** very active or intense: *a vivid imagination. adj.* [*Vivid* is from Latin *vividus,* which comes from *vivere,* meaning "to live."] —**viv′id ly,** *adv.* —**viv′id ness,** *n.*

Check the sentence(s) in which a form of **vivid** is used correctly.

___**a.** Tropical birds are famous for their vivid colors.

___**b.** The old woman was so near death that she was almost vivid.

___**c.** The man was so vivid that he could easily lift a 200-pound weight.

___**d.** She described the scene vividly.

c

216c

sta di um (stā′dē əm), an oval, U-shaped, or round building, usually without a roof. Tiers of seats for spectators surround the playing field. *n.*

Which of the following might be likely to take place in a **stadium?**

___**a.** ballet dance   ___**d.** football game

___**b.** rodeo   ___**e.** circus

___**c.** study period   ___**f.** World Series game

d

241b

The house was set far back from the street, so it was a long walk to the house. The **circular** driveway curved around from the main gate to the house and then back to the gate.

Circular means:

___**a.** having beautiful scenery

___**b.** long and uninteresting

___**c.** round like a circle

___**d.** surrounded by trees

266b

The size of the jackal is **moderate.** It is larger than some dogs but smaller than many.

Moderate means:

___**a.** small

___**b.** usual

___**c.** pleasant

___**d.** not extreme

291a

pic tur esque (pik′ chə resk′)

As the three sailors looked back at the cottages and the busy dock, Bill remarked on the **picturesque** scene. Uncle Robert agreed. Then he stopped suddenly. Bill had been addressing Stephanie, not him.

Write a definition or synonym:

10c

c

a muse ment (ə myüz′mənt), **1** condition of being amused: *The boy's amusement was so great that we all had to laugh with him.* **2** anything that amuses, such as an entertainment or sport. *n.*

ANALOGY **amusement : smile ::**
 __**a.** carnival : clown
 __**b.** entertainment : movies
 __**c.** enjoyment : fun
 __**d.** sport : study
 __**e.** worry : frown

35c

c

gos sip (gos′ip), **1** idle talk, not always true, about other people and their private affairs. **2** repeat what one knows or hears about other people and their private affairs. **3** person who gossips a good deal. 1,3 *n.*, 2 *v.* —**gos′sip-er,** *n.* —**gos′sip ing ly,** *adv.*

ANALOGY **gossip : busybody :: teacher :**
 __**a.** length
 __**b.** instructor
 __**c.** honesty
 __**d.** purpose
 __**e.** column

LESSON 7

b, c, f

Second Sight

For months after the accident in which I lost my sight, I was afraid of everything. I wouldn't even try to get out of bed to take care of myself. And the more I had to be waited on, the more unpleasant life seemed. Then my parents decided to send me to a school for the blind. There, I was given something to replace the vision I had lost—a guide dog named Diana.

86a

e

ro mance (*n.* rō mans′ *or* rō′ mans; *v.* rō mans′)

There was only one problem: the play wasn't intended as a comedy at all. It was supposed to be a **romance**.

Write a definition or synonym:

111a

un like (un līk′)

Sailboats are **unlike** powerboats in many ways.

Write a definition or synonym:

136b

A **hearse** passed us. It was followed by a long procession of cars with their lights on. It was not respectful to break into the funeral procession, so we waited until all 64 cars passed.

Hearse means:
 __**a.** police officer who rides a motorcycle
 __**b.** auto for carrying a dead person
 __**c.** carriage or wagon drawn by a horse
 __**d.** a long line of cars

166c

con stant (kon′stənt), **1** going on without stopping: *Three days of constant rain caused flooding.* **2** continually happening; repeated again and again: *a constant ticking sound.* **3** always the same; not changing: *The ship held a constant course due north.* **4** thing that is always the same; value or quantity that does not change: *The speed of light is an important constant in physics.* **5** faithful; loyal; steadfast: *a constant friend.* 1-3,5 *adj.,* 4 *n.*

Check the sentence(s) in which **constant** is used correctly.
__a. The boat was in constant use.
__b. The constant light of the flashing sign caught our eyes.
__c. We saw it constant.
__d. He was my constant companion.

191b

Many things that I saw during the trip have faded from my mind. I still have a **vivid** picture of the Matterhorn, however, rising in majesty over the little town of Zermatt.

Vivid means:
__a. blurred
__b. beautiful
__c. distinct
__d. souvenir

216b

Although it was still early, the **stadium** was crowded. Everyone expected a good football game.

A **stadium** is:
__a. a large field for athletics
__b. a large vehicle for transportation
__c. a large gymnasium for athletics
__d. space and seats for athletic games

241a

cir cu lar (sér′ kū lər)

We walked up a **circular** driveway to a mansion on Maple Avenue. No one from school had ever been here before. I was sure we would get something interesting.

Write a definition or synonym:

266a

mod er ate (*adj., n.* mod′ ər it; *v.* mod′ ə rāt′)

The jackal is an animal of **moderate** size.

Write a definition or synonym:

LESSON 30 | Romance at Sea

Stephanie met Bill Coolidge last summer during vacation. They made definite plans to meet again this year. Sure enough, Bill was waiting for Stephanie when she ran down to the dock. There was only one problem: Stephanie's Uncle Robert had sailed across the bay just to take Stephanie sailing. She couldn't say no without hurting Uncle Robert's feelings, but she couldn't just sail away from Bill. Uncle Robert temporarily solved the problem by inviting Bill to come along.

e

LESSON Mission to Colombia

The United States government has long understood the need to improve relations with the people of other countries. Back in 1960 plans were made to establish a volunteer force of Americans who would live and work in foreign nations for two years at a time. This idea is still going strong.

b

36a

va ri e ty (və rī′ ə tē)

There is great **variety** in the jobs to be done in a newsroom.

Write a definition or synonym:

61a

dis po si tion (dis′ pə zish′ ən)

During the first few days, I learned about Diana's **disposition**.

Write a definition or synonym:

86b

"We're going to have two people who are truly in love," Linda had said. "They talk poetry to each other. They have beautiful, noble feelings all the time. That's all you need to make a successful **romance**."

Romance means:
___**a.** funny story
___**b.** comedy
___**c.** love story
___**d.** mystery

111b

The shape of a sailboat is **unlike** that of a powerboat. Sailboats are long, low, and sleek, while powerboats are wider, higher, and shorter.

Unlike means:
___**a.** similar to
___**b.** opposite
___**c.** smaller
___**d.** not like

b

136c

hearse (hėrs), automobile, carriage, etc., for carrying a coffin to the cemetery. *n.* —**hearse′like′**, *adj.*

A **hearse** is different from other vehicles. Check the adjective(s) below that describe a **hearse**.
___**a.** colorful   ___**d.** small
___**b.** long   ___**e.** depressing
___**c.** black   ___**f.** sweet

166b

The Chinese laborers in the West were in **constant** competition with the Irishmen, Scots, and Germans working on the eastern end. They never let up in their race toward the meeting place in Utah.

Constant means:
___**a.** never-ending
___**b.** once in a while
___**c.** recent
___**d.** a small amount

191a

viv id (viv′ id)

I have a **vivid** picture in my mind of my first glimpse of the Matterhorn.

Write a definition or synonym:

216a

a, b, e

sta di um (stā′ dē əm)

Saturday afternoon we went to the **stadium** right after lunch.

Write a definition or synonym:

LESSON 25 | A White Elephant

b, d, e

Each year, our school puts on a "White Elephant" sale. People with interesting old things that they have no use for give them to us. We sell them if we can and give the money to the Boy Scouts and the Girl Scouts. The idea is that there is a good use for everything. You just have to put the right things in the hands of the right people. Last weekend, my friend Bette Lou and I went out to collect "white elephants." We got much more than we bargained for.

265c

c

a rouse (ə rouz′), **1** stir to action; excite: *The mystery story aroused my imagination.* **2** awaken: *The barking dog aroused me from my sleep. v.,* **a roused, a rous ing.** —**a rous′a ble,** *adj.* —**a rous′er,** *n.*

Which of the following might possibly **arouse** someone?
___**a.** the sun ___**d.** a storm
___**b.** an attack ___**e.** a vicious crime
___**c.** an alarm clock ___**f.** a horse

290c

d

broad cast (brôd′kast′), **1** something sent out by radio or television; a radio or television program of speech, music, etc. **2** send out by radio or television. **3** a sending out by radio or television. **4** sent out by radio or television. **5** scatter or spread widely. **6** a scattering or spreading far and wide. **7** scattered widely. **8** over a wide surface. 1,3,6 *n.*, 2,5 *v.*, **broad cast** or **broad cast ed** for 2, **broad cast** for 5, **broad cast ing;** 4,7 *adj.*, 8 *adv.* —**broad′cast′er,** *n.* (Definition adapted)

ANALOGY broadcast : TV show :: publish :
___**a.** spelling
___**b.** ideas
___**c.** audience
___**d.** book
___**e.** printing

64

11a

corps (kôr)

The group of volunteers was called the Peace **Corps**.

Write a definition or synonym:

36b

Some reporters were assigned to cover city news, some world news, and some business news. Still others wrote up sports events and features. There was great **variety** in the subjects to be covered.

A synonym for **variety** is:
___**a.** amount
___**b.** difficulty
___**c.** difference
___**d.** interest

61b

When we went walking, Diana never became upset when I made a wrong turn. She would calmly nudge me along the correct path. I began to realize how important it was for a guide dog to have a calm **disposition**.

Disposition means:
___**a.** training
___**b.** cleverness
___**c.** nature
___**d.** skill

86c

c

ro mance (rō mans′ or rō′mans for 1-6; rō mans′ for 7,8), **1** a love story. **2** story of adventure. **3** story or poem telling of heroes. **4** real happenings that are like stories of heroes and are full of love, excitement, or noble deeds. **5** a love affair. **6** a made-up story. **7** make up stories. **8** think or talk in a romantic way. 1-6 n., 7,8 v., **ro manced, ro manc ing. —ro manc′er,** n. **(Definition adapted)**

1. Which of the following appeared in a famous **romance**?
   ___**a.** Tom, Dick, and Harry ___**c.** Romeo and Juliet
   ___**b.** Puss-in-Boots ___**d.** Pinocchio
2. In which of the following would you be most likely to find a **romance**?
   ___**a.** the newspaper ___**c.** a fairy tale
   ___**b.** the dictionary

111c

d

un like (un līk′), **1** not like; different: *The two problems are quite unlike.* **2** different from: *to act unlike others.* 1 adj., 2 prep.

Check the sentence(s) in which **unlike** is used correctly.
___**a.** The twins were as unlike as two peas in a pod.
___**b.** This hat is unlike your other one.
___**c.** The food in India is unlike that in the United States.
___**d.** Why do you unlike him?

137a

b, c, e

sub urb (sub′ érb′)

After two hours, we reached the **suburb** where our relatives live.

Write a definition or synonym:

166a

a, c

con stant (kon′ stənt)

There was **constant** competition between the two groups of builders.

Write a definition or synonym:

LESSON

1. b, c, e
2. b

20

The White Tower

In Switzerland there is a mountain called the Matterhorn. Because it rises almost straight up on all sides, and is nearly always covered with snow, it is often called "The White Tower." I had my first glimpse of this beautiful mountain last year during a trip to Europe.

215c

d

an ni ver sar y (an′ə vėr′sər ē), **1** the yearly return of a special date: *Your birthday is an anniversary you like to have remembered.* **2** celebration of the yearly return of a special date. **3** having to do with an anniversary: *an anniversary dinner.* 1,2 *n., pl.* **an ni ver sa ries;** 3 *adj.*

Which of the following are **anniversaries**?
__a. one's birthday   __d. the first warm day
__b. April Fool's Day   __e. date of a marriage
__c. day of report cards __f. a rainy day

240c

c

co me di an (kə mē′dē ən), **1** actor in comedies. **2** person who amuses others with funny talk and actions. *n.*

A **comedian** does *not* need:
__a. wit
__b. money
__c. a sense of humor
__d. good looks
__e. a stage

265b

Although many people may visit a jackal in a zoo, few remain very long. The odor is overpowering and quickly **arouses** disgust.

A synonym for **arouse** is:
__a. anger
__b. frighten
__c. awaken
__d. change

290b

People received their news by newspaper or by mail in 1860. There was no way for election results to be **broadcast**.

Broadcast means:
__a. read from a paper
__b. report in a loud voice
__c. tell in detail
__d. send out by radio or television

11b

Thousands of young men and women were eager to join the **Corps**. Married couples and older people were accepted too. Those who were finally selected were well qualified for the work they would be doing. I was proud to belong to the Peace **Corps**.

Corps means:
- __**a.** a social club
- __**b.** a journey
- __**c.** an organized group of people
- __**d.** a dead body

36c

c

va ri e ty (və rī′ə tē), **1** lack of sameness; difference or change: *Variety is the spice of life.* **2** number of different kinds: *This shop has a variety of toys.* **3** kind or sort: *Which varieties of cake did you buy?* **4** division of a species. *n., pl.* **va ri e ties.**

Check the sentence(s) in which **variety** is used correctly.
- __**a.** I have a variety of the same books.
- __**b.** John had a variety doing his homework.
- __**c.** There was a variety of flowers in the garden.
- __**d.** The play had a variety of characters.

61c

c

dis po si tion (dis′pə zish′ən), **1** one's habitual ways of acting toward others or of thinking about things; nature: *His cheerful disposition made him popular.* **2** tendency; inclination: *A quarrelsome person has a disposition to start trouble.* **3** a putting in a certain order or position; arrangement: *The teacher changed the disposition of the desks in the classroom.* **4** a disposing; settlement: *What disposition did the court make of the case?* **5** disposal: *She had a large sum of money at her disposition. n.*

Check the sentence(s) in which **disposition** is used correctly.
- __**a.** The generals discussed the disposition of the troops.
- __**b.** The disposition of the case was announced by the lawyer.
- __**c.** I am in a very difficult disposition.
- __**d.** Her disposition to debate made her a good lawyer.

87a

1. c
2. c

vil lain (vil′ ən)

Linda herself wrote most of the lines to be spoken by the **villain**.

Write a definition or synonym:

112a

b, c

in struc tion (in struk′ shən)

People who want to sail should first get some **instruction**.

Write a definition or synonym:

137b

We turned off the turnpike and drove through the winding streets of the **suburb** until we reached my cousin's house.

Suburb means:
- __**a.** boundary of a city
- __**b.** town near a large city
- __**c.** small village in the country
- __**d.** place where many people live

290a

broad cast (brôd′ kast′)

In those days election results were not **broadcast** as they are today.

a, c

Write a definition or synonym:

265a

a rouse (ə rouz′)

The jackal, one kind of wild dog, **arouses** disgust in most people.

a, b, d

Write a definition or synonym:

240b

Sure enough, about half the audience burst out laughing each time Manny drove the bad guys out of town, screaming and holding their ears. They thought the funniest part came when Manny turned up the volume again and destroyed the town. Many might not have intended it, but everyone thought he was a real **comedian!**

A **comedian** is a person who:
__a. makes mistakes
__b. writes plays
__c. makes people laugh
__d. is successful

215b

That day the college was one hundred years old. It was customary to have a small ceremony every year on the college's **anniversary**.

An **anniversary** is:
__a. a celebration
__b. something that happens only once
__c. something that happens every one hundred years
__d. the yearly return of a date

190c

in dus tri ous (in dus′trē əs), working hard and steadily; diligent: *An industrious student usually has good grades.* —in dus′tri ous ly, *adv.* —in dus′tri ous ness, *n.*

b

1. Which of the following are usually thought of as **industrious?**
__a. lion   __d. dog
__b. bee   __e. beaver
__c. ant   __f. deer

2. Which of the following was (were) **industrious?**
__a. Pinocchio
__b. the Seven Dwarfs
__c. Goldilocks

165c

so lu tion (sə lü′shən), 1 the solving of a problem: *That problem was hard; its solution required many hours.* 2 explanation: *The police are seeking a solution of the crime.* 3 mixture formed by combining a solid, liquid, or gas with another solid, liquid, or gas so that the molecules of each are evenly distributed: *Salt and water form a solution.* 4 the forming of such a mixture: *the solution of a gas in a liquid.* 5 (in mathematics) any number which makes an open sentence a true statement, *n.*

d

Check the sentence(s) in which **solution** is used correctly.
__a. The scientist made a solution of several substances.
__b. As the soldiers carried the flag by, we all made a solution to it.
__c. Her solution of the problem won her a prize.

11c

c

corps (kôr), **1** group of soldiers, trained for specialized military service: *the Medical Corps, the Signal Corps.* **2** a military unit made up of two or more divisions plus supporting troops, usually commanded by a lieutenant general. It is smaller than an army. **3** group of people with special training, organized for working together: *A large hospital has a corps of nurses. n., pl.* corps (kôrz).

Check the sentence(s) in which **corps** is used correctly.

___**a.** The corps of robins flew south.
___**b.** A corps of firemen paraded past the mayor.
___**c.** I found the corps of a snake on the trail.
___**d.** "Of corps you may go," said Mary.

37a

c, d

a ware (ə wer′ *or* ə wâr′)

As soon as we walked through the door to the pressroom, we were **aware** of the size and power of the printing presses.

Write a definition or synonym:

62a

a, b, d

cau tious (kô′ shəs)

At the beginning I was very **cautious**.

Write a definition or synonym:

87b

Linda also insisted that the **villain** be dressed in black clothing and wear a thin mustache. "The **villain** must do terrible things all the time," Linda had said. So Linda had the bad guy tie the hero to the railroad tracks. There was only one problem—the script didn't mention trains or railroad tracks.

Villain means:
___**a.** a wild animal
___**b.** a wicked person
___**c.** a person who imitates
___**d.** a soldier

112b

Through **instruction** they will learn about the wind, how to handle the sails, how to care for the boat, and many other things.

Instruction means:
___**a.** understanding
___**b.** equipment
___**c.** teaching
___**d.** speech

137c

b

sub urb (sub′ėrb′), district, town, or village just outside or near a city: *Many people who work in the city live in the suburbs. n.*

Check the sentence(s) in which a form of **suburb** is used correctly.

___**a.** Most farmers live in the suburbs.
___**b.** Many people who work in the city live in the suburbs.
___**c.** The suburbs in the inner city are crowded.
___**d.** There are no neighbors for miles in our suburb.

165b

The builders in California did not have enough men to work on their end of the railroad. Their **solution** of this problem was to import thousands of Chinese laborers.

A **solution** is:
___**a.** a method
___**b.** an opinion
___**c.** a cause
___**d.** a solving

190b

Each day I was surprised to see the many changes the **industrious** workmen had made. It would not be long before the job was completed.

A synonym for **industrious** is:
___**a.** well-paid
___**b.** hard-working
___**c.** commercial
___**d.** strong

215a

b, c, e

an ni ver sar y (an′ ə vēr′ sər ē)

Arlene told me that the college was celebrating its **anniversary**.

Write a definition or synonym:

240a

b, e, f

co me di an (kə mē′ dē ən)

Although the critics were less than complimentary about Manny's film, his fans claimed that their hero proved he was a great **comedian** as well as a great singer.

Write a definition or synonym:

264c

d

muz zle (muz′əl), **1** the nose, mouth, and jaws of a four-footed animal. **2** a cover or cage of straps or wires to put over the head and mouth of an animal to keep it from biting or eating. **3** put such a muzzle on. **4** compel (a person) to keep silent about something: *Fear that they might betray friends muzzled them.* **5** the open front part of the barrel of a gun, pistol, etc. 1,2,5 *n.*, 3,4 *v.*, **muz zled, muz zling. —muz′zler,** *n.*

Check the sentence(s) in which a form of **muzzle** is used correctly.
___**a.** I felt the muzzle of the gun against my shoulder.
___**b.** The gangsters muzzled the witness by threatening her life.
___**c.** The dog wagged his muzzle happily.
___**d.** The vicious dog had to be muzzled.

289c

d

poll (pōl), **1** a voting; collection of votes: *The class had a poll to decide where it would have its picnic.* **2** number of votes cast. **3 polls,** *pl.* place where votes are cast and counted: *The polls will be open all day.* **4** list of persons, especially a list of voters. **5** receive at an election: *The mayor polled a record vote.* **6** vote; cast (a vote). **7** take or register the votes of: *to poll a village.* **8** a survey of public opinion concerning a particular subject. **9** the head, especially the part of it on which the hair grows. 1-4,8,9 *n.*, 5-7 *v.* —**poll′er,** *n.*

When would a **poll** be likely?
___**a.** in deciding how to spend club funds
___**b.** when going fishing
___**c.** in electing a mayor
___**d.** when hiring a worker
___**e.** at a spelling contest
___**f.** in finding out who was correct

12a

b

prep a ra tion (prep′ ə rā′ shən)

I was assigned to Colombia. Before departing, we spent many months in **preparation**.

Write a definition or synonym:

37b

The large newspaper presses were very noisy. It was hard to be **aware** of anything except the noise. I didn't even know that the foreman of the pressroom was near us until he tapped my shoulder.

Aware means:
___**a.** thoughtful
___**b.** conscious
___**c.** afraid
___**d.** alert

62b

When Diana led me into the city streets for the first time, I was very nervous. Before long, I learned how **cautious** Diana was. I walked along the busy streets without worrying at all.

Cautious means:
___**a.** frightened
___**b.** quiet
___**c.** quick
___**d.** careful

87c

b

vil lain (vil′ən), **1** a very wicked person: *The villain stole the money and cast the blame on a friend.* **2** villein. *n.*

Which of the following would be likely to be a **villain**?
___**a.** a criminal ___**d.** a harsh landlord
___**b.** an angel ___**e.** a kind woman
___**c.** a witch ___**f.** an elf

112c

c

in struc tion (in struk′shən), **1** a teaching or educating. **2** knowledge or teaching given; lesson. **3 instructions,** *pl.* directions; orders. *n.*

ANALOGY instruction : instructor ::
___**a.** race : prize
___**b.** water : plant
___**c.** knowledge : ignorance
___**d.** farming : farm
___**e.** invention : inventor

138a

b

bash ful (bash′ fəl)

My cousins have some **bashful** friends.

Write a definition or synonym:

289b

When the results of the **poll** were announced, it turned out that Abraham Lincoln had won.

A **poll** is:
___ **a.** a campaign
___ **b.** a list of questions
___ **c.** a debate
___ **d.** a voting

264b

He was trying to tame the dog. He thought that the **muzzle** would break him of the habit of snapping at people.

A **muzzle** is:
___ **a.** a rope or chain
___ **b.** the front part of the body
___ **c.** a whip
___ **d.** a cover of straps or wires

d

239c

dis may (dis mā'), 1 sudden loss of courage because of fear of danger: *They were filled with dismay when they saw the rattlesnake.* 2 trouble greatly; make afraid: *The thought that she might fail the test dismayed her.* 1 n., 2 v. —**dis-may'ing ly**, adv.

A person who is **dismayed** would be:
___ **a.** unyielding ___ **d.** relaxed
___ **b.** nervous ___ **e.** upset
___ **c.** composed ___ **f.** frightened

c

214c

de vel op ment (di vel'əp mənt), 1 process of developing; growth: *The doctor followed the child's development closely.* 2 outcome; result; new event: *The newspaper described the latest developments in the elections.* 3 a working out in greater and greater detail: *The development of plans for a flight to the moon took many years.* 4 group of similar houses or apartment buildings built on open land or in place of old buildings. n.

Check the phrase(s) in which **development** is used correctly.
___ **a.** development of the dinner
___ **b.** development of his plans
___ **c.** development of the battle
___ **d.** development of the cookies
___ **e.** development of the story
___ **f.** development of lightning

b, c, e, g

190a

in dus tri ous (in dus' trē əs)

Soon the **industrious** workmen would make the property beautiful again.

Write a definition or synonym:

a, c

165a

so lu tion (sə lü' shən)

A pressing labor problem in the West required a quick **solution**.

Write a definition or synonym:

12b

Our **preparation** included training in foreign language and learning about the history and customs of Colombia. A part of the **preparation** that no one enjoyed was the series of shots we were given to protect us from disease.

Preparation means:
__a. an education
__b. a chore
__c. a making ready
__d. condition

37c

b

a ware (ə wer′ *or* ə war′), having knowledge; realizing; conscious: *I was too sleepy to be aware how cold it was. She was not aware of her danger. adj.* —**a ware′ness,** *n.*

ANALOGY aware : unknowing :: awake :
__a. dreaming
__b. tired
__c. asleep
__d. alert
__e. understanding

62c

d

cau tious (kô′shəs), very careful; taking care to be safe; not taking chances: *A cautious driver never drives too fast. adj.* —**cau′tious ly,** *adv.* —**cau′tious ness,** *n.*

Check the time(s) when one would be **cautious.**
__a. crossing a street   __d. using a knife
__b. lighting a fire   __e. singing a song
__c. reading a book

88a

a, c, d

vow (vou)

Linda directed the villain to twirl his mustache when he heard the young lovers, each making a **vow** to the other.

Write a definition or synonym:

113a

e

ac quire (ə kwīr′)

At this time, much knowledge of the sea will be **acquired.**

Write a definition or synonym:

138b

Every time we visit, these **bashful** girls sit in a corner and giggle. They won't even talk to my brother and me.

A synonym for **bashful** is:
__a. tired
__b. little
__c. shy
__d. sad

289a

poll (pōl)

Finally the day came for the great national poll.

Write a definition or synonym:

a, d, e

264a

muz zle (muz' əl)

A man I knew put a muzzle on a wild dog.

Write a definition or synonym:

b, c, e

239b

At first, the cruel sheriff thought that by covering both ears with his hands, he could escape with only a bad headache. To his growing **dismay,** he learned that Manny's music could pass through flesh and bone. Soon, the victim lost his last shred of bravery and began to cry and roll around on the floor.

Dismay means:

__a. make curious
__b. make angry
__c. surprise
__d. make afraid

214b

The **development** of the school from a small college to a great university had taken place rapidly. Many buildings had to be added, for the number of students had almost doubled.

Development means:

__a. foundation
__b. start
__c. growth
__d. change

189c

cav ern (kav'ərn), a large cave. *n.*

a

Which of the following might you find in a cavern?

__a. wildflowers __e. cave explorers
__b. bats __f. furniture
__c. bears __g. bones
__d. a tree

164c

con flict (kon'flikt *for 1,2;* kən flikt' *for 3*), 1 a fight or struggle, especially a long one: *The UN General Assembly discussed the conflict in the Middle East.* 2 active opposition of persons or ideas: *A conflict of opinion arose over the need for a new highway.* 3 be actively opposed; differ in thought or action; clash: *The testimony of the witnesses conflicted on whether the robber had blond or dark hair.* 1,2 *n.,* 3 *v.*

a

Check the sentence(s) in which a form of **conflict** is used correctly.

__a. What he said conflicted with the facts.
__b. The fish conflicted to free himself from the hook.
__c. The conflict over slavery was one cause of the Civil War.

12c

c

prep a ra tion (prep′ə rā′shən), **1** a preparing; making ready: *I sharpened the knife in preparation for carving the meat.* **2** a being ready. **3** thing done to get ready: *He made thorough preparations for his trip by carefully planning which routes to take.* **4** a specially made medicine or food or mixture of any kind. *n.*

1. Which of the following events might call for **preparation**?
   __**a.** a play   __**c.** a party
   __**b.** reading a book   __**d.** sunrise
2. Which of the following is a **preparation**?
   __**a.** air   __**c.** seawater
   __**b.** cough syrup

38a

c

sub scribe (səb skrīb′)

When we were leaving, we told the publisher we would like to **subscribe** to the *Daily Observer*.

Write a definition or synonym:

63a

a, b, d

re ly (ri lī′)

Soon I knew I could **rely** on her.

Write a definition or synonym:

88b

The lovers were supposed to swear that they would love each other forever and a day, until the end of time. When the villain heard this solemn **vow**, he was supposed to rush onto the stage, twirling his mustache.

Vow means:
__**a.** wish
__**b.** suggestion
__**c.** promise
__**d.** order

113b

Beginners usually start with no knowledge of the sea and its ways. During sailing courses, however, they are able to **acquire** information as well as a feeling of confidence.

Acquire means:
__**a.** get by one's own efforts
__**b.** get by a stroke of luck
__**c.** get in great quantity
__**d.** learn by imitating

138c

c

bash ful (bash′fəl), uneasy in the presence of strangers; easily embarrassed; shy: *The child was too bashful to greet us. adj.* —**bash′ful ly,** *adv.* —**bash′ful ness,** *n.*

ANALOGY **bashful : bold :: beautiful :**
__**a.** mild
__**b.** honest
__**c.** handsome
__**d.** pleasant
__**e.** ugly

164b

Conflicts with the Indians occurred all along the way. Railroad workers often had to stop their labors, pick up guns, and defend themselves.

A synonym for **conflict** is:
__a. fight
__b. conference
__c. meeting
__d. race

189b

The original owner had dug a **cavern** behind the cellar. There he concealed slaves who had escaped on the "Underground Railroad" just before the Civil War. A small door in the cellar wall served as the entrance to this hidden space.

A **cavern** is:
__a. a cave
__b. a house
__c. a basement
__d. a cell

214a

e

de vel op ment (di vel′ əp mənt)

As we walked across campus, Arlene insisted on telling me about the **development** of the college.

Write a definition or synonym:

239a

a, c,
d, e

dis may (dis mā′)

Then something happened that **dismayed** the sheriff greatly. Manny hit the first few notes of his "Song of Destruction."

Write a definition or synonym:

263c

a

ac knowl edge (ak nol′ij), **1** admit to be true: *to acknowledge one's own faults.* **2** recognize the authority or claims of: *Parliament acknowledged Elizabeth I to be queen.* **3** make known that one has received (a service, favor, gift, message, etc.): *I acknowledged her letter at once. v.,* **ac knowl edged, ac knowl edg ing. —ac knowl′edge- a ble,** *adj.* **—ac knowl′edged ly,** *adv.* **—ac knowl′edg- er,** *n.*

Which of the following might one **acknowledge**?
__a. a sentence   __d. a trip
__b. a compliment   __e. an invitation
__c. a mistake   __f. an inventor

288c

d

in sure (in shúr′), **1** arrange payment of money in case of loss, accident, or death by paying a certain amount of money at intervals. An insurance company will insure your property, person, or life. **2** make safe from financial loss by paying money to an insurance company: *She insured her car against accident, theft, and fire. v.,* **in- sured, in sur ing.**

Check the sentence(s) in which a form of **insure** is used correctly.
__a. Good study habits will insure good grades.
__b. I am insure as to what is right.
__c. He is a very insure child.
__d. Brushing your teeth will insure fewer cavities.
__e. We are insured against fire and theft.

13a

de part (di pärt′)

We were scheduled to **depart** at 4:00 P.M. When we landed, we would be high in the Andes Mountains of Colombia.

Write a definition or synonym:

38b

Mr. Sandoval thought we could learn a lot by reading the *Daily Observer* each day. He suggested that we **subscribe** to it. We decided to pay the cost out of our class treasury.

Subscribe means:
__a. to become a staff member of an organization
__b. to pay money to receive a newspaper or magazine
__c. to study a newspaper or magazine
__d. to promise to sell a newspaper or magazine

63b

I could **rely** on Diana to lead me anywhere a sighted person would walk. If she stopped, I knew there must be danger ahead.

A synonym for **rely** is:
__a. ask
__b. depend
__c. expect
__d. defend

88c

c

vow (vou), **1** a solemn promise: *a vow of secrecy, marriage vows.* **2** a promise made to God: *a nun's vows.* **3** make a vow: *I vowed never to leave home again.* **4** make a vow to do, give, get, etc.: *vow revenge.* 1,2 *n.,* 3,4 *v.* —**vow′er,** *n.* —**vow′less,** *adj.*

Check the sentence(s) in which **vow** is used correctly.
__a. I made a vow to be true to my country.
__b. The dancer made a vow to the audience.
__c. The hero made a vow that he would marry the young maid.
__d. The vow was made in good faith.
__e. She made a vow that we all leave the room.

113c

a

ac quire (ə kwīr′), come to have; get as one's own; obtain: *I acquired the money for college by working summers.* *v.,* **ac quired, ac quir ing.** —**ac quir′a ble,** *adj.*

Check the sentence(s) in which **acquired** is used correctly.
__a. He has acquired a large stamp collection.
__b. I acquired whether Mrs. Jones was there or not.
__c. She acquired the measles.
__d. Have you acquired the golden badge yet?

139a

e

af fec tion ate (ə fek′ shə nit)

After many hours of visiting, we said an **affectionate** farewell.

Write a definition or synonym:

288b

Generally, people in the North believed with Lincoln that the nation could not be half-slave and half-free. They thought that if Lincoln won, the unity of the country would be **insured**.

Insure means:

___a. prevent
___b. hope for
___c. plan for
___d. make sure

263b

Some people who love dogs don't like to think that dogs are descended from wolves. However, when they study the history of the various breeds, they have to **acknowledge** the fact that dogs and wolves have enough in common to be related.

Acknowledge means:

___a. admit to be true
___b. deny the truth of
___c. find hard to believe
___d. like to think

238c

c

flour ish (flėr′ish), 1 grow or develop with vigor; do well; thrive: *Your radishes are flourishing. Our newspaper business flourished.* 2 wave in the air: *She flourished the letter when she saw us.* 3 a waving about: *He removed his hat with a flourish.* 4 an extra ornament or curve in handwriting. 5 a showy trill or passage in music: *a flourish of trumpets.* 6 a showy display: *The agent showed us about the house with much flourish.* 1,2 v., 3–6 n., pl. **flour ish es.** [*Flourish* can be traced back to Latin *florem,* meaning "a flower."] —**flour′ish ing ly,** *adv.*

Check the sentence(s) in which a form of **flourish** is used correctly.

___a. Flowers flourish in that sunny climate.
___b. He flourished the water down the drain.
___c. She played a flourish on her flute.
___d. The waiter served the meal with a flourish.
___e. The teacher does not appreciate the flourishes in my signature.

213c

a

chef (shef), 1 a head cook: *the chef of a large restaurant.* 2 any cook. *n.*

ANALOGY chef : mushroom ::

___a. carpenter : paint
___b. bank teller : candy
___c. guard : money
___d. secretary : gun
___e. baker : flour

189a

cav ern (kav′ərn)

One laborer discovered a **cavern** in the cellar.

Write a definition or synonym:

164a

b, c

con flict (n. kon′ flikt; v. kən flikt′)

The builders of the railroad soon had another **conflict** on their hands.

Write a definition or synonym:

13b

The plane was late so we didn't **depart** until 4:30 in the afternoon. As soon as we left the ground, a few of the group began to feel homesick. Most of us looked forward to two years of living in the mountains and working with the Colombian people.

A synonym for **depart** is:
__a. meet
__b. hike
__c. arrive
__d. leave

38c

b

sub scribe (səb skrīb′), **1** promise to give or pay (a sum of money): *She subscribed $15 to the hospital fund.* **2** promise to accept and pay for: *We subscribe to a few magazines.* **3** write (one's name) at the end of a document, etc.; show one's consent or approval by signing: *The men who subscribed to the Declaration of Independence are now famous.* **4** give one's consent or approval; agree: *She does not subscribe to my opinion. v.,* **sub scribed, sub scrib ing.**

Check the sentence(s) in which a form of **subscribe** is used correctly.
__a. She will not subscribe to the governor's plan.
__b. The company had its name subscribed on its trucks.
__c. They subscribed a large sum for the new church building.
__d. The note subscribed where the treasure was hidden.

63c

b

re ly (ri lī′), depend or trust: *Rely on your own efforts. I relied upon your promise. v.,* **re lied, re ly ing.**

Check the sentence(s) in which a form of **rely** is used correctly.
__a. Do not rely on your beauty to get good grades.
__b. I can't rely on him for help.
__c. He relied on the furniture.
__d. She relied to the question.

89a

a, c, d

di a logue or **di a log** (dī′ ə lôg)

Unfortunately, the villain forgot his cue. The young lovers had to keep repeating their **dialogue** while the audience laughed and laughed.

Write a definition or synonym:

114a

a, d

ap prov al (ə prü′ vəl)

When beginners learn the names of all the equipment and the parts of a sailboat, they are certain to win their instructor's **approval**.

Write a definition or synonym:

139b

We all kissed my uncle. My mother kissed my aunt. My aunt kissed my father. Everybody was so **affectionate** that I could hardly stand it.

A synonym for **affectionate** is:
__a. big
__b. friendly
__c. hearty
__d. loving

163c

c

hub (hub), **1** the central part of a wheel. **2** center of interest, activity, etc.: *London is the hub of English life. n.*

Check the sentence(s) in which **hub** can be correctly substituted for the word in italics.
— **a.** She placed the bowl in the *center* of the table.
— **b.** The *center* of the wheel was a disk of metal.
— **c.** Washington, D.C. is the *center* of political life in the U.S.A.

188c

d

re mark a ble (ri märˊkə bəl), worthy of notice; unusual: *He has a remarkable memory. adj.* —**re markˊa ble- ness,** *n.*

ANALOGY **remarkable : ordinary ::**
— **a.** breakable : broken
— **b.** reckless : careless
— **c.** famous : unknown
— **d.** breathless : angry
— **e.** noticeable : quiet

213b

"Arlene is a friend of the **chef's**," her roommate explained. "She can walk into the kitchen for snacks between meals."

A synonym for **chef** is:
— **a.** cook
— **b.** dean
— **c.** president
— **d.** policeman

238b

Before starting to play his guitar, Manny **flourished** it with a dramatic wave of his arm. This gave the sheriff and the audience plenty of time to prepare for what was going to happen next.

Flourish means:
— **a.** throw away
— **b.** beat on something
— **c.** wave in the air
— **d.** put away

263a

e

ac knowl edge (ak nolˊ ij)

Scientists **acknowledge** the wolf as the ancestor of the dog.

Write a definition or synonym:

288a

a, c, d

in sure (in shu̇rˊ)

Both men worked hard to **insure** their success in the election.

Write a definition or synonym:

13c

d

de part (di pärt′), **1** go away; leave: *Your flight departs at 6:15.* **2** turn away; change: *She departed from her usual way of working.* *v.*

Check the sentence(s) in which a form of **depart** is used correctly.

___**a.** She arrived in the morning and departed in the afternoon.
___**b.** We departed before the snowball.
___**c.** The ship departed from the dock.
___**d.** He will depart down the street.

39a

a, c

cash ier (ka shir′)

We visited the business office and talked to the **cashier**.

Write a definition or synonym:

64a

a, b

fetch (fech)

Diana loved to **fetch** things for me, just as if she were a regular pet.

Write a definition or synonym:

89b

The hero said, "I'll love you forever and ever." Then the heroine said, "Until the end of time." At that point, the villain was supposed to rush out and twirl his mustache.

When the villain failed to appear, the hero and heroine kept repeating their last two lines of **dialogue**.

A synonym for **dialogue** is:

___**a.** laughter
___**b.** conversation
___**c.** action
___**d.** comedy

114b

A sailing instructor appreciates a student who learns to think and talk like a sailor. This kind of student is likely to progress quickly and receive even more **approval**.

Approval means:

___**a.** careful opinion
___**b.** favorable opinion
___**c.** impression of
___**d.** strong feeling

139c

d

af fec tion ate (ə fek′shə nit), showing or having affection; loving and tender: *an affectionate letter, an affectionate farewell.* *adj.* —**af fec′tion ate ly,** *adv.*

ANALOGY affectionate : friend ::
___**a.** polite : clerk
___**b.** careful : mother
___**c.** calm : criminal
___**d.** nervous : mailman
___**e.** cold : enemy

81

163b

Omaha had been chosen because it was the **hub** of trade between East and West. People traveling from all directions would usually pass through it.

Hub means:
___**a.** beginning
___**b.** cause
___**c.** center
___**d.** passage

188b

It was built one hundred years ago, and its owners had used it as a place to hide runaway slaves. Their courage was **remarkable**, since a Confederate Army camp had been near the house.

A synonym for **remarkable** is:
___**a.** rapid
___**b.** sad
___**c.** sudden
___**d.** unusual

213a

a, c, d

chef (shef)

Arlene seemed to have gained a bit of weight. I mentioned this in my usual considerate way. She agreed and said it was the fault of the college **chef**.

Write a definition or synonym:

238a

c, d

flour ish (flér′ ish)

Manny rode down the dusty street, dragging his electric cord behind him and **flourishing** his deadly guitar.

Write a definition or synonym:

262c

c

hu mane (hyü mān′), not cruel or brutal; kind; merciful: *We believe in the humane treatment of prisoners. adj.* —**hu mane′ly,** *adv.* —**hu mane′ness,** *n.*

ANALOGY humane : civilized :: careful :
___**a.** calm
___**b.** reckless
___**c.** hot-tempered
___**d.** silly
___**e.** thoughtful

287c

b

crit i cal (krit′ə kəl), **1** inclined to find fault or disapprove: *a critical disposition.* **2** coming from one who is skilled as a critic: *a critical judgment, critical essays.* **3** of a crisis; being important to the outcome of a situation: *Help arrived at the critical moment.* **4** full of danger or difficulty: *The patient was in a critical condition. adj.* —**crit′i cal ly,** *adv.* —**crit′i cal ness,** *n.*

Check the sentence(s) in which **critical** is used correctly.
___**a.** At the critical moment of the battle, help arrived.
___**b.** They played a critical game of Ping-Pong.
___**c.** Metal is a critical material in wartime.
___**d.** Her critical manner made her very unpopular.

14a

vis i ble (viz′ ə bəl)

The first streaks of dawn were **visible** as we neared Colombia.

Write a definition or synonym:

a, c

39b

The **cashier** in the *Daily Observer*'s business office was glad to take our money. Evidently not many people paid for six months in advance.

Cashier means:
__a. a person who has charge of taking advertisements
__b. a person who has charge of money
__c. a person who types
__d. a person who sells newspapers

64b

When I woke up in the morning I would call Diana and she would **fetch** my slippers, no matter where I had left them.

Fetch means:
__a. pitch
__b. buy
__c. pick
__d. get

89c

di a logue or **di a log** (dī′ə lôg), **1** conversation: *Two actors had a dialogue in the middle of the stage.* **2** conversation written out: *That book has a good plot and much clever dialogue. n.* [*Dialogue* is from Greek *dialogos*, which comes from *dia-*, meaning "between," and *logos*, meaning "speech."]

Which of the following would be able to take part in a **dialogue**?
__a. man and beast   __d. boy and girl
__b. husband and wife __e. hat and coat
__c. cat and dog

b

114c

ap prov al (ə prü′vəl), **1** favorable opinion; approving; praise: *We all like others to show approval of what we do.* **2** permission; consent: *I have my parents' approval to go on the trip. n.*
on approval, so that the customer can inspect the item and decide whether to buy or return it: *We bought the television set on approval.*

1. Which of the following would be likely to cause a teacher to express **approval**?
__a. high marks   __d. a project well done
__b. talking in class __e. good behavior
__c. running in the hall __f. dirty feet
2. If a store sent you a book **on approval**, you could *not*:
__a. have it free __b. read it __c. send it back

b

140a

mo not o nous (mə not′ n əs)

When it got dark, we started the **monotonous** drive home.

Write a definition or synonym:

287b

Douglas opposed Lincoln for President of the United States in 1860. This was a **critical** year for the country, as it was on the brink of war. Many people felt their whole way of life depended on this election.

Critical means:

__**a.** evil
__**b.** full of danger
__**c.** very exciting
__**d.** sad

262b

Many people feel that with **humane** treatment, a wild dog could eventually be tamed. It is my opinion that this is not likely with most wild dogs. Once a dog is used to the harsh treatment of nature, no amount of kindness will change him.

Humane means:

__**a.** healthful
__**b.** human
__**c.** kind
__**d.** expensive

---

b

237c

ty rant (tī'rənt), **1** person who uses power cruelly or unjustly. **2** a cruel or unjust ruler. **3** an absolute ruler, as in ancient Greece. Some tyrants of Greek cities were mild and just rulers. *n.*

Check the sentences that are true statements.

__**a.** All the Greek tyrants were cruel rulers.
__**b.** All tyrants are kings.
__**c.** An unjust king is a tyrant.
__**d.** A cruel employer can be a tyrant.

---

c

212c

dor mi to ry (dôr'mə tôr'ē), **1** a building with many rooms for sleeping in. Many colleges have dormitories for students whose homes are elsewhere. **2** room for sleeping that has several beds. *n., pl.* **dor mi to ries.**

A **dormitory** would be likely to contain which of the following?

__**a.** beds   __**d.** showers
__**b.** classrooms   __**e.** auditoriums
__**c.** people   __**f.** animals

---

c, e, d,
b, a

188a

re mark a ble (ri mär' kə bəl)

The house had a **remarkable** history.

Write a definition or synonym:

---

a, c

163a

hub (hub)

Omaha was the **hub** of the Middle West.

Write a definition or synonym:

14b

When it was time to land, it was light enough so that the entire airport was **visible**. It looked like all of the other airports I had ever seen.

Visible means:
__a. close
__b. easily available
__c. can be seen
__d. on the ground

39c

b

cash ier[1] (ka shir'), person who has charge of money in a bank, or in any business. *n.* [*Cashier*[1] comes from French *caissier*, meaning "treasurer," and can be traced back to Latin *capsa*, meaning "box."]

cash ier[2] (ka shir'), dismiss from service; discharge in disgrace: *The dishonest officer was deprived of his rank and cashiered. v.* [*Cashier*[2] comes from Dutch *casseren*, and can be traced back to Latin *quassare*, meaning "to shatter, shake violently."]

Where would you be likely to find a **cashier**?
__a. in a restaurant
__b. in a movie theater
__c. in a model house
__d. in a hospital nursery
__e. on a farm

64c

d

fetch (fech), **1** go and get; bring: *Please fetch me my glasses.* **2** cause to come; succeed in bringing: *Her call fetched me at once.* **3** be sold for: *These eggs will fetch a good price. v.* —**fetch'er**, *n.*

fetch ing (fech'ing), attractive; charming: *a fetching new outfit. adj.* —**fetch'ing ly**, *adv.*

Check the sentence(s) in which a form of **fetch** is used correctly.
__a. When did you fetch the groceries?
__b. They fetched him from the jail.
__c. The girl fetched in the river.
__d. I fetched the groceries in the store.
__e. She has a fetching smile.

90a

b, d

fre quent (*adj.* frē' kwent; *v.* fri kwent')

In spite of all the mistakes, there was **frequent** applause from those watching the play.

Write a definition or synonym:

115a

1. a, d, e
2. a

bea con (bē' kən)

Beacons are a great help to sailors.

Write a definition or synonym:

140b

The journey home seemed to take forever. All we saw were thousands of headlights hour after hour. As my father backed the car into our garage he said, "Now, that was a pleasant change from the daily routine!" My brother and I just groaned. Nothing could have been more **monotonous**.

Monotonous means:
__a. not varying
__b. ever changing
__c. very restful
__d. quiet

85

c, d, e

287a

crit i cal (krit' a kal)

Then came the critical election of 1860.

Write a definition or synonym:

---

a, e, f

262a

hu mane (hyū mān)

In this country, tame dogs usually receive **humane treatment.**

Write a definition or synonym:

237b

The sheriff was so mean and had bossed the town for so long that he deserved to be deafened and driven mad by Manny's music. So may it be with all **tyrants!**

A **tyrant** is:

—a. a victim
—b. a cruel ruler
—c. a king
—d. an old man

212b

Arlene's room was on the third floor of the **dormitory.** It was nice enough, but she had to share the room with two other students. When she finally introduced me to one of her roommates, she described me as her "kid sister"!

A **dormitory** is:

—a. a building for studying
—b. a large hotel
—c. a building with sleeping rooms
—d. a building for gym

---

a

187c

ba sic (bā'sik). 1 forming the basis; fundamental: *Addition, subtraction, multiplication, and division are the basic processes of arithmetic.* 2 (in chemistry) being, having the properties of, or containing a base; alkaline. *adj.*

Each item at the left is a **basic** part of an item at the right. Match the items.

a. flour	—	music
b. cream	—	omelet
c. notes	—	steel
d. iron	—	butter
e. egg	—	bread

---

c

162c

as sure (a shur'). 1 tell positively: *They assured me that they would be on time.* 2 make sure or certain: convince: *She assured herself that the bridge was safe before she crossed it.* 3 make safe; secure: *Victory was assured when the team scored in the final seconds of the game.* 4 give or restore confidence to; encourage: *The father assured his frightened son.* v., as sured, as sur ing. —as sur'er, as- su'ror, n.

In which of the following is something or someone being **assured?**

—a. A doctor tells a patient that the operation is not dangerous.
—b. Travelers at a crossroad do not know which way to go.
—c. A home buyer takes out fire insurance.

14c

vis i ble (viz′ə bəl), **1** that can be seen: *The shore was barely visible through the fog.* **2** readily evident; apparent; obvious: *The vagrant had no visible means of support. adj.*

1. Which of the following is (are) likely to be **visible**?
   __**a.** heat   __**c.** wind
   __**b.** cold   __**d.** smoke
2. Which of the following is (are) **visible** on a clear night?
   __**a.** the sun   __**c.** a light
   __**b.** the stars

40a

a, b

com pe ti tion (kom′ pə tish′ ən)

Back at school there was great **competition** for jobs on the school newspaper.

Write a definition or synonym:

65a

a, b, e

be grudge (bi gruj′)

Diana never seemed to **begrudge** the time she spent with me.

Write a definition or synonym:

90b

The audience clapped so often that the assembly period ended before the play was over. From the **frequent** applause, you would have thought Linda's romance was the best comedy ever seen in our school assembly. But Linda didn't agree. She vowed never to direct a play again.

Frequent means:
__**a.** occurring steadily
__**b.** occurring often
__**c.** making a loud noise
__**d.** given gladly

115b

The **beacon** is usually located where there are dangerous rocks or reefs under the water. It can be seen for long distances at night.

Beacon means:
__**a.** a light on water
__**b.** a guiding light
__**c.** a type of boat
__**d.** a weather vane

140c

a

mo not o nous (mə not′n əs), **1** continuing in the same tone: *She spoke in a monotonous voice.* **2** not varying; without change: *monotonous food.* **3** wearying because of its sameness: *monotonous work. adj.* —**mo not′o nous ly,** *adv.* —**mo not′o nous ness,** *n.*

Which of the following might be **monotonous**?
__**a.** driving through the desert
__**b.** visiting an amusement park
__**c.** playing baseball
__**d.** singing the same song over and over
__**e.** Christmas Eve
__**f.** eating ice cream everyday

286c

pub·lic·i·ty (pub lis'a tē) **1** public notice: *the publicity that actors desire.* **2** measures used for getting, or the process of getting, public notice: *I worked on the publici-ty for the concert.* **3** articles, announcements, etc., used to get public notice: *write publicity.* n.

b

Which of the following would *not* desire **publicity?**

___ **a.** a TV star   ___ **d.** a failing student
___ **b.** an opera singer   ___ **e.** a criminal
___ **c.** a baby   ___ **f.** a politician

261c

re·li·a·ble (ri lī'a bal), worthy of trust; able to be depend-ed on: *Send her to the bank for the money; she is reliable.* adj. **—re·li'a·ble·ness,** n.

d

Which of the following can be considered **reliable?**

___ **a.** school records   ___ **d.** spies
___ **b.** rumors   ___ **e.** dictionaries
___ **c.** criminals   ___ **f.** a trained mechanic

237a

ty·rant (tī' rant)

In Manny's movie, the sheriff was nothing but a petty **tyrant.**

b, d

Write a definition or synonym:

212a

dor·mi·to·ry (dôr' ma tôr' ē)

Arlene took me straight to her **dormitory.** She didn't seem interested in introducing me to the dozens of guys who were walking around the campus.

b, d

Write a definition or synonym:

187b

The laborers said that the **basic** structure of the house was so strong and well preserved that it could last another hundred years. The foundation and walls were unusually sturdy.

Basic means:

___ **a.** forming the base
___ **b.** easily done
___ **c.** very difficult
___ **d.** having to do with basements

162b

In 1863 President Lincoln signed a bill fixing Omaha as the eastern end of the railroad. Now those who had wanted the railroad were **assured** that it would come about.

Assure means:

___ **a.** make probable
___ **b.** make possible
___ **c.** make certain
___ **d.** make real

15a

ap prox i mate ly (ə prok′ sə mit lē)

It would take **approximately** two days to reach our village.

Write a definition or synonym:

40b

Mr. Sandoval suggested that we hold a **competition** to see which student would become the first editor of ths school paper. We each wrote a sample and the class voted on the one they liked best. The winner and the new editor turned out to be … me! And the sample is the one you've just finished reading!

A **competition** is:
___**a.** an argument
___**b.** a settlement
___**c.** a contest
___**d.** an agreement

65b

Diana was by my side all day, always calm and friendly. She did not seem to **begrudge** the time she had to wait while I talked with people, attended classes, or went swimming.

Begrudge means:
___**a.** be unhappy
___**b.** be happy to give something
___**c.** be unwilling to give something
___**d.** be wise about something

90c

b

fre quent (frē′kwənt *for 1;* fri kwent′ *for 2*), **1** happening often, near together, or every little while: *In my part of the country storms are frequent in March.* **2** go to often; be often in: *Frogs frequent ponds, streams, and marshes.* 1 *adj.,* 2 *v.* —**fre quent′er,** *n.*

1. Which of the following means about the same as **frequent**?
 ___**a.** not at all
 ___**b.** every little while
 ___**c.** once in a while
2. If you **frequent** your friend's house, you:
 ___**a.** pass by it often
 ___**b.** visit it often
 ___**c.** know where it is

115c

b

bea con (bē′kən), **1** fire or light used as a signal to guide or warn. **2** marker, signal light, or radio station that guides aircraft and ships through fogs, storms, etc. **3** a tall tower for a signal; lighthouse. *n.*

ANALOGY **beacon : guide :: arrow :**
 ___**a.** point
 ___**b.** warn
 ___**c.** stop
 ___**d.** slow
 ___**e.** control

LESSON 15 | The Sky Hawks

In the early days of flying, many pilots earned their livings by flying in air shows. They would perform dangerous loops, spins, and rolls to entertain the crowds below. These pioneers of the air led exciting but dangerous lives.

162a

c

as sure (ə shür′)

Finally the building of a railroad to California was **assured**.

Write a definition or synonym:

187a

a, b

ba sic (bā′ sik)

The **basic** structure of the main house was excellent.

Write a definition or synonym:

211c

b

cam pus (kam′pəs), grounds of a college, university, or school. *n., pl.* **cam pus es.**

Which of the following signs would probably be found on a college **campus**?
__**a.** Do Not Disturb
__**b.** No Parking
__**c.** Quiet
__**d.** Keep Off the Grass
__**e.** Hospital Zone
__**f.** Ring Front Bell

236c

a

as sas si nate (ə sas′n āt), murder by a sudden or secret attack: *President Kennedy was assassinated in 1963. v.,* **as sas si nat ed, as sas si nat ing. —as sas′si na′tor,** *n.*

Who was **assassinated**?
__**a.** Franklin D. Roosevelt
__**b.** Abraham Lincoln
__**c.** George Washington
__**d.** Martin Luther King

261b

Although the tame dogs we have in our homes are quite **reliable**, one can never tell what a wild dog will do next. As a matter of fact, it can be quite dangerous to trust a wild dog.

Reliable means:
__**a.** healthy
__**b.** honest
__**c.** generous
__**d.** worthy of trust

286b

Even though Lincoln lost the 1858 election, the **publicity** he received was important to his career. Before he lost the election, Lincoln was hardly known outside the state of Illinois. Afterwards, the whole country had heard of him.

Publicity means:
__**a.** public duty
__**b.** public notice
__**c.** violent disagreement
__**d.** confusion

15b

Since the village was eighty miles away in the mountains, we were told it would take **approximately** two days to reach it. If the weather was bad, it might take longer.

Approximately means:
__**a.** exactly
__**b.** just
__**c.** about
__**d.** possibly

40c

c

com pe ti tion (kom′pə tish′ən), **1** a trying hard to win or gain something wanted by others; rivalry: *competition among stores for customers. There is competition in many games.* **2** contest: *She won first place in the swimming competition. n.*

Check the situation(s) in which there might be **competition**.
__**a.** in a relay race
__**b.** reading a book
__**c.** in a fishing contest
__**d.** in an election for class president
__**e.** hiking

65c

c

be grudge (bi gruj′), **1** give or allow (something) unwillingly; grudge: *She is so stingy that she begrudges her dog a bone.* **2** envy: *The neighbors begrudge us our swimming pool. v.,* **be grudged, be grudg ing.**

Check the sentence(s) in which a form of **begrudge** is used correctly.
__**a.** I am happy to begrudge her the book.
__**b.** He is so busy he begrudges the time he must spend eating.
__**c.** She begrudged that I meant to cry.
__**d.** I am so begrudged that I lost my bracelet.

LESSON 10 The World of Modern Art

1. b
2. b

The Guggenheim Museum in New York City is one of the most unusual buildings in the world. It is shaped like a huge, white doughnut. Inside, the paintings are hung along a ramp that hugs the building's walls. There is nothing but open space in the middle of the art museum. We took the elevator to the top and walked down along the ramp, studying each picture, until we got back to the ground floor.

116a

buoy (boi *or* bü′ ē)

Buoys may be seen in many harbors.

Write a definition or synonym:

141a

aer o nau tics (er′ ə nô′ tiks *or* ar′ ə nô′ tiks)

The **aeronautics** industry got its start in the 1920s.

Write a definition or synonym:

286a

pub lic i ty (pub lis′ ə tē)

The election of 1858 received much **publicity.**

Write a definition or synonym:

261a

re li a ble (ri lī′ a bəl)

Most people think that all dogs are **reliable.**

Write a definition or synonym:

236b

Many claimed that the only way to get rid of a truly bad guy is to **assassinate** him. Instead of doing the job with a gun or a bow and arrow, Manny plugged in his guitar and turned up the volume until it was louder than the human ear can stand.

Assassinate means:

___ **a.** murder
___ **b.** persuade
___ **c.** frighten
___ **d.** threaten

211b

The wide walks were shaded by tall trees. The **campus** looked green and beautiful in the fall sun.

Campus means:

___ **a.** play area of a school
___ **b.** grounds of a school
___ **c.** field for outdoor gym
___ **d.** entrance of a school

186c

struc ture (struk′chər), 1 something built; a building or construction. Dams, bridges, and tunnels are very large structures; apartment houses are smaller structures. 2 anything composed of parts arranged together: *The human body is a wonderful structure.* 3 manner of building; way parts are put together; construction: *The structure of the school was excellent.* 4 arrangement of parts, elements, etc.: *the structure of a molecule, the structure of a flower, sentence structure, the structure of a story.* 5 make into a structure; build; construct: *to structure a sentence.* 1-4 n., 5 v.

Check the sentence(s) in which **structure** is used correctly.

___ **a.** The scientist described the structure of an atom.
___ **b.** The structure of the bridge was a marvelous combination of beauty and strength.
___ **c.** She composed a new structure for the piano.
___ **d.** The hostess made an attractive structure of flowers in the vase.

161c

crit i cize (krit′ə sīz), 1 find fault with; disapprove of; blame: *Do not criticize him until you know all the circumstances.* 2 judge or speak as a critic: *The editor criticized the author's new novel, comparing it with her last one.* v., crit i cized, crit i ciz ing. —crit′i ciz′er, n.

ANALOGY criticize : praise :: question :

___ **a.** demand
___ **b.** repeat
___ **c.** answer
___ **d.** relax
___ **e.** approve

15c

c

ap prox i mate ly (ə prok′sə mit lē), by a close estimate; nearly; about: *We are approximately 200 miles from home. adv.*

Check the phrase(s) in which **approximately** is used correctly.
__**a.** approximately three feet
__**b.** approximately sweet
__**c.** approximately dead
__**d.** approximately six years

---

a, c, d

LESSON 5 | Suzanne in Spain

My older sister Suzanne took a trip to Spain last summer. Before she left, she promised us all that she would write once a week and tell us everything that happened. My parents had checked her travel plans carefully, so they knew what hotel she was staying in each day and what city was next on her list of places to visit. Still, they couldn't help but worry about her.

66a

b

in ten tion (in ten′ shən)

Only once did I misunderstand Diana's **intentions**.

Write a definition or synonym:

91a

at trac tion (ə trak′ shən)

The Guggenheim Museum of Art is a great **attraction**.

Write a definition or synonym:

116b

The colors of the **buoys** are important. A red **buoy** floating on the surface means the boat should stay to the left of the signal when returning to the harbor. Many buoys have bells so that they can guide a boat at night or in heavy fog.

A **buoy** is:
__**a.** a noisemaker
__**b.** a floating marker
__**c.** a small boat
__**d.** a member of the Coast Guard

141b

The **aeronautics** industry was not yet well developed. Only a few models of planes were made. One of them was a small, two-winged airplane which could be flown almost as easily as a car could be driven.

Aeronautics means:
__**a.** living in the air
__**b.** operating machinery
__**c.** study of the air
__**d.** science of aircraft

285c

o ver come (ō'vər kum'), 1 get the better of; win the victory over; conquer; defeat: *overcome an enemy, overcome difficulties.* 2 make weak or helpless: *Weariness overcame her and she fell asleep.* v., o ver came, o ver come, o ver com ing.

ANALOGY overcome : defeat ::

_a. conquer : lose
_b. battle : escape
_c. prevail : consume
_d. aid : assist
_e. subscribe : demand

a

LESSON 27 | Wild Dogs and Their Relatives

Many people think of the dog as a friendly animal and the ideal family pet. However, these dog lovers probably have never seen a pack of wild dogs on the hunt! I bet they never studied such wild beasts as wolves, jackals, foxes, and coyotes—all near-relatives of the dog. If they knew more about a dog's family background, they might learn to see their beloved pet with new eyes.

a, b

236a

as sas si nate (ə sas' n āt)

The high point of the picture came when everyone learned how Manny was going to confront the crooked sheriff: Manny planned to **assassinate** him with a blast of rock music!

Write a definition or synonym:

a, c, f

211a

cam pus (kam' pəs)

The college **campus** was beautiful.

Write a definition or synonym:

186b

There was an old stable on the property. This **structure**, unlike the others on the property, was so badly rotted that it would have to be torn down.

A synonym for **structure** is:

_a. home
_b. addition
_c. model
_d. building

161b

They **criticized** the plan for many reasons. Some were against it because it would cost too much money. Others felt it would be too difficult to build a railroad through the mountains.

Criticize means:

_a. ignore
_b. discuss
_c. be in favor of
_d. find fault with

16a

a, d

knap sack (nap′ sak′)

We got our **knapsacks** out of our baggage.

Write a definition or synonym:

41a

a broad (ə brôd′)

This was Suzanne's first trip **abroad**.

Write a definition or synonym:

66b

She jumped on me suddenly, pushing me backwards. Of course, I wondered why. For a second, I thought Diana's **intention** was to be playful. Then I heard the screech of automobile brakes. I realized that Diana had knocked me down in order to save my life!

A synonym for **intention** is:
__**a.** hope
__**b.** dream
__**c.** pleasure
__**d.** plan

91b

Because it is so different, it is an **attraction** for thousands of visitors every year. People from all parts of the world come to see this unusual building.

Attraction means:
__**a.** thing that makes people laugh
__**b.** thing that fascinates people
__**c.** thing that makes noise
__**d.** thing that bothers people

116c

b

buoy (boi *or* bü′ē), **1** a floating object anchored on the water to warn against hidden rocks or shallows or to show the safe part of a channel. **2** life buoy. *n.*
buoy up, 1 hold up; keep from sinking: *Life jackets buoyed them up until rescuers came.* **2** support or encourage: *Hope can buoy you up, even when something goes wrong.*

1. Check the phrase(s) in which **buoy** is used correctly.
__**a.** whistle buoy
__**b.** water buoy
__**c.** cold buoy
__**d.** life buoy
2. To **buoy** your courage means the same as:
__**a.** to be brave
__**b.** to find courage
__**c.** to look for courage

141c

d

aer o nau tics (er′ə nô′tiks *or* ar′ə nô′tiks), science or art having to do with the design, manufacture, and operation of aircraft. *n.*

Who of the following would be likely to be interested in **aeronautics**?
__**a.** arithmetic teacher   __**d.** horse trainer
__**b.** airline pilot   __**e.** baggage collector
__**c.** airplane mechanic   __**f.** ticket agent

161a

crit i cize (krit′ ə sīz)

During the 1850s many Americans talked of building a railroad to the West. There were some who **criticized** the plan.

Write a definition or synonym:

186a

a, c, f

struc ture (struk′ chər)

One **structure** would be torn down.

Write a definition or synonym:

LESSON

b, c

22

College Girl

Arlene and I have always been close friends, even though she never lets me forget she is my older sister. Last fall, when she went away to college, I missed having her around the house. I did what any lonely person would do. I wrote her a letter telling her that I was coming up to visit during the big football weekend. Arlene wasn't exactly delighted, but she did meet my train at the station.

235c

b

dra mat ic (drə mat′ik), **1** of drama; having to do with plays: *a dramatic actor.* **2** seeming like a play; full of action or feeling; exciting: *the dramatic reunion of a family separated during wartime.* **3** striking; impressive: *a dramatic use of color. adj.* —**dra mat′i cal ly,** *adv.*

Check the phrase(s) in which **dramatic** is used correctly
___**a.** dramatic pose
___**b.** dramatic television set
___**c.** dramatic scene
___**d.** dramatic kitten
___**e.** dramatic sleep
___**f.** dramatic lessons

260c

b

bo nus (bō′nəs), something extra, given in addition to what is due: *The company gave each worker a vacation bonus. n., pl.* **bo nus es.** [*Bonus* comes from Latin *bonus,* meaning "good."]

In which of the following does someone receive a **bonus**?
___**a.** That store gives a free box of soap when you buy a washing machine.
___**b.** A man gets an extra week's pay at Christmas.
___**c.** A child finds a penny on the street.

285b

As expected, Douglas did **overcome** Abe Lincoln in 1858. Although Lincoln was quite disappointed, he decided to continue his political career.

Overcome means:
___**a.** defeat
___**b.** equal
___**c.** surprise
___**d.** catch up to

16b

We loaded our **knapsacks** with the food and clothing we would need for the trip. The rest of our baggage would be carried to the village by pack mule.

A **knapsack** is:
___**a.** a litter bag
___**b.** a bag for carrying things on the back
___**c.** a bag of heavy brown paper
___**d.** a suitcase

41b

Although Suzanne had traveled about the United States a great deal, she knew she would find many strange and different experiences when she went **abroad**.

Abroad means:
___**a.** in Europe
___**b.** outside one's country
___**c.** on the ocean
___**d.** in a strange place

66c

d

in ten tion (in ten′shən), **1** an intending; purpose; design; plan: *If I hurt your feelings, it was without intention. Your intention to help is good, but first you must learn how.* **2** meaning. *n.*

Check the sentence(s) in which a form of **intention** is used correctly.
___**a.** His intention was to finish the project quickly.
___**b.** We must plan our intentions for the car.
___**c.** Her intention is to attend law school.
___**d.** Do not intention your paragraphs.

91c

b

at trac tion (ə trak′shən), **1** thing that delights or attracts people: *The elephants were the chief attraction at the circus.* **2** act or power of attracting: *the attraction of a magnet for iron filings. Sports have no attraction for him. n.*

Which of the following would be likely to be an **attraction**?
___**a.** oatmeal ___**d.** a magician
___**b.** the city dump ___**e.** a movie star
___**c.** a pile of laundry ___**f.** a rock concert

117a

1. a, d
2. a

boul der (bōl′ dər)

Sometimes a buoy marks the location of an underwater **boulder**.

Write a definition or synonym:

142a

b, c

aer i al (er′ ē əl *or* ar′ ē əl)

In stunt flying, the pilots often made **aerial** loops.

Write a definition or synonym:

LESSON 17

The Iron Trail

c

One of the most interesting stories in the history of the Old West is the story of the Union Pacific Railroad. It was the first line to connect East with West, stretching all the way from Omaha, Nebraska to Sacramento, California.

185c

b

la·bor·er (lā′bər ər), 1 person who does work that requires strength rather than skill or training. 2 worker, n.

Where would a **laborer** be least likely to work?

__a. at a tea party   __d. in a field
__b. in a factory   __e. in an orchard
__c. at a dog show   __f. in a college classroom

210c

d

re·solve (ri zolv′), 1 make up one's mind; determine; decide: *I resolved to do better work in the future.* 2 thing determined on; thing decided: *He kept his resolve to do better.* 3 firmness in carrying out a purpose: determination: *Helen Keller was a woman of resolve.* 4 decide by vote: *It was resolved that our class should have a picnic.* 5 answer and explain; solve: *The letter resolved our doubts.* 6 break into parts; break up: *Some chemical compounds resolve when heated.* 7 change: *The assembly resolved itself into a committee.* 1,4-7 *v.*

Resolve applies to which of the following?

__a. putting parts together to make a whole
__b. making up one's mind to study harder
__c. explaining a puzzling situation
__d. being uncertain which route to follow

235b

Many wanted the scene to be so **dramatic** that the audience would be sitting on the edge of their seats, breathless with suspense.

Another word for **dramatic** is:

__a. concluding
__b. exciting
__c. frightening
__d. unreal

260b

Strange as it may seem, I had so much fun learning about Daniel Boone that I forgot I was writing the paper for a grade. When I was given an A, I considered it a **bonus.** Doing a good job was enough of a reward.

A **bonus** is:

__a. a surprise
__b. something extra
__c. something good
__d. pleasure trip

285a

b, d

o ver come (ō′ vər kum′)

In 1858 it appeared that Lincoln would not be able to **overcome** his opponent in the race for a seat in the U.S. Senate. Senator Douglas was clearly the choice of the people.

Write a definition or synonym:

16c

b

knap sack (nap′sak′), a canvas or leather bag with two shoulder straps, used for carrying clothes, equipment, etc., on the back; rucksack. *n.*

ANALOGY **knapsack : back :: shoes :**
 __a. necktie
 __b. clothing
 __c. feet
 __d. bag
 __e. legs

41c

b

a broad (ə brôd′), **1** outside one's country; to a foreign land: *I am going abroad next year to study in Italy.* **2** out in the open air; outdoors: *My grandfather walks abroad only on warm days.* **3** far and wide; widely: *The news that the circus was coming quickly spread abroad.* **4** going around; in motion; current: *A rumor is abroad that school will close.* 1-3 *adv.,* 4 *adj.*

1. If you lived in Chicago, which of the following places would be **abroad**?
 __a. New York __d. London
 __b. Paris __e. California
 __c. Dallas __f. Madrid
2. Which of the following would be **abroad** at night?
 __a. a newspaper __c. a robin
 __b. an owl __d. a bat

67a

a, c

bruise (brüz)

During this incident, I received a number of **bruises**.

Write a definition or synonym:

92a

d, e, f

sit u at ed (sich′ ü ā′ tid)

The museum is conveniently **situated**.

Write a definition or synonym:

117b

If a sailor runs a boat into an underwater **boulder**, the boat could sink in a matter of minutes.

Boulder means:
 __a. pile of stones
 __b. wooden pier
 __c. sandpile
 __d. large rock

142b

Sometimes **aerial** loops were dangerous because the plane could easily go out of control. As the plane turned round and round, the crowd below held its breath. One pilot set a record of over a thousand loops in one flight.

Aerial means having to do with:
 __a. sight
 __b. weather
 __c. the air
 __d. the ground

160c

b

im pris on (im priz′n), **1** put in prison; keep in prison. **2** confine closely; restrain. *v.*

ANALOGY **imprison : release ::**
___**a.** attack : destroy
___**b.** confine : punish
___**c.** fasten : loosen
___**d.** run : retreat
___**e.** catch : break

185b

Many **laborers** started to work on the house. They began to remove broken windows and floors. Others started on the grounds around the house. The grounds were to become the beautiful gardens they had been a hundred years ago.

A synonym for **laborer** is:
___**a.** designer
___**b.** worker
___**c.** person
___**d.** manufacturer

210b

I also **resolved** to visit Egypt someday and see the Great Pyramids for myself. When I wrote Anouk about this decision, I realized something else. I made up my mind that becoming friends does not depend on age or sex or country of national origin.

Resolve means:
___**a.** dream
___**b.** think
___**c.** wish
___**d.** determine

235a

a, b,
d, e

dra mat ic (drə mat′ ik)

One of the most **dramatic** scenes in the movie occurs when Manny and the other good guys meet the crooked sheriff and his gang for a showdown.

Write a definition or synonym:

260a

a, c

bo nus (bō′ nəs)

The excellent grade I received for my paper almost seemed like a **bonus.**

Write a definition or synonym:

284c

c

a chieve ment (ə chēv′mənt), **1** thing achieved; some plan or action carried out with courage or unusual ability; accomplishment; feat: *Landing astronauts on the moon was a great achievement.* **2** an achieving: *the achievement of success. n.*

Which of the following can be considered **achievements?**
___**a.** swatting a mosquito
___**b.** building a rocket
___**c.** beginning a long walk
___**d.** winning a scholarship
___**e.** eating dinner

17a

c

con sume (kən süm′)

We each **consumed** a thick steak before we left the airport.

Write a definition or synonym:

42a

1. b, d,
f
2. b, d

in de pend ent (in′ di pen′ dənt)

The days passed and we received no cards or letters from Suzanne. Father kept reminding us that Suzanne had always been a very **independent** girl.

Write a definition or synonym:

67b

I couldn't see the **bruises,** of course. But I could certainly feel them! It took more than a week before I could get around with comfort again.

Bruise means:
__**a.** bump on the head
__**b.** cut that bleeds a lot
__**c.** injury that changes color of the skin
__**d.** hole that breaks the skin

92b

We learned that it is **situated** on Fifth Avenue, near Central Park. We could take a bus that would stop only one block east of its location.

Situated means:
__**a.** built
__**b.** located
__**c.** visited
__**d.** planned

117c

d

boul der (bōl′dər), a large rock, rounded or worn by the action of water and weather. *n.*

ANALOGY boulder : pebble :: tree :
__**a.** sky
__**b.** bush
__**c.** weather
__**d.** birds
__**e.** branch

142c

c

aer i al (er′ē əl *or* ar′ē əl), **1** a long wire or set of wires or rods used in television or radio for sending out or receiving electromagnetic waves; antenna. **2** having to do with or done by aircraft: *aerial photography, aerial warfare.* **3** growing in air instead of in soil. **4** of or having to do with the air; atmospheric: *aerial currents.* 1 *n.,* 2-4 *adj.* —**aer′i al ly,** *adv.*

Check the phrase(s) in which **aerial** is used correctly.
__**a.** aerial earthworm   __**d.** aerial games
__**b.** aerial house   __**e.** television aerial
__**c.** aerial pencil   __**f.** aerial stunt

160b

When the jury decided that Herman was guilty as charged, Judge Wayne cleared her throat. Then she sentenced Herman to be **imprisoned** for one year for his crime. Many of us felt that Herman should have been sent to jail for ten years, but we were glad he had been found guilty.

Imprison means:

__a. give punishment
__b. put in prison
__c. release from prison
__d. teach a lesson

185a

d

la bor er (lā' bar ar)

Write a definition or synonym:

In less than a week, **laborers** came to the site.

210a

b, c

re solve (ri zolv')

Write a definition or synonym:

I **resolved** to write to Anouk that night.

234c

c

com pose (kəm pōz'), 1 make up; form: *The ocean is composed of salt water. Our party was composed of three grown-ups and four children.* 2 put together. To compose a story or poem is to construct it from words. To compose a piece of music is to invent the tune and write down the notes. To compose in a printing office is to set up type to form words or sentences. To compose a picture is to arrange the things in it artistically. 3 make calm: *Stop crying and compose yourself.* 4 settle; arrange: *The union and the company composed their differences and agreed on a contract.* v., com posed, com pos ing.

Which of the following can be composed?

__a. an opera
__b. oneself
__c. a pair of curtains
__d. a plot
__e. a front page

259c

b

man u script (man'yə skript), book or paper written by hand or with a typewriter. Before printing was invented, all books and papers were handwritten manuscripts. n.

In which of the following sentences is **manuscript** used *incorrectly?*

__a. I read the manuscript in the newspaper.
__b. The manuscript for her book lay on the desk for some time.
__c. They printed thousands of copies of the manuscript.
__d. A manuscript is corrected after it is written.

284b

His most important **achievement** was the Kansas-Nebraska Bill of 1854, which Douglas worked tirelessly to get Congress to pass the bill, which allowed Western settlers to decide for themselves whether they wanted slavery in their own states.

Achievement means:

__a. plan for the future
__b. difficult task
__c. thing accomplished
__d. preparation for action

17b

We wanted to have one last meal of familiar food. We each **consumed** a tremendous amount of steak. I insisted on having a milkshake for dessert.

Consume means: (Check two)
___a. cook
___b. use up
___c. eat or drink up
___d. empty

42b

Of course, Suzanne did not fear traveling alone. She has looked after herself for years. She has always been a very **independent** person.

Independent means:
___a. having a great deal of money
___b. wanting no help from others
___c. wanting to help others
___d. brave and strong

67c

c

bruise (brüz), **1** injury to the body, caused by a fall or a blow, that breaks blood vessels without breaking the skin: *The bruise on my arm turned black and blue.* **2** injury to the outside of a fruit, vegetable, plant, etc. **3** injure the outside of: *Rough handling bruised the apples before they could be sold.* **4** hurt; injure: *Your harsh words bruised my feelings.* **5** become bruised: *My flesh bruises easily.* 1,2 *n.*, 3-5 *v.*, **bruised, bruis ing.**

Check the sentence(s) in which **bruise** is used correctly.
___a. The bandage was soaked with blood from the bruise.
___b. The bruise turned black as coal.
___c. He received a bruise when the ball hit him.
___d. Do not bring the bruise with you.

92c

b

sit u at ed (sich′ü ā′tid), **1** placed; located: *New York is a favorably situated city.* **2** in a certain financial or social position: *The doctor was quite well situated. adj.*

Check the sentence(s) in which **situated** is used correctly.
___a. I was situated after eating.
___b. Probably it was situated.
___c. Who was situated in the game?
___d. The barn was situated at the far end of the property.

118a

b

snarl (snärl)

No sailor likes to **snarl** a line.

Write a definition or synonym:

143a

d, e, f

al ti tude (al′ tə tüd *or* al′ tə tyüd)

It is fun to watch a plane gain **altitude**.

Write a definition or synonym:

160a

b

im pris on (im priz′ n)

As usual, the jury believed Sergeant Salinger's version of the facts. If the jury found Herman guilty, the judge would have to decide whether or not to **imprison** him.

Write a definition or synonym:

184c

c

dwell (dwel), make one's home; live: *They dwell in the country but work in the city.* v., **dwelt** or **dwelled, dwelling.** —**dwell′er,** n.
dwell on or **dwell upon, 1** think, write, or speak about for a long time: *Her mind dwelt on the pleasant day she had spent in the country.* **2** put stress on: *The speaker dwelt especially on the great need for teachers.*

ANALOGY dwell : home :: drive :
    __**a.** tent
    __**b.** house
    __**c.** road
    __**d.** car
    __**e.** live

209c

d

re mark (ri märk′), **1** say in a few words; state; comment: *She remarked that it was a beautiful day.* **2** something said in a few words; short statement: *The president made a few remarks.* **3** notice; observe: *Did you remark that strange cloud?* **4** act of noticing; observation. 1,3 *v.*, 2,4 *n.* —**re mark′er,** *n.*

Check the sentence(s) in which a form of **remark** is used correctly.
    __**a.** "We are having remarked weather," she said.
    __**b.** The police officer remarked the man's odd behavior.
    __**c.** Her remarks were very funny.
    __**d.** I remarked that TV program every week.

234b

For the first time in years, Manny's throat was tight and his hands were cold and damp. He did his best to **compose** himself so that no one would notice how nervous he was.

Compose means:
    __**a.** assure
    __**b.** train
    __**c.** calm
    __**d.** convince

259b

I was careful to keep the **manuscript** neat. To be sure, I even typed it.

Manuscript means:
    __**a.** one's life story written by oneself
    __**b.** book or paper handwritten or typed
    __**c.** printed material
    __**d.** page of a book

284a

c, d, e

a chieve ment (ə chēv′ mənt)

Douglas's **achievements** in the Senate were important.

Write a definition or synonym:

17c

b, c

con sume (kən süm′), **1** use up; spend: *A student consumes much time in studying. I consumed almost all the money I earned last summer.* **2** eat or drink up: *We will each consume at least two sandwiches on our hike.* **3** destroy; burn up: *A huge fire consumed the entire forest.* *v.,* **con sumed, con sum ing.** —**con sum′ing ly,** *adv.*

Check the thing(s) that you might **consume**.
__a. clocks
__b. garbage
__c. water
__d. rugs

42c

b

in de pend ent (in′di pen′dənt), **1** not influenced by others; thinking or acting for oneself: *an independent voter, an independent thinker.* **2** not under another's rule or control; ruling, guiding, or governing oneself: *The United States is an independent country.* **3** not connected with others; separate or distinct: *an independent investigation, independent work.* **4** not depending on others for one's support: *Now that I have a better-paying job, I can be completely independent.* **5** enough to live on without working: *an independent income.* **6** person who is independent in thought or behavior. **7** person who votes without regard to party. 1-5 *adj.,* 6,7 *n.* —**in′de pend′ent ly,** *adv.*

Check the sentence(s) in which **independent** is used correctly.
__a. A baby is a very independent person.
__b. She was so poor she could afford to be independent.
__c. After he found a job, he became very independent.
__d. She says she is an independent, voting sometimes for one party, sometimes for another.

68a

b, c

suf fi cient (sə fish′ ənt)

At last, Diana and I had received **sufficient** training.

Write a definition or synonym:

93a

d

com pete (kəm pēt′)

The museum **competes** with other museums in the city.

Write a definition or synonym:

118b

If the lines become **snarled,** the sailor will lose control of the sails, and the boat may turn over.

A synonym for **snarl** is:
__a. break
__b. tangle
__c. lose
__d. throw

143b

None of the early planes could fly at a very high **altitude.** None went so high that the air became thin or the pilot needed special equipment.

Altitude means:
__a. high rate of speed
__b. a great distance
__c. height above the earth
__d. width of a circle

159c

b

al i bi (al′ə bī), **1** the statement that an accused person was somewhere else when an offense was committed: *Immediately after the robbery the gang scattered to establish alibis.* **2** INFORMAL. an excuse: *What is your alibi for failing to do your homework?* **3** INFORMAL. make an excuse: *She alibied that she was very busy when they asked her why she didn't visit them.* 1,2 *n., pl.* **al i bis;** 3 *v.,* **al i bied, al i bi ing.** [*Alibi* comes from Latin *alibi,* meaning "else-where."]

Which of the following could be described as an **alibi**?
__**a.** a note to a friend saying you cannot attend her party
__**b.** telling your teacher you were talking in class only because your friend kept asking you questions
__**c.** having to stay home from school with measles

184b

When the park was completed, the caretaker and his family would **dwell** in the bungalow. By living right next to the place where he worked, the caretaker could watch over the museum twenty-four hours a day.

A synonym for **dwell** is:
__**a.** remain
__**b.** vacation
__**c.** live
__**d.** work

209b

"It was interesting," I **remarked**. Then I added, "Even if Anouk thought she was writing to a boy, I'm going to answer it right away!"

A synonym for **remark** is:
__**a.** agree
__**b.** think
__**c.** shout
__**d.** say

234a

b, c, d, e

com pose (kəm pōz′)

When the cameras were rolling and Manny was ready to make his first appearance, he tried hard to **compose** himself.

Write a definition or synonym:

259a

b,d,g

man u script (man′ yə skript)

My parents liked my finished **manuscript** and so did my teacher.

Write a definition or synonym:

283c

c

qual i fi ca tion (kwol′ə fə kā′shən), **1** that which makes a person fit for a job, task, office, etc.: *A knowledge of trails is one qualification for a guide.* **2** that which limits, changes, or makes less free and full: *His enjoyment of the trip had one qualification; his friends could not enjoy it, too.* **3** modification; limitation; restriction: *The statement was made without any qualification. n.*

Check the phrase(s) in which a form of **qualification** is used correctly.
__**a.** tired qualification
__**b.** wealthy qualification
__**c.** many qualifications
__**d.** poor qualification
__**e.** outstanding qualification

18a

c

en thu si asm (en thü′ zē az′ əm)

At the end of our journey the people of the little village in Colombia greeted us with **enthusiasm**.

Write a definition or synonym:

43a

c, d

lug gage (lug′ ij)

When Suzanne left, she had almost no **luggage**.

Write a definition or synonym:

68b

There was no longer any need to remain at school. Diana and I each had received **sufficient** training—as much as was necessary to lead a full life on our own.

A synonym for **sufficient** is:
__**a.** good
__**b.** enough
__**c.** much
__**d.** any

93b

Other museums have many modern paintings. The Guggenheim **competes** with them to attract visitors. One way it does this is by having frequent special showings of the works of famous artists.

Compete means:
__**a.** share
__**b.** be a rival
__**c.** unite
__**d.** enter business

118c

b

snarl[1] (snärl), **1** growl sharply and show one's teeth: *The dog snarled at the stranger.* **2** a sharp, angry growl. **3** say or express with a snarl; speak harshly in a sharp, angry tone: *snarl a nasty threat.* **4** a sharp, angry tone or remark: *A snarl was her only reply.* 1,3 *v.*, 2,4 *n.* —**snarl′er,** *n.* —**snarl′ing ly,** *adv.*
snarl[2] (snärl), **1** a tangle: *I combed the snarls out of my hair.* **2** confusion: *Their legal affairs were in a snarl.* **3** to tangle or become tangled: *The kitten snarled the yarn by playing with it. Her hair snarls easily.* **4** confuse. 1,2 *n.*, 3,4 *v.*

1. Which of the following would be easily **snarled**?
   __**a.** rubber ball   __**d.** twine
   __**b.** chair   __**e.** knitting yarn
   __**c.** hair
2. Which of the following would be likely to **snarl**?
   __**a.** a leopard   __**c.** a gangster
   __**b.** a baby   __**d.** an eagle

143c

c

al ti tude (al′tə tüd *or* al′tə tyüd), **1** height above the earth's surface: *What altitude did the airplane reach?* **2** height above sea level: *The altitude of Denver is 5300 feet.* **3** a high place: *At some altitudes snow never melts.* **4** the vertical distance from the base of a geometrical figure to its highest point. **5** the angular distance of a star, planet, etc., above the horizon. *n.*

Check the sentence(s) in which **altitude** is used correctly.
__**a.** The dog had an altitude of 104°.
__**b.** The helicopter was flying at a low altitude.
__**c.** What is your altitude toward him?
__**d.** The plane fell from a high altitude.

159b

Herman's **alibi** fell apart when Salinger proved that Herman's friends were seen in many different parts of town that night. Herman could no longer claim that he was nowhere near the scene of the crime.

An **alibi** is:
_**a.** a lie
_**b.** an excuse
_**c.** an untrue story
_**d.** a rude remark

184a

a, c,
d, e

dwell (dwel)

The future caretaker would **dwell** there.

Write a definition or synonym:

209a

c, e

re mark (ri märk′)

When I read Anouk's letter to my class, my teacher **remarked** that it was certainly interesting.

Write a definition or synonym:

233c

b

vague (vāg), not definite; not clear; not distinct: *In a fog everything looks vague. His vague statement confused them.* adj., **va guer, va guest.** —**vague′ly,** adv. —**vague′- ness,** n.

Which of the following might be described as **vague**?
_**a.** a mud puddle
_**b.** an inscription on an ancient tomb
_**c.** a face seen through a thick veil
_**d.** a faint impression
_**e.** a slight recollection

258c

b

fad (fad), something everybody is very much interested in for a short time; fashion or craze: *No one plays that game anymore; it was only a fad. n.*

Which of the following might be called **fads**?
_**a.** test   _**e.** reading
_**b.** hula hoops _**f.** television
_**c.** cleanliness _**g.** the "Hustle"
_**d.** granny glasses

283b

Douglas's excellent **qualifications** had already made him highly respected in the U. S. Senate. His ability and energy had made it possible for him to become a leader of his party in the Senate.

A **qualification** is that which:
_**a.** describes a person's appearance
_**b.** a person is born with
_**c.** makes a person fit for a job
_**d.** can be acquired by education

18b

The people showed a lot of **enthusiasm** when we arrived. They had a huge party to celebrate our coming. At the feast we had some of the spiciest food I had ever tasted. The main dish was seasoned with chili peppers.

Enthusiasm means:
___**a.** laughter
___**b.** eager interest
___**c.** noisy cheers
___**d.** relief

43b

Suzanne didn't want to be slowed down by heavy suitcases. She limited her **luggage** to one backpack.

A synonym for **luggage** is:
___**a.** clothes
___**b.** hatboxes
___**c.** baggage
___**d.** packages

68c

b

suf fi cient (sə fish′ənt), as much as is needed; enough: *sufficient proof. They did not have sufficient clothing for winter. adj.* —**suf fi′cient ly,** *adv.*

ANALOGY sufficient : lacking :: agreeable :
___**a.** expensive
___**b.** fortunate
___**c.** delicious
___**d.** unpleasant
___**e.** thirsty

93c

b

com pete (kəm pēt′), **1** try hard to win or gain something wanted by others; be rivals; contend: *She competed against many fine athletes for the gold medal. It is difficult for a small grocery store to compete with a supermarket.* **2** take part (in a contest): *Will you compete in the final race? v.,* **com pet ed, com pet ing.**

At which of the following events might one be likely to **compete**?
___**a.** stargazing ___**d.** archery contest
___**b.** canoe race ___**e.** lunch
___**c.** circus ___**f.** spelling bee

119a

1. c, d, e
2. a, c

budge (buj)

Sometimes a sailor cannot **budge** the anchor.

Write a definition or synonym:

144a

b, d

in struct (in strukt′)

In those days, there were few people who could **instruct** beginners.

Write a definition or synonym:

159a

a, d

al i bi (al′ ə bī)

When Sergeant Salinger took the stand, he made Herman's **alibi** look ridiculous.

Write a definition or synonym:

183c

b

bun ga low (bung′gə lō), a small one-story house. *n.* [*Bungalow* comes from Hindustani *banglā*, meaning "of Bengal." These houses were first observed in India, when it was part of the British Empire.]

In which of the following places would you be likely to find a **bungalow**?
___**a.** in a residential area   ___**d.** in the country
___**b.** in the Arctic   ___**e.** at the seashore
___**c.** in a housing development

208c

b

leg i ble (lej′ə bəl), **1** able to be read. **2** easy to read; plain and clear: *legible handwriting. adj.*

Check the phrase(s) in which **legible** is used correctly.
___**a.** legible for the football team
___**b.** legible flying conditions
___**c.** legible letter
___**d.** legible water
___**e.** legible penmanship

233b

Manny knew just what he wanted when it came to songs, costumes, and action. But he had very unclear ideas about what message he was trying to get across, and only a **vague** notion of why the good guys were fighting the bad.

Vague means:
___**a.** very strong
___**b.** not definite
___**c.** familiar
___**d.** distinct

258b

The **fad** for coonskin caps started when a song about Davy Crockett became popular. If there is ever a popular song about Daniel Boone, perhaps everyone will want to wear big, black felt hats the way Boone did.

A **fad** is something that:
___**a.** people have always done
___**b.** everyone is interested in for a short time
___**c.** is required by the authorities
___**d.** is required for membership in an organization

283a

b,c,d

qual i fi ca tion (kwol′ ə fə kā′ shən)

At first glance, Douglas had much better **qualifications** than Lincoln did.

Write a definition or synonym:

b

18c

en thu si asm (en thü′zē az′əm), eager interest; zeal: *The pep talk filled the team with enthusiasm. n.*

ANALOGY enthusiasm : boredom ::
___a. intermission : intersection
___b. responsibility : joy
___c. accomplishment : task
___d. admiration : contempt
___e. punishment : pain

c

43c

lug gage (lug′ij), baggage. *n.* —lug′gage less, *adj.*

Which of these objects could be called **luggage**?
___a. a purse   ___d. a hair dryer
___b. a suitcase   ___e. a suit
___c. a shopping bag   ___f. a knapsack

d

69a

e ven tu al ly (i ven′ chü ə lē)

Eventually, it seemed that Diana could read my mind.

Write a definition or synonym:

b,d,f

94a

bleak (blēk)

One painting we saw was of a **bleak** country scene.

Write a definition or synonym:

119b

When the anchor won't **budge**, a sailor may have to swim down to it and free it from the mud or rock that is holding it.

A synonym for **budge** is:
___a. break
___b. move
___c. pull
___d. repair

144b

Many of the stunt flyers would **instruct** pupils in their spare time. This was not difficult, for in those days not much was really known about aeronautics. It didn't take long to learn to fly a plane.

A synonym for **instruct** is:
___a. learn
___b. study
___c. test
___d. teach

282c

op po nent (ə pōʹnənt), 1 person who is on the other side in a fight, game, or discussion; person fighting, struggling, or speaking against another: *She defeated her opponent in the election.* 2 opposing. *1 n., 2 adj.*

b

In which of the following would you be likely to have an opponent?

__a. choir __d. tennis
__b. boxing match __e. ice skating
__c. checkers __f. piano lesson

258a

fad (fad)

b,d,e

Years ago, coonskin caps were a big **fad** in our town.

Write a definition or synonym:

233a

vague (vāg)

a, c

When people asked what the importance or the meaning of his movie might be, Manny tended to be rather **vague**.

Write a definition or synonym:

208b

Wind and sand have worn away some of the picture writings so that they cannot be made out. Others are **legible**, however. Experts who have learned the language have been able to tell us much about the ancient Egyptians.

Legible means:

__a. like new
__b. can be read
__c. long lasting
__d. in good condition

183b

The **bungalow** would be made more modern inside, but it would not be enlarged. A small family could squeeze into it now. They would be glad enough not to have to climb any stairs.

A **bungalow** is:

__a. a house having two or more stories
__b. a house of one or one-and-a-half stories
__c. a one-room cottage
__d. a house with an attached garage

158c

gang ster (gangʹstər), member of a gang of criminals or racketeers. *n.*

a

Check the sentence(s) in which a form of **gangster** is used correctly.

__a. Large cities usually have more gangsters than small towns.
__b. The gangsters gave a party for the mayor.
__c. He showed gangster ability at an early age.
__d. Gangsters should be punished.

19a

d

in di ges tion (in′ də jes′ chən)

We were warned about **indigestion**.

Write a definition or synonym:

44a

b, f

a wait (ə wāt′)

As the days turned into weeks, we all anxiously **awaited** Suzanne's first letter.

Write a definition or synonym:

69b

After we had been working together for a long time, Diana and I seemed to understand each other perfectly. **Eventually,** we knew each other so well that we could do almost anything together.

A synonym for **eventually** is:
___**a.** once
___**b.** finally
___**c.** often
___**d.** always

94b

It showed a dark deserted farmhouse with a dead tree standing beside it. The scene was made to look even more **bleak** by being painted in various shades of gray. It was oddly beautiful.

Bleak means:
___**a.** different
___**b.** frightening
___**c.** ugly
___**d.** dismal

119c

b

budge (buj), move even a little: *The stone was so heavy that we could not budge it. I was too tired to budge from my chair.* v., **budged, budg ing.**

Check the sentence(s) in which a form of **budge** is used correctly.
___**a.** The dog refused to budge from his house.
___**b.** I budged the line in.
___**c.** Look out or you'll budge the glass!
___**d.** I was not able to budge the boulder.

144c

d

in struct (in strukt′), **1** give knowledge to; show how to do; teach; train; educate: *We have one teacher who instructs us in reading, English, history, and arithmetic.* **2** give directions to; order: *The doctor instructed him to go to bed and rest. The owner of the house instructed her agent to sell it.* **3** inform; tell: *The family lawyer instructed them that the contract would be signed Monday.* v. —**in struct′i ble,** *adj.*

Check the sentence(s) in which a form of **instruct** is used correctly.
___**a.** Who will instruct you in swimming?
___**b.** The doctor instructed her patient to get plenty of sleep.
___**c.** I was instructed by the knife.
___**d.** He instructed his lesson before he went to bed.

282b

The two men admired and respected each other. They were political **opponents**, however, because they held such differing opinions about the future of slavery. Douglas believed that each state should decide for itself whether or not to have slavery. Lincoln wanted to see slavery ended in the entire country.

An **opponent** is one who:

- __a. runs for office
- __b. is on the other side
- __c. defeats another
- __d. resembles another

257c

mer it (mer'it), 1 worth or value; goodness: *Students will be graded according to the merit of their work.* 2 something that deserves praise or reward. 3 deserve: *Your excellent work merits praise.* 4 Usually, **merits**, *pl.* actual facts or qualities, whether good or bad: *The judge will consider the case on its merits.* 1,2,4 *n.,* 3 *v.* —**mer'it less,** *adj.*

Check the sentence(s) in which **merit** can be correctly substituted for the word in italics.

- __a. Can you tell me the *value* of that diamond?
- __b. He felt his deed did not *deserve* such applause.
- __c. The witness was told to stick to *fact.*
- __d. They got just what they *deserve!*
- __e. You will be graded according to the *worth* of your paintings.

232c

pro fes sion al (prə fesh'ə nal), 1 of a profession; appropriate to a profession: *Our doctor has a professional seriousness unlike her ordinary joking manner.* 2 engaged in a profession: *A lawyer or a doctor is a professional person.* 3 making a business or trade of something which others do for pleasure: *a professional ballplayer, professional musicians.* 4 a person who does this. 5 undertaken or engaged in by professionals rather than amateurs: *a professional ball game.* 1-3 *adj.,* 4 *n.* —**pro fes'sion al ly,** *adv.*

Check the sentence(s) in which a form of **professional** is used correctly.

- __a. Professionals are not allowed to enter an amateur competition.
- __b. His professional is medicine.
- __c. She became a professional tennis player because she needed the money.

208a

leg i ble (lej' ə bal)

Anouk told me that there are ancient picture writings on stone that are **legible** today.

Write a definition or synonym:

183a

bun ga low (bung' gə lō)

Behind the main house, almost hidden by the thick bushes, was a **bungalow**.

Write a definition or synonym:

155b

Herman begged the jury to be kind to him. "How can I be a **gangster**?" he asked. "I never was arrested before. I meant no harm. My friends and I were all playing cards that night!"

The meaning of **gangster** is:

- __a. member of a gang of criminals
- __b. one who has served a prison sentence
- __c. person who dislikes other people
- __d. person who breaks the law

19b

Sure enough, a few of the group were bothered by **indigestion**. They said that the food they ate felt like a lump of lead in their stomachs. The next day, however, they felt fine.

Indigestion means:
__a. difficulty in swallowing food
__b. choking
__c. difficulty in changing food for body use
__d. difficulty in staying thin

44b

Two weeks passed without a letter. Then a third week went by. Now we **awaited** word from Suzanne or from the Spanish authorities. What could have happened to her?

Await means:
__a. hope for
__b. wait for
__c. expect
__d. want

69c

b

e ven tu al ly (i ven′chü ə lē), in the end; finally: *We waited more than an hour for them but eventually we had to leave without them. adv.*

ANALOGY eventually : initially ::
__a. once : final
__b. death : birth
__c. meat : potatoes
__d. past : future
__e. age : wealth

94c

d

bleak (blēk), **1** swept by winds; bare: *The rocky peaks of high mountains are bleak.* **2** chilly; cold: *The bleak winter wind made us shiver.* **3** cheerless and depressing; dismal: *A prisoner's life is bleak. adj.* —**bleak′ly**, *adv.* —**bleak′- ness**, *n.*

ANALOGY bleak : cozy :: harsh :
__a. gentle
__b. foreign
__c. chilly
__d. wind
__e. bare

120a

a, d

sol i tar y (sol′ ə ter′ ē)

One often sees **solitary** sailors.

Write a definition or synonym:

145a

a, b

bach e lor (bach′ ə lər)

Many of the pilots in the early days were **bachelors**.

Write a definition or synonym:

158a

c

gang ster (gang′ stər)

When it was Herman's turn to speak in his own defense, he made his position quite clear. "I'm a businessman," he stated, "not a **gangster**! Show some respect!"

Write a definition or synonym:

182c

c

res i den tial (rez′ə den′shəl), **1** of or suitable for homes or residences: *They live in a large residential district outside the city.* **2** having to do with residence: *The city is considering the adoption of a residential requirement for all city employees to live within the city limits. adj.* —**res′i-den′tial ly,** *adv.*
res i dence (rez′ə dəns), **1** the place where a person lives; house; home; abode: *The President's residence is the White House in Washington, D.C.* **2** a residing; living; dwelling: *Long residence in France made them very fond of the French.* **3** period of residing in a place: *They spent a residence of ten years in France. n.*

ANALOGY **residential : family :: commercial :**
___a. downtown
___b. wealthy
___c. business
___d. dwelling
___e. office

207c

b

cof fin (kô′fən), box into which a dead person is put to be buried; casket. *n.*

ANALOGY **coffin : ground ::**
___a. balloon : basket
___b. submarine : water
___c. cemetery : church
___d. train : station
___e. car : repairs

232b

Manny had to turn down a lot of his friends who wanted parts in his movie. "You may be very talented," Manny told them, "and you may learn the business of acting, but I can't afford to have anything go wrong. Every actor and actress in my show must be a **professional**."

Professional means:
___a. engaged in for pleasure
___b. engaged in the study of
___c. having a great interest in
___d. engaged in for business

257b

The **merit** of Boone's achievements was recognized by the government of the United States. He was rewarded with a gold medal.

A synonym for **merit** is:
___a. interest
___b. ability
___c. worth
___d. humor

282a

b, c

op po nent (ə pō′ nənt)

Although both men were against the spread of slavery, they were political **opponents**.

Write a definition or synonym:

19c

c

in di ges tion (in/də jes/chən), inability to digest food; difficulty in digesting food: *The rich food we ate gave us indigestion. n.*

After which of the following events would a person be most likely to suffer **indigestion**?
_a. a horse show
_b. a dinner with spicy food
_c. watching a relay race
_d. watching a basketball game

44c

b

a wait (ə wāt/), **1** wait for; look forward to: *I shall await your answer to my letter with eagerness.* **2** be ready for; be in store for: *Many pleasures await you on your trip. v.*

Check the sentence(s) in which a form of **await** is used correctly.
_a. Shall I await on the tables?
_b. He has awaited the money for a week.
_c. I awaited the decision of the judges.
_d. You await for the job.

70a

b

balk (bôk)

Diana **balked** only twice in all the time she has been with me.

Write a definition or synonym:

95a

a

bur lap (bér′ lap)

It was painted on **burlap**.

Write a definition or synonym:

120b

Some sailboats can be easily handled by one person, and there are many people who prefer **solitary** sailing. Such people seem to find the sound of the wind and water a pleasant change from the sound of human voices and the hubbub of daily work.

Solitary means:
_a. unfriendly
_b. alone
_c. interesting
_d. quiet

145b

Many of these **bachelor** pilots were too busy traveling to settle in one place, marry, and raise a family. The goal of many was to set some sort of flying record.

A **bachelor** is:
_a. a young man
_b. a man who has not married
_c. a person whose husband or wife has died
_d. a middle-aged person

157c

in di vid u al (in′də vij′ü əl), **1** person: *an extremely unpleasant individual.* **2** a single person, animal, or thing. **3** for or by one only; single; particular; separate: *Each student was given individual attention.* **4** belonging to or marking off one person or thing specially: *an individual style of writing.* 1,2 *n.*, 3,4 *adj.*

c

ANALOGY **individual : group** ::
___**a.** part : apart
___**b.** one : alone
___**c.** animal : herd
___**d.** farm : explorer
___**e.** alone : many

182b

The house would be furnished, but would no longer be used for **residential** purposes. It would be used as a museum to show how people lived at the time of the Civil War.

Residential means:
___**a.** having to do with business
___**b.** having to do with land
___**c.** having to do with homes
___**d.** having to do with people

207b

After a corpse was prepared, it was placed in a **coffin**. The coffin was sometimes carved to fit the shape of the Pharaoh it contained.

A **coffin** is:
___**a.** a statue of a dead person
___**b.** a box for a dead body
___**c.** a large tomb
___**d.** a small house or hut

232a

e

pro fes sion al (prə fesh′ ə nəl)

Manny wanted the acting, the directing, and even the costumes to be handled by **professionals**.

Write a definition or synonym:

257a

b

mer it (mer′ it)

Boone performed many deeds of **merit**.

Write a definition or synonym:

281c

d

ri val ry (rī′vəl rē), effort to obtain something another person wants; competition: *There is rivalry among business firms for trade. n., pl.* **ri val ries.**

Check the sentence(s) in which a form of **rivalry** is used correctly.
___**a.** He entered the painting rivalry.
___**b.** The rivalry between the two teams was keen.
___**c.** There is no rivalry in our family.
___**d.** There are many quiz rivalries on television.

20a

b

suit a ble (sü′ tə bəl)

After the celebration, we met with the villagers to plan a **suitable** project.

Write a definition or synonym:

45a

b, c

a pol o gize (ə pol′ ə jīz)

Finally, we received our first letter. In it, Suzanne **apologized** at great length. Then she went on to explain.

Write a definition or synonym:

70b

Once Diana **balked** when I wanted to go up a narrow wooden stairway. She insisted on waiting at the bottom until some movers had managed to get a piano down the stairs. We probably would have been hurt if Diana had let me go ahead when I wanted to.

Balk means:
__a. trip and fall
__b. appear frightened
__c. fall and get up
__d. stop short and refuse to go on

95b

The artist had painted on **burlap** because its coarse weave would produce an interesting-looking surface.

Burlap is:
__a. fine cloth
__b. heavy paper
__c. rough cloth
__d. silk

120c

b

sol i tar y (sol′ə ter′ē), **1** alone; single; only: *A solitary rider was seen in the distance.* **2** without companions; away from people; lonely. *adj.* —**sol′i tar′i ly**, *adv.* —**sol′i tar′i ness**, *n.*

1. A person who leads a **solitary** life might be:
   __a. a hermit
   __b. a storekeeper
   __c. a shepherd
   __d. an explorer
   __e. a teacher
2. Can a group of people lead a **solitary** life together?
   Yes__   No__

145c

b

bach e lor (bach′ə lər), **1** man who has not married. **2** person who has the first degree of a college or university. *n.*

Which of the following phrases might apply to a **bachelor**?
__a. at graduation   __d. on a date
__b. in a freshman class __e. with his wife
__c. in a suit of armor   __f. in his crib

157b

Herman's lawyer said that Herman was not the type of man who would steal or cheat when acting alone, as an **individual**. According to the lawyer, Herman had fallen in with a bad crowd.

An **individual** is:
___**a.** an example
___**b.** a type
___**c.** a person
___**d.** a criminal

182a

a, c

res i den tial (rez′ ə den′ shəl)

After the house became a museum, it would no longer be considered **residential**.

Write a definition or synonym:

207a

d

cof fin (kô′ fən)

The **coffins** of some of the Pharaohs were made of stone.

Write a definition or synonym:

231c

b

dra ma (drä′mə *or* dram′ə), **1** a play such as one sees in a theater; story written to be acted out by actors on the stage. **2** the art of writing, acting, or producing plays: *He is studying drama.* **3** series of happenings in real life that seem like those of a play: *The history of America is a thrilling drama. n., pl.* **dra mas.**

ANALOGY drama : acts :: novel :
___**a.** reason
___**b.** pages
___**c.** author
___**d.** characters
___**e.** chapters

256c

d

ab surd (ab sėrd′), plainly not true or sensible; foolish; ridiculous: *The idea that the number 13 brings bad luck is absurd. adj.* [*Absurd* comes from Latin *absurdus,* meaning "out of tune, senseless."] —**ab surd′ly,** *adv.* —**ab surd′- ness,** *n.*

ANALOGY absurd : reasonable ::
___**a.** plain : true
___**b.** simple : fancy
___**c.** natural : expensive
___**d.** funny : laughable
___**e.** right : correct

281b

Their **rivalry** was especially keen in 1858, when both were running for the Senate. Lincoln and Douglas were both excellent public speakers. People came from miles around to hear them debate.

A synonym for **rivalry** is:
___**a.** fighting
___**b.** campaign
___**c.** hatred
___**d.** competition

20b

We decided that building a well would be a **suitable** project. Not only was it badly needed, but it was something that could be handled easily with the equipment that was available.

Another word for **suitable** is:
_ **a.** easy
_ **b.** enjoyable
_ **c.** fitting
_ **d.** necessary

45b

She had met a wonderful old friend and had changed her travel plans completely. She was sorry that she had not written sooner, but she had been busy. She **apologized** for the delay, and promised that in the future she would write once a week.

Apologize means:
_ **a.** ignore
_ **b.** feel anxious
_ **c.** arm oneself
_ **d.** express regret

70c

d

balk (bôk), **1** stop short and stubbornly refuse to go on: *My horse balked at the fence.* **2** prevent from going on; hinder: *The police balked the robber's plans.* **3** hindrance. **4** (in baseball) an illegal motion made by a pitcher, especially one in which a throw that has been started is not completed. 1,2 *v.*, 3,4 *n.* Also **baulk.—balk′er,** *n.*

Which of the following could be correctly described by the word **balk**?
_ **a.** A prisoner is stopped from escaping by a guard.
_ **b.** A cow refuses to cross a road.
_ **c.** A baseball player throws in a fast pitch.
_ **d.** A boy misses a good opportunity to earn a reward.

95c

c

bur lap (bėr′lap), a coarse fabric made from jute or hemp, used to make bags. A finer grade of burlap is used for curtains, wall coverings, and upholstery. *n.*

Burlap would be best suited for which of the following?
_ **a.** making an evening dress
_ **b.** drying one's face
_ **c.** wrapping up a baby
_ **d.** decorating a house

LESSON 13   The Desert Called Rub' al Khali

1. a,c, d
2. No

Sally Wainwright left America six months ago. Her father, who is an engineer, had taken a job in Saudi Arabia. Sally's first letters showed that she was a little homesick. Then her letters became cheerful. Sally explained that her family was living on the edge of a desert near the border of Saudi Arabia and Yemen called Rub' al Khali. It is also known as the Great Sandy Desert. Sally became interested in exploring the desert.

146a

a,c,d

de scend (di send′)

Some daring pilots could **descend** to within three or four feet of the ground.

Write a definition or synonym:

281a

ri val ry (rī' val rē)

Abe Lincoln, the Republican candidate, challenged Douglas, the Democratic candidate, to a series of debates. The **rivalry** between the two men attracted the attention of the whole country.

Write a definition or synonym:

256b

Like many who would follow him to the frontier lands in Kentucky, Boone couldn't spell! It seems **absurd** to think a strong man and a great explorer could not perform as well as a small child when he tried to write his name.

Absurd means:

—a. annoying
—b. not plain or clear
—c. very embarrassing
—d. foolish

231b

Instead of a story which simply strung together his musical numbers, Manny chose a real **drama**. He wanted good actors and actresses to make the audience care about what was happening to the characters; and he wanted plenty of action and suspense.

A **drama** is:

—a. an opera
—b. a play
—c. a performance
—d. a story

206c

a

fab ric (fab′rik). 1 woven or knitted material; cloth. Velvet, canvas, linen, and flannel are fabrics. 2 way in which a thing is put together; frame or structure: *The fabric of a person's character may be weak or strong. n.*

ANALOGY fabric : cotton :: wood :

—a. hard
—b. knotted
—c. carved
—d. pine
—e. broken

181c

c

do nate (dō'nāt), give money or help, especially to a fund or institution; contribute: *She donated $20 to the community chest. v.,* **do nat ed, do nat ing.** —do'na-tor, n.

Check the sentence(s) in which a form of **donate** is used correctly.

—a. I will donate some of my old books to the fair.
—b. He ate many donates.
—c. The Red Cross often donates food and clothing.
—d. The dog donated her paw.

157a

1, c,d,
e

2, a,b

in di vid u al (in' də vij' ü al)

Nevertheless, Herman's lawyer told the jury many times that Herman was an honest **individual**.

Write a definition or synonym:

20c

suit a ble (sü′tə bəl), right for the occasion; fitting; proper: *Plain clothes are suitable for school wear. The park gives the children a suitable playground. adj.* —**suit′a ble- ness,** *n.*

Check the sentence(s) in which **suitable** is used correctly.
__a. We decorated the house in a suitable way for the holidays.
__b. She wore suitable clothes for play.
__c. It was a suitable fit.
__d. There was not a wave on the suitable ocean.

45c

a pol o gize (ə pol′ə jīz), **1** make an apology; say one is sorry; offer an excuse: *I apologized for being so late.* **2** defend an idea, argument, belief, etc., in speech or writing. *v.,* **a pol o gized, a pol o giz ing.** —**a pol′o- giz′er,** *n.*

For which of the following things would you be likely to **apologize**?
__a. hitting someone __d. spilling milk
__b. winning a prize __e. planting a tree
__c. studying hard __f. singing a song

LESSON 8 | Manny Spellbinder Plays Underwater Music

When Manny Spellbinder was just starting out, no one had ever heard of him or his strange music. But Manny wanted his name and his music to become so familiar that people would shiver and clap their hands over their ears whenever they heard the name "Spellbinder." That's why he was willing to play for nothing. And that's why he gave his free concerts everwhere—even on the cliffs at Foster's Beach.

96a

dis pute (dis pyüt′)

Along the ramp we overheard a **dispute**.

Write a definition or synonym:

121a

bar ren (bar′ ən)

Sally wrote a series of letters to help me understand what life was like in the desert. Like most people, I had assumed that the desert was completely **barren**.

Write a definition or synonym:

146b

After they had **descended** from the clouds, they would thrill people by flying under bridges and through tunnels. One pilot even flew in and out through the open doors of a building!

Descend means:
__a. go up from a lower place
__b. go around in a circle
__c. go down from a higher place
__d. turn right side up

LESSON 29 | "The Little Giant"

During the 1840s and '50s, two men from the state of Illinois were building their political careers. One was Abraham Lincoln. Lincoln's political opponent was short, plump, and a masterful politician. Because Stephen A. Douglas was a man of great talent with a physically small frame, he was affectionately known as "The Little Giant."

256a

ab surd (ab sėrd')

There was one fact about Boone's life that seems almost **absurd** today.

Write a definition or synonym:

231a

dra ma (drä′ mä or dram′ ə)

Manny selected a **drama** with a serious message for his first movie.

Write a definition or synonym:

206b

Before the body was buried, strips of **fabric** were carefully wrapped around it. Many, many yards of fine linen were used for this purpose.

A synonym for **fabric** is:

__a. cloth
__b. paper
__c. design
__d. clothing

181b

The owners wanted to do something for the city where they lived, so they **donated** the whole property to the city government. In accepting the gift, the city agreed to turn the old house into a museum and the grounds into a park.

A synonym for **donate** is:

__a. sell
__b. send
__c. give
__d. carry

156c

ve hi cle (vē′ə kəl), **1** any means of carrying, conveying, or transporting, such as a car, carriage, cart, wagon, sled, etc. Automobiles and trucks are motor vehicles. Rockets and satellites are space vehicles. **2** a means or medium by which something is communicated, shown, done, etc.: *Language is the vehicle of thought.* **3** (in painting) a liquid into which pigment is mixed to apply color to a surface: *Linseed oil is a vehicle for paint. n.*

1. **Vehicle** is *not* usually used to describe:

__a. a wagon   __d. an airplane
__b. a bicycle   __e. a parachute
__c. a ship

2. A **vehicle** for expressing a feeling is:

__a. a speech   __c. your ears
__b. a poem

a, b

LESSON

A Different Kind of Career Education

Every so often, someone at school gave a talk on careers and career preparation. For a while, I listened very carefully. I even took notes and discussed all the choices that seemed open to me. But I was never able to make up my mind until one day last summer. Then I knew what my career choice had to be, and it was nothing like the ones I had imagined.

46a

a, d

bal let (bal′ ā *or* ba lā′)

In her next letter, Suzanne said she had been attending the **ballet** with her friend during their week in the city of Madrid. My parents wished Suzanne had said something more about this mysterious "friend."

Write a definition or synonym:

71a

bask (bask)

When Labor Day weekend began, Manny Spellbinder expected to find thousands of people **basking** in the sun at Foster's Beach.

Write a definition or synonym:

96b

The **dispute** concerned a strange painting which showed a light gray square on a dark gray square. One person liked it and the other thought it was terrible.

Dispute means:
___**a.** a criticism
___**b.** a disagreement
___**c.** a fight
___**d.** a conversation

121b

Sally explained that the desert is dotted with water holes called oases. The desert is not completely **barren** because there is a wide variety of plant life growing near each oasis.

Barren means:
___**a.** rocky
___**b.** not healthy
___**c.** different from others
___**d.** not producing anything

146c

c

de scend (di send′), 1 go or come down from a higher to a lower place. 2 go or come down from an earlier to a later time. 3 go from greater to less numbers; go from higher to lower on any scale. 4 make a sudden attack. 5 be handed down from parent to child. 6 come down or spring from. 7 lower oneself; stoop. *v.* —**de scend′a ble, de scend′i ble,** *adj.* —**de-scend′er,** *n.* (Definition adapted)

ANALOGY **descend : climb ::**
___**a.** lower : move
___**b.** drop : lift
___**c.** search : discover
___**d.** lay : set
___**e.** belong : attack

125

156b

The stolen **vehicle** was a baby carriage. It wasn't new, but it was quite expensive. Herman had specialized in stealing rare or custom-built trucks, cars, and baby carriages.

Vehicle means:
- __a. thing for carrying people or goods on land
- __b. something that has wheels
- __c. means of transportation used by businesses
- __d. an object that has been taken without permission

181a

do nate (dō′ nāt)

One day we learned that the house and land had been **donated** to the city.

Write a definition or synonym:

206a

c

fab ric (fab′ rik)

After the corpse was prepared it was wrapped in **fabric**.

Write a definition or synonym:

a, c

LESSON 24

The Electric Cowboy

Sooner or later it was bound to happen. Manny Spellbinder made a movie! Manny's albums were selling so well that people came in spite of the bad reviews from the critics. But even Manny's fans were a little confused by what they saw. Whoever heard of a western movie where all the good guys were unshaven and wore black hats? And whoever heard of a singing cowboy with an electric guitar and a huge loudspeaker with a battery strapped onto his saddle? Well, there's a first time for everything.

255c

a

re side (ri zīd′), **1** live (in or at a place) for a long time; dwell: *This family has resided in our town for 100 years.* **2** be; exist: *The power to declare war resides in Congress.* *v.,* **re sid ed, re sid ing. —re sid′er,** *n.*

ANALOGY reside : dwell :: eat :
- __a. await
- __b. blunder
- __c. consume
- __d. approve
- __e. hoist

280c

c

san i tar y (san′ə ter′ē), **1** of or having to do with health; favorable to health; preventing disease: *sanitary regulations in a hospital.* **2** free from dirt and filth: *Food should be kept in a sanitary place. adj.* **—san′i tar′i ly,** *adv.* **—san′i tar′i ness,** *n.*

ANALOGY sanitary : filthy ::
- __a. raw : cooked
- __b. free : noisy
- __c. ill : sick
- __d. fine : grand
- __e. know : realize

21a

oc cu py (ok′ yə pī)

Most of my spare time was **occupied** with baseball that summer.

Write a definition or synonym:

46b

She wrote that the dancing was very much like that in our American **ballet**, although the dancers presented the story of a Moorish princess who had lived in the Alhambra.

Ballet means:
___**a.** a play on a stage
___**b.** a dance by a group
___**c.** a dance by teen-agers
___**d.** a folk dance of a country

71b

Although it was nearly fall, it was very warm at the beach. It was still pleasant to **bask** there in the sun.

Bask means:
___**a.** play
___**b.** get hot
___**c.** warm oneself
___**d.** bathe in water

96c

b

dis pute (dis pyüt′), **1** give reasons or facts for or against something; argue; debate; discuss. **2** argument; debate. **3** quarrel. **4** a quarrel. **5** disagree with (a statement); declare to be false or wrong; call in question. **6** fight for; fight over; contest. **7** try to win. 1,3,5-7 *v.*, **dis put ed, dis put ing;** 2,4 *n.* —**dis put′er,** *n.* (**Definition adapted**)

In which of the following sentences is **dispute** used correctly?
___**a.** They had a dispute about the money.
___**b.** He would dispute the picture.
___**c.** Disputes are usually friendly and quiet.
___**d.** The dispute between the two women showed that they agreed with each other.
___**e.** The dispute was settled with guns.

121c

d

bar ren (bar′ən), **1** not able to produce offspring: *a barren fruit tree, a barren animal.* **2** not able to produce much: *a barren desert.* **3** without interest; unattractive; dull. **4** of no advantange; unprofitable: *the barren victories of war.* **5 barrens,** *pl.* a barren stretch of land. 1-4 *adj.*, 5 *n.* —**bar′ren ly,** *adv.* —**bar′ren ness,** *n.*

Which of the following might be **barren**?
___**a.** rocks   ___**d.** flower garden
___**b.** beach   ___**e.** desert
___**c.** green lawn   ___**f.** apple pie

147a

b

com mer cial (kə mér′ shəl)

There were few **commercial** planes.

Write a definition or synonym:

280b

That infection kept me on the bench for weeks. Now I am so careful about **sanitary** precautions that the boys are talking about buying me some rubber gloves and a mask!

Sanitary means having to do with:

__**a.** courage
__**b.** sports
__**c.** health
__**d.** medicine

255b

It was impossible for Boone to **reside** with his family when he was exploring the wilderness of Kentucky. Because he was away for such long periods, he was able to visit his family only rarely. Then he was more than a guest than a member of the family.

Reside means:

__**a.** live in
__**b.** remain
__**c.** was content
__**d.** own land

230c

c

pos·sess (pə zes'/), **1** have as belonging to one; own: *My aunt possessed great intelligence and determination.* **2** hold as property; hold; occupy. **3** control; influence strongly: *She was possessed by the desire to be rich.* **4** control by an evil spirit: *He fought like one possessed.* v.

Check the sentence(s) in which a form of **possess** is used correctly.

__**a.** Do you possess a bicycle?
__**b.** He possessed her how to do card tricks.
__**c.** She possessed a great talent for music.
__**d.** Did you possess the arithmetic test or did you fail?

205c

c

corpse (kôrps), a dead human body. *n.*

Check the sentence(s) in which a form of **corpse** is used correctly.

__**a.** The lifeguard was proud of his handsome corpse.
__**b.** She joined the Marine Corpse.
__**c.** Murder cannot be proved unless a corpse is found.
__**d.** We admired the marble corpses in the museum.

LESSON 19 | Haunted House

a, c

Around the corner from the street where I live, there's an old, empty house with trees and tall bushes growing all around it. Once it was probably quite attractive, but now the paint is peeling, the windows are broken, and there are big holes in the roof. We used to make up all sorts of exciting stories about the people who had once lived and died there. What we didn't know was that the truth was much stranger than our fiction.

156a

a,d,f

ve·hi·cle (vē' ə kəl)

Herman was accused of altering and reselling a **vehicle** that he had stolen from a young mother.

Write a definition or synonym:

21b

I had a pretty busy summer. Part of each day I ran errands for the local drugstore. Baseball **occupied** the rest of my time.

The meaning of **occupy** is:
__a. consist of
__b. own
__c. reserve
__d. take up

46c

b

bal let (bal′ā *or* ba lā′), **1** an elaborate dance by a group on a stage. A ballet tells a story through the movements of the dancing and is accompanied by music often written especially for it. **2** the dancers in a ballet. *n.*

If a person wanted to be in a **ballet**, he or she would have to do which of the following well?
__a. sing   __d. laugh
__b. dance   __e. run
__c. speak

71c

c

bask (bask), **1** warm oneself pleasantly: *The cat basks before the fire.* **2** feel great pleasure: *The author basked in the praise of the critics. v.*

Which of the following would enable a person to **bask**?
__a. sun   __e. sand
__b. snow   __f. grass
__c. fire   __g. warmth
__d. water

97a

a, e

baf fle (baf′ əl)

Another man thought the painting was **baffling**.

Write a definition or synonym:

122a

a, b, e

hint (hint)

In some parts of the desert, it is hard to find a **hint** of life.

Write a definition or synonym:

147b

Today's **commercial** planes make it possible to fly from Chicago to Los Angeles in about three hours. Air transportation is something that most people can afford.

Commercial means:
__a. having to do with amusement
__b. having to do with business
__c. common
__d. having to do with government

155c

d

re cit al (ri sī′tl), 1 a reciting; telling facts in detail: *I hope that my lengthy recital of my problems hasn't bored you.* 2 story; account. 3 a musical entertainment, given usually by a single performer: *My music teacher will give a piano recital Tuesday afternoon. n.*

Which of the following might be part of a **recital**?
__a. facts   __d. a musician
__b. scenery   __e. a pet
__c. pencil   __f. music

180c

c

con sid er ate (kən sid′ər it), thoughtful of others and their feelings: *She is considerate enough to tell her parents where she is going and with whom. adj.* —**con sid′er ate ly,** *adv.* —**con sid′er ate ness,** *n.*

Check the sentence(s) in which **considerate** is used correctly.
__a. How considerate of you to give me part of your dessert!
__b. She gave her considerate opinion of the book.
__c. His behavior in the auditorium showed he was not considerate of others.

205b

The **corpse** was treated so as to preserve it. The ancient Egyptians believed that people did not really die, but lived forever. Therefore, the Pharaoh would continue to need his body after burial.

A **corpse** is:
__a. a human body
__b. a person's belongings
__c. a dead body
__d. a soul

230b

Most TV viewers **possess** good sense, but they don't always use what they have. Fortunately, most people don't treat their neighbors as the Hatfields and McCoys did on "Fighting Families." I would never throw a smoke bomb at the Simpsons or the Santinis, though goodness knows, they deserve it!

A synonym for **possess** is:
__a. recognize
__b. acquire
__c. have
__d. show

255a

b,d,e

re side (ri zīd′)

For many years Boone did not **reside** in any one place.

Write a definition or synonym:

280a

a, c

san i tar y (san′ ə ter′ ē)

Now I am the most **sanitary** member of the football team.

Write a definition or synonym:

21c

d

oc cu py (ok′yə pī), **1** take up; fill: *The building occupies an entire block. The lessons occupy the morning.* **2** keep busy; engage; employ: *Composing music occupied her attention.* **3** take possession of: *The enemy occupied our fort.* **4** have; hold: *A judge occupies an important position.* **5** live in: *Two families occupy the house next door.* *v.*, **oc cu pied, oc cu py ing.**

Which of the following things could be **occupied**?
__a. a house
__b. a seat
__c. a dinner
__d. a fire

47a

b

boul e vard (bùl′ ə värd)

In her next letter, Suzanne wrote about the **boulevards** in Madrid. She said that both she and her "friend" had admired them.

Write a definition or synonym:

72a

a,c,g

a quar i um (ə kwer′ ē əm)

The members of the band didn't care for their new name: Manny Spellbinder and the Dead Fish. They said it made them feel like they belonged inside an **aquarium**.

Write a definition or synonym:

97b

The painting **baffled** him because he could not understand why someone would go to the trouble of painting squares.

Baffle means:
__a. fill with amazement or delight
__b. be too hard for a person to solve
__c. play a trick on
__d. make a fool of

122b

Desert creatures are skilled at escaping the midday heat. In some parts of the desert it is difficult to find a **hint** of life, even when you are searching for it.

Hint means:
__a. complete description
__b. slight sign
__c. answer
__d. explanation

147c

b

com mer cial (kə mėr′shəl), **1** having to do with trade or business: *a store or other commercial establishment.* **2** made to be sold for a profit: *Anything you can buy in a store is a commercial product.* **3** supported by an advertiser or sponsor: *a commercial television program.* **4** an advertising message on radio or television, broadcast between or during programs. 1-3 *adj.*, 4 *n.* —**com mer′cial ly,** *adv.*

Check the phrase(s) in which **commercial** is used correctly.
__a. commercial traveler   __d. commercial art
__b. commercial goodness   __e. commercial TV
__c. commercial senator   __f. commercial fair

131

279c

dis in fect ant (dis'in fek'tant), 1 substance used to destroy disease germs. Alcohol and iodine are disinfectants. 2 used to destroy disease germs: *a disinfectant soap.* 1 *n.,* 2 *adj.*

b

A disinfectant might be used:
__a. to clean a bathroom
__b. to wash a bicycle
__c. to clean a wound
__d. to keep one's hair in place
__e. to drink

254c

fic tion (fik'shən), 1 novels, short stories, and other prose writings that tell about imaginary people and happenings. 2 something imagined or made up: *They exaggerate so much in telling about their experiences that it is impossible to separate fact from fiction. n.*

c

Which of the following would be *least* likely to be or contain **fiction?**
__a. the story of Cinderella
__b. a newspaper article
__c. comic books
__d. a biography
__e. a mathematics textbook
__f. *Gulliver's Travels*

230a

pos sess (pə zes')

d

I just don't know what **possessed** the millions of people who thought "Fighting Families" was the best new TV show of the season!

Write a definition or synonym:

205a

corpse (kôrps)

a, b, f

The **corpse** of a Pharaoh was prepared in a special way.

Write a definition or synonym:

180b

That was the kind of information that Linda appreciated. She was pleased at meeting someone **considerate** enough to pay attention to her feelings. Linda looked and felt so good that she easily won the part.

Considerate means:
__a. businesslike
__b. tireless
__c. thoughtful of others
__d. full of fun

155b

Then they listened to Herman's **recital** of the events of the night of the crime. Herman carefully described everything that had happened. But what he said was completely different from what the other witnesses described.

Recital means:
__a. made-up story
__b. point of view
__c. monotonous story
__d. telling facts in detail

22a

a, b

un for tu nate (un fôr′ chə nit)

One day an **unfortunate** accident occurred. Between innings, while I was looking around, I saw my dog Shep on the other side of the street.

Write a definition or synonym:

47b

Suzanne wrote that the **boulevards** in Madrid are so filled with traffic that it is dangerous to cross them. They are quite different from the little side streets, which are too narrow for even a single automobile.

Boulevard means:
___a. park
___b. broad street
___c. city square
___d. alley

72b

"You guys are definitely not inside an **aquarium**," Manny declared. "There is no glass tank around us, no fish food, and nobody to take care of you. Besides, dead fish don't belong in an **aquarium**, only live ones do. If you want to stay healthy, you'd better do what I say!"

Aquarium means:
___a. board for mounting stuffed fish
___b. collection of pictures of fish
___c. place for keeping live fish
___d. lake or pond containing fish

97c

b

baf fle (baf′əl), **1** hinder (a person) by being too hard to understand or solve; bewilder: *This puzzle baffles me. The absence of clues baffled the police.* **2** device for hindering or changing the flow of air, water, or sound waves: *a baffle for a jet engine.* 1 *v.,* **baf fled, baf fling;** 2 *n.* —**baf′fle ment,** *n.* —**baf′fler,** *n.*

ANALOGY **baffling : problem :: amusing :**
___a. difficulty
___b. trouble
___c. joke
___d. entertain
___e. screen

122c

b

hint (hint), **1** a slight sign; indirect suggestion: *A small black cloud gave a hint of a coming storm.* **2** give a slight sign of; suggest indirectly: *She hinted that she was tired by yawning several times.* 1 *n.,* 2 *v.* —**hint′er,** *n.*

ANALOGY **hint : clue :: command :**
___a. suggest
___b. order
___c. persuade
___d. guess
___e. sign

148a

a, d,
e, f

rou tine (rü tēn′)

Commercial flights today are **routine**.

Write a definition or synonym:

155a

a,c,d

re cit al (ri si′ tl)

The members of the jury listened to the **recital** of each witness.

Write a definition or synonym:

180a

e

con sid er ate (kən sid′ ər it)

The assistant director, who was a more **considerate** person, told Linda about another movie that had parts for young actresses like Linda. Tryouts were being held that day.

Write a definition or synonym:

204c

b

bur i al (ber′ē əl), **1** act of putting a dead body in a grave, in a tomb, or in the sea; burying: *The sailor was given a burial at sea.* **2** having to do with burying: *a burial service.* 1 *n.,* 2 *adj.*

A **burial** is connected with which of the following?
___**a.** the hiding of a bone by a dog
___**b.** the covering of a house by a blizzard
___**c.** the exploring of the ocean by a skin diver
___**d.** the painting of a house
___**e.** the mowing of a lawn
___**f.** the hiding of treasure by pirates

229c

a

hor rid (hôr′id), **1** causing great fear; terrible; frightful. **2** very unpleasant: *a horrid person, a horrid day. adj.* —**hor′rid ly,** *adv.* —**hor′rid ness,** *n.*

ANALOGY **horrid : fear :: annoying :**
___**a.** amusement
___**b.** laughter
___**c.** terror
___**d.** anger
___**e.** pleasure

254b

It is difficult to believe that a man could have escaped death as often as Daniel Boone did. A writer of **fiction** could not invent more exciting stories than the events in Boone's life.

Fiction means:
___**a.** adventure stories
___**b.** writing about true experiences
___**c.** writings about made-up people or events
___**d.** poetry

279b

She frowned when I shook my head. "You should always wash a cut and treat it with a **disinfectant**," she said. "Now the germs that you allowed to stay in that cut have multiplied."

A **disinfectant** is something that:
___**a.** cleans
___**b.** kills germs
___**c.** covers
___**d.** deadens pain

22b

When I saw Shep, I whistled to him. Shep spotted me at the same time and started running toward me. He picked an **unfortunate** time to run across the street—a car was coming straight toward him!

A synonym for **unfortunate** is:
__a. accidental
__b. unusual
__c. unhappy
__d. unlucky

47c

b

boul e vard (bùl/ə värd), a broad street or avenue, often planted with trees. *n.*

ANALOGY **boulevard : avenue ::**
__a. artery : vein
__b. truck : bicycle
__c. barn : house
__d. paint : crayon
__e. tree : building

72c

c

a quar i um (ə kwer/ē əm), **1** tank or glass bowl in which living fish or other water animals, and water plants are kept. **2** building used for showing collections of living fish, water animals, and water plants. *n., pl.* **a quar i-ums, a quar i a** (ə kwer/ē ə). [*Aquarium* is from Latin *aquarium,* meaning "a watering place (for cattle)," which comes from *aqua,* meaning "water."]

Which of the following might be kept in an **aquarium**?
__a. a snail   __d. sand
__b. water plants __e. leaves
__c. dirt   __f. bricks

98a

c

pose (pōz)

As a joke, I **posed** as an art expert.

Write a definition or synonym:

123a

b

de sir a ble (di zī′ rə bəl)

It isn't **desirable** to travel on the desert during the day.

Write a definition or synonym:

148b

But in early flying almost no flight was **routine**. The pilot could always expect some trouble with the weather, the engine, or the plane itself.

Routine means:
__a. fixed; regular
__b. out of the ordinary
__c. dull; monotonous
__d. lasting a long time

279a

b, d

dis in fect ant (dis'in fek'tənt)

"Did you use a **disinfectant?**" the doctor asked.

Write a definition or synonym:

254a

d, e

fic tion (fik'shən)

Some stories about Daniel Boone's adventures seem like works of **fiction.**

Write a definition or synonym:

229b

d

I thought it was extremely unpleasant to see neighbors lying, stealing, shooting, and bombing each other. The worst part was the laughter each attack provoked in the audience. Considering the poor acting and the unbelievable story line, I would say the show was **horrid.**

A synonym for **horrid** is:
__a. terrible
__b. boring
__c. poor
__d. stupid

204b

b

Anouk had seen the Pyramids and could tell me much about them. They were constructed for the **burial** of ancient Egyptian kings, or Pharaohs. They had to be built long in advance of the king's death.

A synonym for **burial** is:
__a. worship
__b. burying
__c. ceremonial
__d. burning

179c

c

com pli ment (kom'plə mənt *for 1,2,4;* kom'plə ment *for 3*), 1 something good said about one; something said in praise of one's work: *She received many compliments on her science project.* 2 a courteous act: *The town paid the old artist the compliment of a large attendance at his exhibit.* 3 pay a compliment to; congratulate: *The coach complimented the winner of the race.* 4 **compliments,** pl. greetings: *In the box of flowers was a card saying "With the compliments of a friend." 1,2,4 n., 3 v.*

ANALOGY compliment : criticism ::
__a. warning : blessing
__b. praise : laughter
__c. helping : serving
__d. believing : trusting
__e. honor : insult

154c

b

es cort (es'kôrt *for 1-3;* e skôrt' *for 4*), 1 person or group of persons going with another to give protection, show honor, etc.: *An escort of several city officials accompanied the famous visitor.* 2 one or more ships or airplanes serving as a guard. 3 man who goes on a date with a woman: *Her escort to the party was a tall young man.* 4 go with as an escort: *Three police cars escorted the governor's limousine in the parade. I enjoyed escorting my cousin to the movies.* 1-3 n., 4 v.

Check the sentence(s) in which a form of **escort** is used correctly.
__a. I escorted him to the platform.
__b. She escorted the ball down the street.
__c. There is no need for you to escort me to the party.
__d. Her father acted as her escort.

22c

d

un for tu nate (un fôr′chə nit), **1** not lucky; having bad luck. **2** not suitable; not fitting: *an unfortunate choice of words*. **3** an unfortunate person. 1,2 *adj.*, 3 *n*. —**un-for′tu nate ly**, *adv*.

ANALOGY **unfortunate : lucky ::**
 __**a.** suitable : fitting
 __**b.** warm : mild
 __**c.** high : slow
 __**d.** rich : poor
 __**e.** easy : amusing

48a

a

con trast (*n.* kon′ trast; *v.* kən trast′)

Suzanne went on to tell us that there was a great **contrast** among the peoples of Spain, just as there is in other countries.

Write a definition or synonym:

73a

a,b,d

dis card (*v.* dis kärd′; *n.* dis′ kärd)

The Dead Fish knew that Manny would **discard** them if they didn't start playing immediately. So the free concert at the beach began.

Write a definition or synonym:

98b

I decided to see if I could explain the painting to the baffled man. It wasn't easy to **pose** as an expert, however, since I didn't understand the painting either. Somehow I was able to convince the man that I knew what I was talking about.

Pose means:
 __**a.** tell a lie
 __**b.** make a false pretense
 __**c.** give a short talk
 __**d.** earn a living

123b

Traveling in the heat of the day is extremely uncomfortable for those who are not used to it. Sally said it was **desirable** to travel only at night when the sun has gone down and the sands have cooled.

Desirable means:
 __**a.** amusing
 __**b.** good
 __**c.** requested
 __**d.** necessary

148c

a

rou tine (rü tēn′), **1** a fixed, regular method of doing things; habitual doing of the same things in the same way: *Getting up and going to bed are parts of your daily routine.* **2** using routine: *routine methods. a routine operation.* **3** average or ordinary; run-of-the-mill: *a routine show with routine performances.* 1 *n.*. 2,3 *adj.* —**rou-tine′ly**, *adv*.

ANALOGY **routine : unusual :: modern :**
 __**a.** safe
 __**b.** expensive
 __**c.** new
 __**d.** regular
 __**e.** ancient

154b

They **escorted** him from his cell to the courtroom and up to the witness stand. Then they left the room.

Escort means:
_a. push
_b. go with
_c. carry
_d. direct

179b

No one had any words of praise or encouragement about Linda's acting ability. One man, in fact, suggested that Linda try fashion modeling instead of acting. "You don't have to say a word," the man said. "You'll do fine." Linda didn't think that was a **compliment** at all!

A **compliment** is:
_a. a statement that is not true
_b. the opinion of a particular person
_c. something good said about one
_d. a statement made with great feeling

204a

b,c,d

bur i al (ber′ ē əl)

I had asked Anouk to tell me something about the Great Pyramids. We had learned at school that they were used as places of **burial** thousands of years ago.

Write a definition or synonym:

229a

b

hor rid (hôr′ id)

I thought the new TV show was just **horrid**. Unfortunately, very few people agreed.

Write a definition or synonym:

253c

c

bal lad (bal′əd), **1** a simple song. **2** poem that tells a story in a simple verse form, especially one that tells a popular legend. Ballads are often sung. **3** a folk song. *n.*

Check the sentence(s) in which a form of **ballad** is used correctly.
_a. I marked my ballad and put it in the box.
_b. The ballad lasted for two hours.
_c. The dancing in the ballad was lovely.
_d. The minstrel sang ballads for the king.
_e. He is a writer of ballads.

278c

c

ag o ny (ag′ə nē), very painful suffering; very great anguish: *the agony of a severe toothache. The loss of their child filled them with agony. n., pl.* **ag o nies.**

Which of the following might cause **agony**?
_a. a mosquito bite   _d. an automobile accident
_b. a famine   _e. missing breakfast
_c. indigestion   _f. a traffic jam

23a

d

mel an chol y (mel′ ən kol′ ē)

Shep was hit! I ran to him. He lay in the road looking at me with the most **melancholy** expression.

Write a definition or synonym:

48b

Suzanne said that the wealthy people seem to be very rich and the poor people seem very poor. The **contrast** between them is so great it seemed startling.

Contrast means:
__**a.** unusual sight
__**b.** wealth
__**c.** great difference
__**d.** extreme poverty

73b

Manny had "discovered" each member of his band. He kept them because they were willing to play his kind of music and do what he said. But he wouldn't hesitate to **discard** them if they failed to obey. He would toss them out and forget all about them if he thought they were no longer useful.

Discard means:
__**a.** put in a safe place
__**b.** destroy completely
__**c.** handle gently
__**d.** throw aside

98c

b

pose[1] (pōz), **1** position of the body; way of holding the body: *a natural pose, a pose taken in exercising.* **2** hold a position: *He posed an hour for his portrait.* **3** put in a certain position: *The photographer posed her before taking her picture.* **4** attitude assumed for effect; pretense; affectation: *Her interest in other people is quite real; it is not just a pose.* **5** put on an attitude for effect; make a false pretense: *They posed as a rich couple although they had little money.* **6** put forward for discussion; state: *pose a question.* 1,4 *n.,* 2,3,5,6 *v.,* **posed, pos ing.**
pose[2] (pōz), puzzle completely. *v.,* **posed, pos ing.**

Check the sentence(s) in which a form of **pose** is used correctly.
__**a.** The roses made a fine pose.
__**b.** The store detective posed as a customer.
__**c.** The teacher posed a subject for discussion.
__**d.** She moved the picture to a new pose on the wall.
__**e.** I was flattered when the art teacher asked me to pose.

123c

b

de sir a ble (di zī′rə bəl), worth wishing for; worth having; pleasing; good: *The creek valley was a very desirable location for the state park. adj.* —**de sir′a ble ness,** *n.*

ANALOGY desirable : wanted ::
__**a.** breakable : beautiful
__**b.** pleasant : expensive
__**c.** unattractive : rejected
__**d.** worthy : helpful
__**e.** excellent : pleasing

149a

e

am a teur (am′ ə chər *or* am′ ə tər)

Some **amateur** flyers later became well known.

Write a definition or synonym:

154a

b, f

es cort (*n.* es′ kôrt; *v.* e skôrt′)

Two guards **escorted** the accused.

Write a definition or synonym:

179a

a, c, e

com pli ment (kom′ plə mənt)

Linda had to be satisfied with **compliments** on her gorgeous outfit.

Write a definition or synonym:

203c

d

ba zaar or **ba zar** (bə zär′), **1** street or streets full of small shops and booths in Oriental countries. **2** place for the sale of many kinds of goods. **3** sale of things contributed by various people, held for some charity or other special purpose. *n.* [*Bazaar* comes from Persian *bāzār.*]

Where would you be most likely to find a **bazaar**?
__a. London   __d. Cairo
__b. India   __e. in a museum
__c. at a church or school fair

228c

c

dis a gree a ble (dis′ə grē′ə bəl), **1** not to one's liking; unpleasant: *A headache is disagreeable.* **2** not friendly; bad-tempered; cross: *People often become disagreeable when they're tired. adj.* —**dis′a gree′a ble ness,** *n.*

ANALOGY **disagreeable : enjoyable ::**
__a. pleasant : wasteful
__b. uncertain : sure
__c. likely : probably
__d. messy : sloppy
__e. angry : cross

253b

Of course, not all **ballads** can be taken for the truth, as they are written or sung mainly for entertainment. Many, however, are based on real people and actual events.

A **ballad** is:
__a. a short story
__b. a true story
__c. a poem that tells a story
__d. a poem about an actual person

278b

My thumb had become badly infected. It was so sore that even the doctor's gentle touch filled me with **agony**.

Agony means:
__a. bleeding
__b. great fear
__c. great pain
__d. fainting

23b

If dogs could cry tears I'm sure Shep would have shed a few. Instead, he just looked **melancholy**, as if he were sorry to have caused me any trouble.

Melancholy means:
__**a.** frightened
__**b.** sad
__**c.** pained
__**d.** angry

48c

c

con trast (kon′trast *for 1,2;* kən trast′ *for 3,4*), **1** a great difference; difference: *the contrast between night and day. There is a great contrast between life now and life a hundred years ago.* **2** person, thing, event, etc., that shows differences when compared with another: *Her dark hair is a sharp contrast to her sister's light hair.* **3** compare (two things) so as to show their differences: *to contrast birds with fishes.* **4** show differences when compared or put side by side: *The black and the gold contrast well in that design.* 1,2 *n.,* 3,4 *v.* —**con trast′a ble,** *adj.* —**con-trast′ing ly,** *adv.*

1. Which of the following pairs of words show **contrast**?
__**a.** large and small __**d.** slim and slender
__**b.** smooth and rough __**e.** clean and dirty
__**c.** hard and tough
2. If two things do *not* **contrast**, they might:
__**a.** differ
__**b.** match
__**c.** oppose

73c

d

dis card (dis kärd′ *for 1,4;* dis′kärd *for 2,3,5*), **1** give up as useless or not wanted; throw aside: *discard a broken toy, discard a belief.* **2** act of throwing aside as useless or not wanted: *The discard of superstition comes with learning.* **3** thing or things thrown aside as useless or not wanted: *That old book is a discard from the library.* **4** get rid of (playing cards not wanted) by throwing them aside or playing them. **5** the cards thrown aside or played as not wanted. 1,4 *v.,* 2,3,5 *n.*

ANALOGY discard : save :: spend :
__**a.** throw
__**b.** keep
__**c.** allow
__**d.** use
__**e.** play

99a

b,c,e

a dor a ble (ə dôr′ ə bəl)

I heard a woman describe one painting as **adorable**.

Write a definition or synonym:

124a

c

ex ceed ing ly (ek sē′ ding lē)

The Great Sandy Desert is not **exceedingly** large.

Write a definition or synonym:

149b

Many competitions were held where **amateur** flyers would try to set speed, distance, and time records. Many of these **amateur** flyers later went to work for the commercial airlines. What began as fun for many became a life's work.

An **amateur** is a person who:
__**a.** does something well
__**b.** is learning a skill
__**c.** does something for a living
__**d.** does something for pleasure

153c

d

judg ment (juj′mənt), **1** result of judging; opinion or estimate: *In my judgment dogs make better pets than cats.* **2** ability to form sound opinions; power to judge well; good sense: *Since she has judgment in such matters, we will ask her.* **3** act of judging, especially a decision, decree, or sentence given by a judge in a court of law. **4** decision made by anybody who judges. **5** criticism; condemnation: *pass judgment on one's neighbors. n.* Also, **judgement.**

Which of the following would be helpful in making a fair **judgment**?

__a. opinions   __d. gifts
__b. facts   __e. hatred
__c. dreams   __f. experience

178c

b

bliss (blis), great happiness; perfect joy: *What bliss it is to plunge into the cool waves on a hot day! n.*

Check any of the following that would likely **result** if a person were in a state of **bliss**.

__a. I didn't feel my arm scrape the door.
__b. My headache kept me awake for hours.
__c. Even my baby brother didn't annoy me.
__d. I argued for a long time with my mother.
__e. Everything seemed to look new and colorful.

203b

She went to the **bazaar** to look for a present to send me. She explained that she had gone up and down the narrow streets and looked into shop after shop in the **bazaar**. She could not decide what to buy.

A **bazaar** is:

__a. a large city
__b. a large department store
__c. the center of a town or city
__d. a group of streets with shops

228b

While trying to escape from the kidnappers, she got herself trapped in a trash barrel. What a **disagreeable** way to end the day!

A synonym for **disagreeable** is:

__a. sad
__b. unhappy
__c. unpleasant
__d. hard

253a

1. b
2. Yes

bal lad (bal′ əd)

I also found a collection of **ballads** about the pioneers.

Write a definition or synonym:

278a

1. a, d
2. b

ag o ny (ag′ ə nē)

Actually, I was in **agony**.

Write a definition or synonym:

23c

b

mel an chol y (mel′ən kol′ē), **1** low spirits; sadness; tendency to be sad. **2** sad; gloomy: *a melancholy person.* **3** causing sadness; depressing: *a melancholy scene.* 1 *n.,* 2,3 *adj.*

When would someone be likely to be **melancholy**?
___**a.** on losing a pet
___**b.** on tripping over a log
___**c.** during a long rainy spell
___**d.** while reading the comics
___**e.** after failing an important test

49a

1. a, b,
   e
2. b

at trac tive (ə trak′ tiv)

Then Suzanne said that she found the Spanish people to be quite **attractive**. "That's just what I'm afraid of," said Mother. "Suzanne and some Spanish boy have fallen in love!"

Write a definition or synonym:

74a

b

sub merge (səb mérj′)

When the people heard the first, earsplitting notes of Manny's music, they rushed over to the tall rocks where the band was playing. Everybody forgot that those rocks would soon be completely **submerged**!

Write a definition or synonym:

99b

The painting was of a large white cat. She gushed on in a foolish way about the cat in the painting. I couldn't see anything **adorable** about that painting. I might have felt differently if the painting had been of a playful kitten.

A synonym for **adorable** is:
___**a.** expensive
___**b.** small
___**c.** lovable
___**d.** gentle

124b

The Sahara desert in Africa has an area of over three million square miles. Compared with the Great Sandy Desert, the Sahara is **exceedingly** large.

Exceedingly means:
___**a.** easily seen
___**b.** very greatly
___**c.** too much
___**d.** somewhat

149c

d

am a teur (am′ə chər *or* am′ə tər), **1** person who does something for pleasure, not for money or as a profession: *Only amateurs can compete in Olympic games.* **2** person who does something unskillfully or in an inexpert way: *This painting is the work of an amateur; it shows very little skill.* **3** of or by amateurs: *an amateur orchestra.* **4** being an amateur: *an amateur golfer.* 1,2 *n.,* 3,4 *adj.* [*Amateur* was borrowed from French *amateur*, which came from Latin *amator*, meaning "lover."]

Check the phrase(s) in which **amateur** is used correctly.
___**a.** amateur student   ___**d.** amateur goat
___**b.** amateur doctor   ___**e.** amateur singer
___**c.** amateur football player ___**f.** amateur hat

143

277c

c

re tort (ri tôrt'), 1 reply quickly or sharply: *"It's none of your business," I retorted.* 2 a sharp or witty reply: *"Why are your teeth so sharp?" asked Red Ridinghood. "The better to eat you with," was the wolf's retort.* 3 return in kind; turn back on: *I told her what I thought of her, and she retorted insult for insult.* 1,3 *v.,* 2 *n.*
re tort² (ri tôrt'), container used for distilling or separating substances by heat. *n.*

1. If you are to **retort**, you must be which of the following?
—**a.** alert —**c.** dizzy
—**b.** slow —**d.** quick
2. You would be likely to find a **retort** in:
—**a.** a lunch counter
—**b.** a laboratory

252c

d

bi og ra phy (bī og'rə fē), an account of a person's life. *n., pl.* **bi og ra phies.**

1. Which of the following would be most important in a **biography**?
—**a.** color —**c.** jokes
—**b.** facts —**d.** pictures
2. Only people who are famous are likely to have **biographical** books written about them.
Yes— No—

228a

a, c

dis a gree a ble (dis'ə grē'ə bəl)

When she attempted to escape, Plain Jane Hatfield came to a **disagreeable** end.

Write a definition or synonym:

203a

a,b,d

ba zaar or **ba zar** (bə zär')

In her letter, Anouk told me she had been to a **bazaar**.

Write a definition or synonym:

178b

Later Moira told reporters she felt as if she were walking on air. She had never felt quite so overjoyed. It was a state of pure **bliss**!

Bliss means:
—**a.** state of sadness
—**b.** state of happiness
—**c.** great anger
—**d.** hurt pride

155b

They would not make their **judgment** until the end of the trial. At that time they would be locked in the jury room until they all agreed on what to do.

Judgment means:
—**a.** thinking
—**b.** note-taking
—**c.** speech
—**d.** decision

24a

a,c,e

ma jor i ty (mə jôr′ ə tē)

I didn't know what to do first. The **majority** of my friends thought I should take Shep to an animal hospital.

Write a definition or synonym:

49b

She said that everyone she met was courteous and cheerful. Each day she made several new friends. She was delighted to be with such **attractive** people.

A synonym for **attractive** is:
__a. happy
__b. pleasing
__c. kind
__d. busy

74b

The tide comes in quickly at Foster's Beach. At low tide, all the rocks are out of the water. But when the water comes rushing in, even the biggest rocks are **submerged**. Soon Manny would be playing underwater music on his electric guitar!

Submerge means:
__a. cover with sand
__b. cover with water
__c. hide
__d. stick out

99c

c

a dor a ble (ə dôr′ə bəl), **1** worthy of being adored.
2 INFORMAL. attractive; delightful: *an adorable kitten. adj.*
—**a dor′a ble ness,** *n.*

Which of the following could be described as **adorable**?
__a. a string of fish __d. a table
__b. a little puppy __e. a worm
__c. a book __f. a baby

124c

b

ex ceed ing ly (ek sē′ding lē), very greatly; to an unusu-al degree; very: *Yesterday was an exceedingly hot day. adv.*

Check the phrase(s) in which **exceedingly** is used correctly.
__a. exceedingly sad __d. exceedingly hungry
__b. exceedingly much __e. exceedingly more
__c. exceedingly a little __f. exceedingly chaired

150a

c, e

feat (fēt)

Some **feats** of pioneer flyers are well known today.

Write a definition or synonym:

277b

When she asked me if my hand hurt, I retorted,
"Only when I smash rocks with my fist."

Retort means:

___ **a.** answer carefully
___ **b.** reply slowly
___ **c.** reply quickly
___ **d.** talk back

252b

The **biography** was written by a man who admired
Boone greatly. His descriptions of the "little things"
in Boone's life made me feel that I had known
Daniel Boone myself.

A **biography** is:

___ **a.** a written story about a dead person
___ **b.** the story of one's life written by oneself
___ **c.** the story of an imaginary person
___ **d.** the written story of a person's life

227c

d

blun der (blun/dər), 1 a stupid mistake: *Misspelling the
title of a book is a silly blunder to make in a book report.*
2 make a stupid mistake: *Someone blundered in sending
you to the wrong address.* 3 move clumsily or blindly;
stumble: *I blundered through the dark house.* 1 n., 2,3 v.

Which of the following are examples of **blundering**?

___ **a.** saying something you regret immediately
___ **b.** moving a heavy piano
___ **c.** knocking over a tray of glasses
___ **d.** being blinded by a brilliant light

202c

a

re mote (ri mōt/), 1 far away; far off: *The North Pole is a
remote part of the world.* 2 out of the way; secluded: *Mail
comes to this remote village only once a week.* 3 distant: *He
is a remote relative.* 4 slight; faint: *I haven't the remotest
idea what you mean.* adj., re mot er, re mot est. —re-
mote/ly, adv. —re mote/ness, n.

Which of the following are **remote**?

___ **a.** Mars   ___ **c.** one's school
___ **b.** Mt. Everest   ___ **e.** one's best friends
___ **d.** a slight hope ___ **f.** a sure thing

178a

e

bliss (blis)

Moira Morris, the actress who was given the part,
felt nothing but **bliss**.

Write a definition or synonym:

153a

b,c,e

judg ment (juj/mənt)

None of the members of the jury knew Herman or
had heard anything about him. They were chosen
because they could be fair in their **judgment** of
his case.

Write a definition or synonym:

24b

A few of my friends said I should take Shep straight home. Most of them thought I should take my dog to an animal hospital first. I agreed with the **majority**.

Majority means:
__a. older
__b. less than half
__c. more than half
__d. younger

49c

b

at trac tive (ə trak′tiv), 1 winning attention and liking; pleasing: *an attractive young couple.* 2 attracting: *the attractive power of a magnet. adj.* —**at trac′tive ly,** *adv.* —**at trac′tive ness,** *n.*

ANALOGY **attractive : unpleasant ::**
__a. mild : afraid
__b. winning : fighting
__c. costly : cheap
__d. pushing : shoving
__e. finding : rewarding

74c

b

sub merge (səb mėrj′), 1 put under water; cover with water: *A big wave submerged us. At high tide this path is submerged.* 2 cover; bury: *His talent was submerged by his shyness.* 3 sink under water; go below the surface: *The submarine submerged to escape attack. v.,* **sub merged, sub merg ing.**

1. Which of the following might be **submerged**?
   __a. rocks __c. stars __e. boat
   __b. shells __d. cloud __f. Mars
2. Which of the following expressions describe(s) something that is **submerged**?
   __a. "in the wild blue yonder"
   __b. "in the briny deep"
   __c. "in the depths of the earth"
   __d. "in Davy Jones' locker"

100a

b, f

no ti fy (nō′ tə fī)

I have **notified** my friends of my trip to the Guggenheim Museum.

Write a definition or synonym:

125a

a, d

dis tin guish (dis ting′ gwish)

It is difficult for one to **distinguish** some desert animals from their surroundings.

Write a definition or synonym:

150b

Charles Lindbergh's **feat** of skill and daring is probably the best known of all flyers' performances. His flight from New York to Paris in 1927 convinced many people that flying was safe.

Feat means:
__a. foolish act
__b. act showing great skill
__c. flight in space
__d. unexpected trip

152c

c

dis hon est (dis on′ist), **1** showing lack of honesty or fair play: *Lying, cheating, and stealing are dishonest.* **2** ready to cheat; not upright: *A person who lies or steals is dishonest.* **3** arranged to work in an unfair way: *dishonest scales weighted to cheat the customer. adj.* —**dis hon′est ly,** *adv.*

Check the phrase(s) in which **dishonest** is used correctly.
__**a.** dishonest dog   __**d.** dishonest heat
__**b.** dishonest behavior __**e.** dishonest scheme
__**c.** dishonest person   __**f.** dishonest food

177c

b

chat (chat), **1** easy, familiar talk: *The two friends had a pleasant chat about old times.* **2** talk in an easy, familiar way: *We sat chatting by the fire after supper.* **3** any of several birds with a chattering cry. 1,3 *n.,* 2 *v.,* **chat ted, chat ting.** —**chat′ta ble,** *adj.* —**chat′ting ly,** *adv.*

ANALOGY chat : speech ::
    __**a.** talk : listen
    __**b.** remind : forget
    __**c.** story : movie
    __**d.** breakfast : lunch
    __**e.** snack : meal

202b

I had never before received a letter from anywhere farther away than a few hundred miles. It was a thrill to receive an envelope that had traveled from such a **remote** place as Egypt.

Another meaning for **remote** is:
__**a.** faraway
__**b.** backward
__**c.** strange
__**d.** foreign

227b

The movers seized clubs and started swinging. The Hatfields grabbed their guns and started shooting. The gunshots were the biggest **blunder** of all. Somebody called the police, and soon the whole family was arrested! Even John had to admit that shooting the movers was a dumb thing to do!

Blunder means:
__**a.** bloody battle
__**b.** unfortunate accident
__**c.** big argument
__**d.** stupid mistake

252a

b,d,e

bi og ra phy (bī og′ rə fē)

I found what I was looking for: a **biography** of Daniel Boone.

Write a definition or synonym:

277a

d

re tort (ri tôrt′)

I tried to make a clever **retort.**

Write a definition or synonym:

24c

ma jor i ty (mə jôr′ə tē), **1** the larger number or part; more than half: *A majority of the children chose red covers for the books they had made.* **2** the number by which the votes on one side are more than those on the other: *He had 18 votes, and she had 12; so he had a majority of 6.* **3** the legal age of responsibility. Under the varying laws of the states of the United States, a person reaches his or her majority at the age of 18 in some states, at 21 in others. *n., pl.* **ma jor i ties.**

Check the sentence(s) in which **majority** is used correctly.
___**a.** The army majority had his new medal pinned to his uniform.
___**b.** The majority of the children went to the movies.
___**c.** He was a majority of the group.
___**d.** The majority of people are honest.

50a

spry (sprī)

Finally Suzanne wrote about the eighty-year-old friend who had shared her travels. "I never met anyone so **spry**," Suzanne said. My parents just looked at each other. What on earth did that mean?

Write a definition or synonym:

75a

brit tle (brit′ l)

If Manny had known anything about the sea, he would have picked a place to play where the rocks were completely dry and the seaweed was **brittle**. But Manny thought only about forcing people to listen to his music.

Write a definition or synonym:

100b

I don't always insist on telling my friends about everything that happens in my life. But the trip to the world of modern art was so fascinating that I sent out postcards to **notify** everyone who might be interested.

Notify means:
___**a.** threaten
___**b.** warn
___**c.** let know
___**d.** educate

125b

Some lizards change color to match their surroundings. This protects them by making them hard to see. It is sometimes almost impossible to **distinguish** a lizard from part of a rock.

Distinguish means:
___**a.** divide
___**b.** separate from
___**c.** tell apart
___**d.** remove

150c

feat (fēt), a great or unusual deed; act showing great skill, strength, or daring. *n.*

Which of the following would be a **feat**?
___**a.** taking a bath   ___**d.** talking loudly
___**b.** picking apples   ___**e.** figure skating
___**c.** walking a tightrope ___**f.** reading a book

276c

a

fear·less (fîr'lis), without fear; afraid of nothing; brave; daring, *adj.* —**fear'less·ly**, *adv.* —**fear'less·ness**, *n.*

ANALOGY fearless : cowardly :: daring :
__ **a.** comfortable
__ **b.** caring
__ **c.** quiet
__ **d.** cautious
__ **e.** lucky

251c

a

en·cy·clo·pe·di·a (en·si'klə·pē/dē·ə), **1** book or set of books giving information on all branches of knowledge, with its articles arranged alphabetically. **2** book treating one subject very thoroughly, with its articles arranged alphabetically: *an encyclopedia of art. n., pl.* **en·cy·clo·pe·di·as.** [*Encyclopedia* comes from the Greek phrase *enkyklios paideia,* meaning "general education."]

For which of the following might you refer to an encyclopedia?
__ **a.** current public opinion
__ **b.** the size of a country
__ **c.** the weather tomorrow
__ **d.** the date of a famous person's birth
__ **e.** the products grown in Brazil

227a

a,c,d

blun·der (blun' dər)

When Dirty John returned and saw his furniture being loaded on the truck, he started to fight with the movers. What a **blunder** that was!

Write a definition or synonym:

202a

b, e

re·mote (ri·mōt')

It was exciting to receive a letter from such a **remote** country.

Write a definition or synonym:

177b

d

No one knows just what was said during that little **chat.** But when the talking was over, Linda knew that it takes more than good looks and good clothes to get a good part.

Chat means:
__ **a.** speech
__ **b.** easy talk
__ **c.** difficult explanation
__ **d.** question and answer period

152b

Herman had lied, stolen, and cheated in his youth. Yet he had not been caught before at his **dishonest** deeds.

Dishonest means:
__ **a.** evil
__ **b.** ungrateful
__ **c.** not honest
__ **d.** cruel

25a

b, d

ca pac i ty (kə pas′ ə tē)

On the way to the animal hospital, I discovered that Shep has a great **capacity** to bear pain.

Write a definition or synonym:

50b

In spite of her age, Suzanne explained, Mrs. Carson had traveled through each country in Europe. She had explored many of the remote villages in each country. She must really be **spry** to get around so easily! Leave it to Suzanne, I thought, to find a traveling companion.

A synonym for **spry** is:
__a. happy
__b. active
__c. busy
__d. curious

75b

When seaweed stays in the sun long enough, it dries out completely. It becomes so **brittle** that it falls to pieces when you pick it up. Like the seaweed, Manny and his band were now getting quite wet! But of course, they kept playing.

Brittle means:
__a. very old
__b. easily broken
__c. of little use
__d. in poor condition

100c

c

no ti fy (nō′tə fī), give notice to; let know; announce to; inform: *Our teacher notified us that there would be a test on Monday. v.,* **no ti fied, no ti fy ing.**

Check the sentence(s) in which a form of **notify** is used correctly.
__a. I was notified that the book had arrived.
__b. She was to notify the class when it was time for gym.
__c. I notified that she had a bruise on her arm.
__d. The falling leaves notified that winter would soon be here.

125c

c

dis tin guish (dis ting′gwish), **1** see or show the differences in; tell apart: *Can you distinguish silk from nylon?* **2** see or show the difference: *to distinguish between right and wrong.* **3** see or hear clearly; make out plainly: *On a clear, bright day you can distinguish things far away.* **4** make different; be a special quality or feature of: *A trunk distinguishes the elephant.* **5** make famous or well known: *She distinguished herself by winning three prizes. v.*

Check the sentence(s) in which a form of **distinguish** is used correctly.
__a. I couldn't distinguish his features in the fog.
__b. She couldn't distinguish what dress to wear.
__c. Driving on the left distinguishes British driving from that of many other countries.
__d. It is easy to distinguish between those particular twins.

c, e

LESSON 16

Justice Is Done

Everyone in our town hated Herman Blau. Most of the police officers I knew would have just loved to put old Herman behind bars. But the police needed evidence of wrongdoing that would stand up in court. It took Sergeant Salinger to catch Herman snatching the purse of a young woman and stealing her baby's carriage. Soon Herman would have his day in court.

151

276b

I was not as **fearless** as I pretended to be. When the doctor reached for a needle, I drew back my hand. I was ashamed of myself for being a coward. "You're not afraid, are you?" the doctor asked with a smile.

Fearless means:

—a. brave
—b. showing off
—c. rude
—d. in a hurry

251b

I often become sidetracked when using an encyclopedia, for there is so much interesting information in it.

An **encyclopedia** is:

—a. a book or books giving information on a great number of subjects
—b. a file or list containing the names of books
—c. a building or room containing many books
—d. a book of words, their meanings, and how to pronounce them

b

226c

au·thor·i·ty (ə thôr′ə tē), 1 power to enforce obedience; right to command or act: *Parents have authority over their children. The police have the authority to arrest speeding drivers.* 2 person or group who has such power or right. 3 the authorities, the officials in control: *Who are the proper authorities to give permits to hunt or fish?* 4 source of correct information or wise advice: *A good dictionary is an authority on the meanings of words.* 5 an expert on some subject: *She is an authority on the Revolutionary War.* n., pl. au·thor·i·ties.

Who of the following has a position with **authority**?

—a. President
—b. schoolboy
—c. teacher
—d. mother
—e. singer
—f. peddler

d

201c

cor·re·spond·ent (kôr′ə spon′dənt), 1 person who exchanges letters with another: *My cousin and I are correspondents.* 2 person employed by a newspaper, magazine, radio or television network, etc., to send news from a particular place or region: *reports from correspondents in China and Great Britain.* 3 person or company that has regular business with another in a distant place: *Many American banks have correspondents in European cities.* 4 in agreement; corresponding. 1-3 n., 4 adj.

Check the sentence(s) in which **correspondent** is used correctly.

—a. I had carried on a correspondent with her for years.
—b. While in Italy, he was a poor correspondent.
—c. I have never written a correspondent letter.
—d. The sad woman was correspondent.
—e. She worked as a correspondent abroad.

c, d

177a

chat (chat)

The director told Linda he wanted to have a little chat.

Write a definition or synonym:

a, c, f

152a

dis·hon·est (dis on′ ist)

It was well known around town that Herman was a **dishonest** person, but no one had managed to prove it in a court of law before.

Write a definition or synonym:

25b

Shep had such a great **capacity** to bear pain that he could be badly injured without showing it.

Capacity means:
- _**a.** amount held
- _**b.** ability
- _**c.** decision
- _**d.** intelligence

50c

b

spry (sprī), active; lively; nimble: *The spry old woman traveled all over the country. adj.,* **spry er, spry est** or **spri er, spri est. —spry′ly,** *adv.* **—spry′ness,** *n.*

Check the sentence(s) in which **spry** is used correctly.
- _**a.** I had a very spry time on my birthday.
- _**b.** The spry old man danced a jig.
- _**c.** Nathan Hale was hanged as a spry.
- _**d.** I have been very spry about my examinations.

75c

b

brit tle (brit′l), very easily broken; breaking with a snap; apt to break: *Thin glass is brittle. adj.* **—brit′tle ness,** *n.*

Which of the following are *not* likely to be **brittle**?
- _**a.** newspaper
- _**d.** green grass
- _**b.** stone
- _**e.** diamond
- _**c.** dead tree branch
- _**f.** dried fern

a, b

LESSON 11

Safecracker on the Side of the Law

The huge safe at the First National Bank was locked and sealed tight at the end of each working day. At seven one Friday morning, Pauline Cuomo, the bank manager, pushed the button on the lock that would open the heavy metal door to the safe. The door didn't open! Something must have happened to the lock! Pauline notified the police and the main office of the bank. Then she put a call through to the company that made the safe and asked for Mr. Lucas Sandoz.

126a

a,c,d

spec i men (spes′ ə mən)

Sally began to photograph **specimens** of desert life.

Write a definition or synonym:

151a

pre side (pri zīd′)

Judge Cynthia Wayne **presided** at the trial of Herman Blau.

Write a definition or synonym:

151c

c

pre side (pri zīd′), **1** hold the place of authority; have charge of a meeting: *preside at an election.* **2** have authority; have control: *The manager presides over the business of this store.* v., **pre sid ed, pre sid ing. —pre sid′er,** *n.*

Who would be most likely to **preside** at something?
__a. president __d. football player
__b. dishwasher __e. flea killer
__c. chairperson __f. manager

176c

d

com plaint (kəm plānt′), **1** a complaining; a voicing of dissatisfaction; finding fault: *His letter is filled with complaints about the food at camp.* **2** accusation; charge: *The judge heard the complaint and ordered an investigation.* **3** a cause for complaining: *Her main complaint is that she has too much work to do.* **4** illness: disease: *A cold is a very common complaint. n.*

Check the sentence(s) in which **complaint** is used correctly.
__a. You must complaint with the rules.
__b. Do not complaint in class.
__c. The policeman filed a complaint against the man.
__d. I do not want to hear a complaint about the meal.

201b

Anouk and I were off to a good start as **correspondents**. She replied immediately to my first letter. She had many interesting things to tell about Egypt and was interested in finding out more about the United States.

A **correspondent** is:
__a. a person who is a close friend
__b. a person who resembles another
__c. a person who supplies information
__d. a person who exchanges letters with another

226b

With Dirty John away, none of the Hatfields felt they had the **authority** to send the movers away. In the Hatfield family, Dirty John kept all power to make decisions to himself.

Authority means:
__a. power to see
__b. right to command
__c. right to give
__d. intelligence

251a

en cy clo pe di a (en sī′ klə pē′ dē ə)

The first step in my project was to go to the **encyclopedia**.

Write a definition or synonym:

276a

1. a, c, d
2. Yes

fear less (fir′ lis)

I tried to act **fearless**.

Write a definition or synonym:

25c

b

ca pac i ty (kə pas′ə tē), **1** amount of room or space inside; largest amount that can be held by a container. **2** ability to receive and hold. **3** ability to learn or do; power or fitness. **4** position or relation. **5** capacitance. *n., pl.* **ca pac i ties.** (Definition adapted)

Which of the following would have a **capacity**?
__a. flowers   __d. a stick
__b. a liter bottle __e. a student
__c. an auditorium

Go back to page 1 and continue on frame 26a.

LESSON ⑥ | Too Expensive to Keep—Too Wonderful to Lose

b

The Christmas that Amanda Wayne got her own horse was the happiest time of her life. She called the horse Ranger and spent every possible minute with him. Then one February day her father had bad news. Their farm was losing money and Ranger would have to be sold. Several days later, Amanda's heart sank when she saw a strange car approaching .

Go back to page 1 and continue on frame 51a.

76a

a, b,
d, e

o ver head (*adv.* ō′ vər hed′; *adj., n.* ō′ vər hed′)

Suddenly we heard a loud noise **overhead**. It was even louder than Manny's rock music.

Write a definition or synonym:

Go back to page 1 and continue on frame 76b.

101a

sat is fac tor y (sat′ i sfak′ tər ē)

The bank had always received **satisfactory** service from the company that manufactured and sold the safe.

Write a definition or synonym:

Go back to page 1 and continue on frame 101b.

126b

One day she photographed a beautiful **specimen** of flowering cactus. This one plant interested her so much that she decided to concentrate on the cactus family.

Specimen means:
__a. only one of its kind
__b. group of any things
__c. one of a group
__d. animal

Go back to page 1 and continue on frame 126c.

151b

Judge Wayne sat on a high chair behind her tall desk. She looked quite stern as she **presided** at Herman's trial. Occasionally, she rapped her gavel to quiet the room, or gave instructions to the witnesses and the jury.

Preside means:
__a. make an appearance
__b. make decisions
__c. be in charge
__d. be present

Turn the book upside down and continue on frame 151c.

EDL WORD CLUES MASTERY TESTS*

Carolyn A. Hill
Rumson-Fair Haven (N.J.) Regional High School

When you finish each Word Clues lesson, how well do you remember the meanings of the words you have studied? The Word Clues Mastery Tests will help you answer this question.

There is one test for each lesson in the book. Each test has ten questions, one on each word taught in the lesson. These target words are set in **boldface** type.

Five kinds of questions are used in the tests. Here are the directions for each kind.

Definitions in Context: Choose the best meaning of the target word in each sentence.

Synonyms or Similar Meanings: Select the word or phrase that is closest in meaning to the target word.

Antonyms or Opposite Meanings: Select the word or phrase that is most nearly opposite in meaning to the target word.

Words in Context: Choose the word that best completes the sentence.

Analogies: Choose the word or phrase that best completes each analogy.

Answer all questions as directed by your instructor. Caution: Pay attention to the headings because the kinds of questions are not always in the same order.

---

*The authors of the Word Clues Mastery Tests for the various levels are as follows:

G	Carolyn A. Hill	**K**	Joseph J. Dignan
H	Marie H. Hughes	**L**	Paul A. Fuchs and
I	Margaret B. Holton		Mary Ellen Grassin
J	Elinor H. Kinney	**M**	William A. Speiser

NOTE: This edition of Word Clues G contains a final posttest. For this test, 25 words have been randomly chosen as representative of the total number of words taught. Students who score 80% or higher can move to the next higher book.

WORD CLUES MASTERY TEST G-2

DEFINITIONS IN CONTEXT

11. It takes me **approximately** an hour to get home from here.
   a. exactly
   b. just
   c. possibly
   d. about
   e. beyond

12. He took his **knapsack** with him.
   a. carrying bag
   b. sleeping bag
   c. litter bag
   d. lunch pail
   e. suitcase

WORDS IN CONTEXT

13. After eating hot peppers, she had ____ .
   a. preparation
   b. excursion
   c. indigestion
   d. cancellation
   e. location

14. Do you have ____ shoes for the long walk?
   a. visible
   b. displeasing
   c. protected
   d. marine
   e. suitable

SYNONYMS OR SIMILAR MEANINGS

15. **enthusiasm**
   a. laughter
   b. zeal
   c. relief
   d. punishment
   e. confusion

16. **visible**
   a. proper
   b. protected
   c. apparent
   d. close
   e. available

ANTONYMS OR OPPOSITE MEANINGS

17. **depart**
   a. meet
   b. hike
   c. leave
   d. separate
   e. arrive

18. **consume**
   a. cook
   b. use
   c. eat
   d. save
   e. share

ANALOGIES

19. **pamphlet : booklet :: preparation :**
   a. newspaper
   b. study guide
   c. getting ready
   d. repair
   e. magazine

20. **site : location :: corps :**
   a. dead body
   b. army
   c. group of people
   d. vision
   e. portion

WORD CLUES MASTERY TEST G-1

DEFINITIONS IN CONTEXT

1. The travel bureau gave us a **pamphlet** to use as a guide on our trip.
   a. booklet
   b. map
   c. card
   d. pattern
   e. ticket

2. We saw an exhibit of **marine** animals.
   a. able to swim
   b. captured
   c. very large
   d. of the sea
   e. rare

SYNONYMS OR SIMILAR MEANINGS

3. **label**
   a. copy
   b. tag
   c. sample
   d. covering
   e. picture

4. **site**
   a. hill
   b. scene
   c. place
   d. land
   e. building

5. **excursion**
   a. trip
   b. operation
   c. walk
   d. visit
   e. argument

ANTONYMS OR OPPOSITE MEANINGS

6. **displeased**
   a. sad
   b. ill
   c. tired
   d. glad
   e. annoyed

7. **gigantic**
   a. tiny
   b. frightening
   c. strong
   d. open
   e. huge

WORDS IN CONTEXT

8. We had to ____ the picnic because of rain.
   a. label
   b. offend
   c. improve
   d. continue
   e. cancel

ANALOGIES

9. **postpone : delay :: label :**
   a. notice
   b. recognize
   c. name
   d. store
   e. use

10. **home : residence :: amusement :**
   a. entertainment
   b. concert
   c. study
   d. family
   e. laughter

WORD CLUES MASTERY TEST **G-4**

DEFINITIONS IN CONTEXT
31. The editor was supposed to **supervise** the reporters.
   a. teach
   b. study
   c. correct
   d. direct
   e. improve

32. A column of **gossip** would make our newspaper more lively.
   a. current events
   b. talk about people
   c. comics and cartoons
   d. falsehoods
   e. advice to people

SYNONYMS OR SIMILAR MEANINGS
33. competition
   a. contest
   b. argument
   c. agreement
   d. comparison
   e. imitation

34. accuracy
   a. skill
   b. cleverness
   c. speed
   d. capacity
   e. correctness

ANTONYMS OR OPPOSITE MEANINGS
35. aware
   a. unafraid
   b. cruel
   c. unconscious
   d. knowing
   e. opposite

36. variety
   a. difference
   b. sameness
   c. amount
   d. difficulty
   e. interest

WORDS IN CONTEXT
37. We paid the ____ for our tickets to the concert.
   a. publisher
   b. marine
   c. corps
   d. lobby
   e. cashier

38. We decided to ____ to the magazine for one year.
   a. supervise
   b. cancel
   c. subscribe
   d. describe
   e. prohibit

ANALOGIES
39. site : place :: policy :
   a. belief
   b. leadership
   c. honesty
   d. important decision
   e. plan of action

40. producer : film :: publisher :
   a. book
   b. author
   c. printer
   d. actor
   e. agent

WORD CLUES MASTERY TEST **G-3**

DEFINITIONS IN CONTEXT
21. The **majority** of the apples were rotten.
   a. greater part
   b. lesser part
   c. half
   d. oldest
   e. smallest

22. She has a great **capacity** to bear pain.
   a. bravery
   b. ability
   c. decision
   d. intelligence
   e. amount held

SYNONYMS OR SIMILAR MEANINGS
23. occupy
   a. delay
   b. complete
   c. fill
   d. purchase
   e. reserve

24. acute
   a. unusual
   b. sudden
   c. frightening
   d. loud
   e. sharp

ANTONYMS OR OPPOSITE MEANINGS
25. unfortunate
   a. lucky
   b. sick
   c. accidental
   d. poor
   e. usual

26. melancholy
   a. frightened
   b. pained
   c. happy
   d. angry
   e. sad

WORDS IN CONTEXT
27. Several people were sitting in the ____, waiting for the doctor.
   a. majority
   b. lobby
   c. corps
   d. capacity
   e. physician

28. The ____ cleaned the wound and sewed it up.
   a. majority
   b. lobby
   c. corps
   d. puncture
   e. physician

ANALOGIES
29. depart : arrive :: prohibit :
   a. arrive
   b. label
   c. criticize
   d. permit
   e. separate

30. indigestion : rich food :: puncture :
   a. postpone
   b. hole
   c. criticize
   d. flat tire
   e. sharp nail

WORD CLUES MASTERY TEST **G-6**

DEFINITIONS IN CONTEXT

51. The workers could barely **hoist** the heavy blocks of stone.
    a. lift up
    b. push out
    c. drag down
    d. carry away
    e. move in

52. When I met the President, I expressed my **admiration**.
    a. relief
    b. regret
    c. amazement
    d. horror
    e. approval

SYNONYMS OR SIMILAR MEANINGS

53. **incident**
    a. time
    b. accident
    c. trouble
    d. event
    e. mistake

54. **apparently**
    a. curiously
    b. noisily
    c. naturally
    d. hardly
    e. seemingly

ANTONYMS OR OPPOSITE MEANINGS

55. **extremely**
    a. very
    b. uncomfortably
    c. slightly
    d. carefully
    e. approximately

56. **sensible**
    a. improper
    b. unwise
    c. unusual
    d. cautious
    e. thoughtful

WORDS IN CONTEXT

57. The ____ between the two yards is marked by a fence.
    a. forest
    b. incident
    c. marine
    d. distance
    e. boundary

58. The soldiers will be punished if they ____ their captain.
    a. disobey
    b. await
    c. supervise
    d. postpone
    e. gossip

ANALOGIES

59. **page : pamphlet :: tread :**
    a. piano
    b. swing
    c. puncture
    d. staircase
    e. ladder

60. **contrast : difference :: commotion :**
    a. admiration
    b. resemblance
    c. capacity
    d. annoyance
    e. disturbance

WORD CLUES MASTERY TEST **G-5**

DEFINITIONS IN CONTEXT

41. I eagerly **await** your first letter.
    a. expect
    b. want
    c. hope for
    d. look forward to
    e. weigh

42. The performers in the **ballet** were excellent.
    a. opera
    b. dance
    c. play
    d. comedy
    e. movie

WORDS IN CONTEXT

43. As children grow up, they long to be ____ of their parents.
    a. acute
    b. approximate
    c. enthusiastic
    d. accurate
    e. independent

44. The bus driver ____ for delaying us.
    a. displeased
    b. apologized
    c. awaited
    d. prohibited
    e. postponed

SYNONYMS OR SIMILAR MEANINGS

45. **luggage**
    a. clothes
    b. hatboxes
    c. packages
    d. waste
    e. baggage

46. **spry**
    a. old
    b. smart
    c. active
    d. thin
    e. curious

ANTONYMS OR OPPOSITE MEANINGS

47. **contrast**
    a. differ
    b. oppose
    c. match
    d. appear
    e. improve

48. **attractive**
    a. unhappy
    b. unkind
    c. unusual
    d. ugly
    e. unexpected

ANALOGIES

49. **book : pamphlet :: boulevard :**
    a. alley
    b. ballet
    c. competition
    d. cashier
    e. policy

50. **unpleasant : displeasing :: abroad :**
    a. trip
    b. flight
    c. unhappy
    d. plan
    e. overseas

WORD CLUES MASTERY TEST G-8

DEFINITIONS IN CONTEXT

71. We **probably** will visit the beach again.
   a. more likely than not
   b. all together
   c. certainly
   d. with luck
   e. eventually

72. I walked along the shore, looking for something for my **aquarium**.
   a. collection of sea pictures
   b. board for mounting stuffed fish
   c. collection of rocks
   d. necklace of shells
   e. place for keeping live fish

SYNONYMS OR SIMILAR MEANINGS

73. submerge
   a. bathe
   b. come
   c. float
   d. bury
   e. combine

74. conceal
   a. damage
   b. wet
   c. hide
   d. follow
   e. tell

75. massive
   a. hard
   b. big
   c. sharp
   d. rough
   e. attractive

ANTONYMS OR OPPOSITE MEANINGS

76. discard
   a. handle gently
   b. destroy completely
   c. put in a safe place
   d. throw aside
   e. cut in half

WORDS IN CONTEXT

77. The dead seaweed appeared to be quite _____ .
   a. massive
   b. brittle
   c. cautious
   d. sensible
   e. marine

78. The cat ____ before the fire.
   a. discarded
   b. submerged
   c. basked
   d. concealed
   e. balked

ANALOGIES

79. knapsack : luggage :: helicopter :
   a. aircraft
   b. visible
   c. capacity
   d. variety
   e. excursion

80. outside : inside :: overhead :
   a. far
   b. boundary
   c. beyond
   d. basement
   e. underneath

WORD CLUES MASTERY TEST G-7

WORDS IN CONTEXT

61. Grandfather never seemed to ____ the time he spent with us.
   a. begrudge
   b. rely
   c. balk
   d. fetch
   e. consume

62. My horse ____ before jumping the fence.
   a. bruised
   b. balked
   c. begrudged
   d. fetched
   e. relied

DEFINITIONS IN CONTEXT

63. One cannot **rely** on the weather report.
   a. ask
   b. expect
   c. balk
   d. believe
   e. depend

64. Those harsh words will **bruise** her feelings.
   a. displease
   b. hurt
   c. occupy
   d. puncture
   e. tread

SYNONYMS OR SIMILAR MEANINGS

65. eventually
   a. once
   b. often
   c. finally
   d. always
   e. surprisingly

66. intention
   a. hope
   b. dream
   c. pleasure
   d. plan
   e. dent

ANTONYMS OR OPPOSITE MEANINGS

67. cautious
   a. suspicious
   b. shy
   c. noisy
   d. slow
   e. careless

68. fetch
   a. sell
   b. choose
   c. buy
   d. remove
   e. succeed

ANALOGIES

69. suitable : fitting :: sufficient :
   a. good
   b. much
   c. enough
   d. any
   e. lacking

70. admiration : approval :: disposition :
   a. nature
   b. problem
   c. interview
   d. contrast
   e. preparation

WORD CLUES MASTERY TEST G-10

DEFINITIONS IN CONTEXT
91. Our teacher **notified** us that there would be a test on Monday.
    a. threatened
    b. informed
    c. warned
    d. displeased
    e. concealed

92. There are many **attractions** at Disneyland.
    a. things that make people laugh
    b. things that make noise
    c. things that bother people
    d. things that cause fear
    e. things that fascinate people

SYNONYMS OR SIMILAR MEANINGS
93. **situated**
    a. built
    b. visited
    c. planned
    d. located
    e. changed

94. **bleak**
    a. dismal
    b. different
    c. frightening
    d. ugly
    e. weak

ANTONYMS OR OPPOSITE MEANINGS
95. **dispute**
    a. criticism
    b. agreement
    c. fight
    d. conversation
    e. refusal

96. **adorable**
    a. expensive
    b. small
    c. large
    d. hateful
    e. delightful

WORDS IN CONTEXT
97. The store detective _____ as a customer.
    a. posed
    b. baffled
    c. situated
    d. disputed
    e. competed

98. An injury kept him from _____ in the race.
    a. posing
    b. baffling
    c. situating
    d. disputing
    e. competing

ANALOGIES
99. **villain : hero :: burlap :**
    a. sack
    b. satin
    c. rough cloth
    d. curtain
    e. canvas

100. **vow : promise :: baffle :**
    a. annoy
    b. rely
    c. memorize
    d. hinder
    e. cancel

WORD CLUES MASTERY TEST G-9

DEFINITIONS IN CONTEXT
81. The actors had to **memorize** their lines.
    a. remember well
    b. study hard
    c. learn by heart
    d. look at carefully
    e. read on stage

82. Our play was based on a **romance**.
    a. funny story
    b. mystery story
    c. true story
    d. serious story
    e. love story

SYNONYMS OR SIMILAR MEANINGS
83. **assembly**
    a. meeting
    b. school
    c. class
    d. show
    e. parade

84. **allegiance**
    a. honor
    b. loyalty
    c. praise
    d. joining
    e. promise

ANTONYMS OR OPPOSITE MEANINGS
85. **frequently**
    a. seldom
    b. often
    c. steadily
    d. loudly
    e. gladly

86. **villain**
    a. criminal
    b. hero
    c. giant
    d. horse
    e. corps

WORDS IN CONTEXT
87. He _____ never to leave home again.
    a. memorized
    b. submerged
    c. vowed
    d. fetched
    e. elaborated

88. The _____ between the two men in the play was very funny.
    a. vow
    b. villain
    c. allegiance
    d. assembly
    e. dialogue

ANALOGIES
89. **gigantic : small :: elaborate :**
    a. complex
    b. open
    c. simple
    d. unwise
    e. strong

90. **puncture : flat tire :: comedy :**
    a. theater
    b. laughter
    c. play
    d. actors
    e. director

WORD CLUES MASTERY TEST G-12

DEFINITIONS IN CONTEXT

111. **Buoys** may be seen in many harbors.
    a. noise makers
    b. floating markers
    c. small boats
    d. young sailors
    e. warning lights

112. An alert crew will gain the captain's **approval**.
    a. careful opinion
    b. unfavorable opinion
    c. instant opinion
    d. strong opinion
    e. favorable opinion

SYNONYMS OR SIMILAR MEANINGS

113. **solitary**
    a. alone
    b. unfriendly
    c. interesting
    d. quiet
    e. private

114. **instruction**
    a. understanding
    b. teaching
    c. equipment
    d. speech
    e. system

ANTONYMS OR OPPOSITE MEANINGS

115. **boulder**
    a. reef
    b. shyness
    c. dam
    d. dock
    e. pebble

116. **unlike**
    a. different
    b. opposite
    c. similar
    d. smaller
    e. pleasant

WORDS IN CONTEXT

117. I have ____ a large stamp collection.
    a. snarled
    b. situated
    c. instructed
    d. acquired
    e. budged

118. The dog refused to ____ from his house.
    a. snarl
    b. situate
    c. occupy
    d. acquire
    e. budge

ANALOGIES

119. **recipe : cook :: beacon :**
    a. pamphlet
    b. guide
    c. sailor
    d. eggs
    e. policy

120. **conceal : hide :: snarl :**
    a. tangle
    b. smile
    c. roar
    d. straighten
    e. annoy

WORD CLUES MASTERY TEST G-11

DEFINITIONS IN CONTEXT

101. I couldn't have found your house without the **assistance** of a map.
    a. relief
    b. strength
    c. observation
    d. advice
    e. help

102. When we arrived, we were surprised to find the door **ajar**.
    a. wide open
    b. unlocked
    c. slightly open
    d. knocked down
    e. broken

SYNONYMS OR SIMILAR MEANINGS

103. **remainder**
    a. part
    b. majority
    c. end
    d. remark
    e. rest

104. **satchel**
    a. suitcase
    b. handbag
    c. knapsack
    d. trunk
    e. baggage

ANTONYMS OR OPPOSITE MEANINGS

105. **satisfactory**
    a. pleasing
    b. dishonest
    c. friendly
    d. excellent
    e. inadequate

106. **customary**
    a. ordinary
    b. unusual
    c. unnecessary
    d. required
    e. bothersome

WORDS IN CONTEXT

107. My parents ____ me for my good grades.
    a. assisted
    b. announced
    c. injected
    d. satisfied
    e. congratulated

108. The ____ appeared in the newspaper.
    a. satisfaction
    b. satchel
    c. announcement
    d. injection
    e. remainder

ANALOGIES

109. **symptom : physician :: clue :**
    a. detective
    b. baffle
    c. publisher
    d. hint
    e. sign

110. **dispute : agreement :: injection :**
    a. competition
    b. removal
    c. insertion
    d. argument
    e. memory

WORD CLUES MASTERY TEST G-14

DEFINITIONS IN CONTEXT
131. It took us ten minutes to get our **sedan** out of the garage.
- **a.** a closed auto seating four or more
- **b.** an auto having no back seat
- **c.** a small truck
- **d.** an open car seating two people
- **e.** a car for carrying a dead person

132. We drove off and headed for the **turnpike**.
- **a.** a highway through the country
- **b.** a road on which toll is paid
- **c.** a place where several roads meet
- **d.** a road on which there is no speed limit
- **e.** a four-lane highway

WORDS IN CONTEXT
133. Because the traffic moved so slowly, we didn't have to watch the ____ .
- **a.** sedan
- **b.** landscape
- **c.** speedometer
- **d.** turnpike
- **e.** hearse

134. At least I could enjoy looking at the ____ as we drove along.
- **a.** sedan
- **b.** landscape
- **c.** speedometer
- **d.** turnpike
- **e.** hearse

SYNONYMS OR SIMILAR MEANINGS
135. **exceed**
- **a.** ignore
- **b.** break
- **c.** surpass
- **d.** equal
- **e.** speed

136. **affectionate**
- **a.** big
- **b.** friendly
- **c.** hearty
- **d.** loving
- **e.** active

ANTONYMS OR OPPOSITE MEANINGS
137. **bashful**
- **a.** bold
- **b.** happy
- **c.** tired
- **d.** big
- **e.** frightened

138. **monotonous**
- **a.** quiet
- **b.** restful
- **c.** long
- **d.** boring
- **e.** varying

ANALOGIES
139. **desert : barren :: hearse :**
- **a.** corps
- **b.** bleak
- **c.** black
- **d.** vehicle
- **e.** funeral

140. **alley : boulevard :: suburb :**
- **a.** village
- **b.** city
- **c.** small
- **d.** friendly
- **e.** highway

WORD CLUES MASTERY TEST G-13

DEFINITIONS IN CONTEXT
121. We had to look carefully to find a **hint** of life on the desert.
- **a.** complete description
- **b.** good example
- **c.** full explanation
- **d.** slight sign
- **e.** little piece

122. The Sahara is **exceedingly** large.
- **a.** extremely
- **b.** visibly
- **c.** eventually
- **d.** apparently
- **e.** slightly

SYNONYMS OR SIMILAR MEANINGS
123. **selection**
- **a.** handling
- **b.** case
- **c.** approval
- **d.** attraction
- **e.** choice

124. **vary**
- **a.** shrink
- **b.** move
- **c.** grow
- **d.** change
- **e.** improve

ANTONYMS OR OPPOSITE MEANINGS
125. **desirable**
- **a.** unnecessary
- **b.** good
- **c.** unappealing
- **d.** amusing
- **e.** requested

126. **abundant**
- **a.** ordinary
- **b.** scarce
- **c.** plentiful
- **d.** frequent
- **e.** favorable

WORDS IN CONTEXT
127. I couldn't ____ his features in the fog.
- **a.** vary
- **b.** hint
- **c.** distinguish
- **d.** budge
- **e.** select

128. We asked permission to take a ____ of plant life for our collection.
- **a.** hint
- **b.** boulder
- **c.** competition
- **d.** specimen
- **e.** disposition

ANALOGIES
129. **sometimes : often :: occasional :**
- **a.** approximate
- **b.** solitary
- **c.** frequent
- **d.** probable
- **e.** never

130. **unlike : similar :: barren :**
- **a.** bare
- **b.** fruitful
- **c.** ajar
- **d.** different
- **e.** empty

WORD CLUES MASTERY TEST G-16

DEFINITIONS IN CONTEXT

151. Judge Black will **preside** at the trial.
    - **a.** give consent
    - **b.** win out
    - **c.** be in charge
    - **d.** be present
    - **e.** take notes

152. Usually, there are more **gangsters** in cities than in small towns.
    - **a.** persons who steal money
    - **b.** people in prison
    - **c.** members of criminal groups
    - **d.** persons who break the law
    - **e.** members of clubs

WORDS IN CONTEXT

153. The troopship had a(n) _____ of three warships.
    - **a.** recital
    - **b.** vehicle
    - **c.** judgment
    - **d.** escort
    - **e.** alibi

154. The jury listened to the _____ of events that took place the night of the crime.
    - **a.** recital
    - **b.** vehicle
    - **c.** judgment
    - **d.** escort
    - **e.** alibi

SYNONYMS OR SIMILAR MEANINGS

155. **judgment**
    - **a.** thinking
    - **b.** speech
    - **c.** rule
    - **d.** decision
    - **e.** hesitation

156. **alibi**
    - **a.** lie
    - **b.** absence
    - **c.** excuse
    - **d.** crime
    - **e.** act

ANTONYMS OR OPPOSITE MEANINGS

157. **dishonest**
    - **a.** evil
    - **b.** honorable
    - **c.** ungrateful
    - **d.** cruel
    - **e.** brave

158. **individual**
    - **a.** sample
    - **b.** expert
    - **c.** member
    - **d.** person
    - **e.** crowd

ANALOGIES

159. **supervise : worker :: imprison :**
    - **a.** guilty
    - **b.** innocent
    - **c.** jail
    - **d.** laborer
    - **e.** criminal

160. **sedan : vehicle ::**
    - **a.** amateur : feat
    - **b.** speedometer : mile
    - **c.** marine : whale
    - **d.** puncture : hole
    - **e.** enthusiasm : punishment

WORD CLUES MASTERY TEST G-15

DEFINITIONS IN CONTEXT

141. In stunt flying, the pilot often makes **aerial** loops.
    - **a.** within sight
    - **b.** in the air
    - **c.** on the ground
    - **d.** out of sight
    - **e.** over a crowd

142. There were few **commercial** planes in the early days of flying.
    - **a.** having to do with amusement
    - **b.** having to do with government
    - **c.** having to do with business
    - **d.** having to do with war
    - **e.** having to do with many people

SYNONYMS OR SIMILAR MEANINGS

143. **instruct**
    - **a.** learn
    - **b.** study
    - **c.** test
    - **d.** warn
    - **e.** teach

144. **routine**
    - **a.** unusual
    - **b.** monotonous
    - **c.** long
    - **d.** regular
    - **e.** occasional

ANTONYMS OR OPPOSITE MEANINGS

145. **bachelor**
    - **a.** youth
    - **b.** widow
    - **c.** husband
    - **d.** uncle
    - **e.** orphan

146. **descend**
    - **a.** stoop
    - **b.** turn
    - **c.** proceed
    - **d.** hurry
    - **e.** climb

WORDS IN CONTEXT

147. It is fun to watch a plane gain _____ .
    - **a.** altitude
    - **b.** feat
    - **c.** routine
    - **d.** aeronautics
    - **e.** aerial

148. Charles Lindbergh's _____ of skill and daring is well known.
    - **a.** altitude
    - **b.** feat
    - **c.** routine
    - **d.** aeronautics
    - **e.** aerial

ANALOGIES

149. **businessman : profit :: amateur :**
    - **a.** pleasure
    - **b.** professional
    - **c.** salary
    - **d.** athlete
    - **e.** beginner

150. **medicine : physician :: aeronautics :**
    - **a.** mathematics
    - **b.** prescription
    - **c.** aircraft
    - **d.** villain
    - **e.** pilot

WORD CLUES MASTERY TEST G-18

DEFINITIONS IN CONTEXT

171. Of the two hats that fit me, this one is **preferable**.
- **a.** less costly
- **b.** of higher quality
- **c.** better-looking
- **d.** more useful
- **e.** more desirable

172. Our neighbors were very **considerate**.
- **a.** businesslike
- **b.** tireless
- **c.** thoughtful of others
- **d.** full of fun
- **e.** pleasant in appearance

WORDS IN CONTEXT

173. I thought the colors used in the painting were too ____.
- **a.** extreme
- **b.** preferable
- **c.** considerate
- **d.** commercial
- **e.** alteration

174. Mother said she would have a(n) ____ with Father.
- **a.** alteration
- **b.** chat
- **c.** complaint
- **d.** bliss
- **e.** compliment

SYNONYMS OR SIMILAR MEANINGS

175. stylish
- **a.** inexpensive
- **b.** colorful
- **c.** fashionable
- **d.** common
- **e.** beautiful

176. alteration
- **a.** discussion
- **b.** argument
- **c.** hesitation
- **d.** change
- **e.** growth

ANTONYMS OR OPPOSITE MEANINGS

177. positive
- **a.** glad
- **b.** insisting
- **c.** pretending
- **d.** calm
- **e.** unsure

178. bliss
- **a.** happiness
- **b.** sadness
- **c.** anger
- **d.** pride
- **e.** conflict

ANALOGIES

179. complaint : compliment ::
- **a.** gossip : bachelor
- **b.** enthusiasm : hub
- **c.** admiration : beacon
- **d.** appropriate : climax
- **e.** blame : praise

180. chat : discuss ::
- **a.** insure : vehicle
- **b.** escort : feat
- **c.** instruct : student
- **d.** sniffle : sob
- **e.** monotonous : varied

WORD CLUES MASTERY TEST G-17

DEFINITIONS IN CONTEXT

161. Can you **assure** me that there is no danger?
- **a.** make probable
- **b.** make possible
- **c.** make certain
- **d.** make real
- **e.** make necessary

162. There was **constant** competition between the two groups.
- **a.** once in a while
- **b.** recent
- **c.** a small amount
- **d.** sufficient
- **e.** never-ending

SYNONYMS OR SIMILAR MEANINGS

163. hub
- **a.** beginning
- **b.** cause
- **c.** place
- **d.** passage
- **e.** center

164. conflict
- **a.** fight
- **b.** conference
- **c.** meeting
- **d.** race
- **e.** accident

ANTONYMS OR OPPOSITE MEANINGS

165. appropriate
- **a.** alike
- **b.** special
- **c.** unusual
- **d.** unsuitable
- **e.** unnecessary

166. distinguished
- **a.** political
- **b.** intelligent
- **c.** unknown
- **d.** poor
- **e.** removed

WORDS IN CONTEXT

167. The ____ of our day was the visit to the zoo.
- **a.** hub
- **b.** conflict
- **c.** vehicle
- **d.** solution
- **e.** climax

168. The Union Pacific Railroad was ____ finished.
- **a.** exceedingly
- **b.** actually
- **c.** constantly
- **d.** occasionally
- **e.** satisfactory

ANALOGIES

169. solution : problem ::
- **a.** gangster : judgment
- **b.** answer : question
- **c.** vehicle : recital
- **d.** medicine : physician
- **e.** dishonest : alibi

170. criticize : fault ::
- **a.** imprison : commercial
- **b.** descend : climb
- **c.** marine : corps
- **d.** displease : knapsack
- **e.** correct : error

WORD CLUES MASTERY TEST G-20

DEFINITIONS IN CONTEXT
191. The **conquest** of their old enemy was discussed everywhere.
- **a.** threat
- **b.** danger
- **c.** search
- **d.** presence
- **e.** defeat

192. We took a picture of the little **cemetery**.
- **a.** town
- **b.** park
- **c.** monument
- **d.** graveyard
- **e.** church

SYNONYMS OR SIMILAR MEANINGS
193. **trophy**
- **a.** victory
- **b.** contest
- **c.** battle
- **d.** end
- **e.** prize

194. **leisure**
- **a.** happy
- **b.** lazy
- **c.** unemployed
- **d.** free
- **e.** tired

ANTONYMS OR OPPOSITE MEANINGS
195. **favorable**
- **a.** unpromising
- **b.** happy
- **c.** lucky
- **d.** favorite
- **e.** pleasant

196. **vivid**
- **a.** beautiful
- **b.** angry
- **c.** distinct
- **d.** alive
- **e.** dull

WORDS IN CONTEXT
197. A lucky ____ in oil stock made his fortune.
- **a.** conquest
- **b.** trophy
- **c.** venture
- **d.** communication
- **e.** crevice

198. There was no ____ between the enemy tribes.
- **a.** conquest
- **b.** trophy
- **c.** venture
- **d.** communication
- **e.** crevice

ANALOGIES
199. **puncture : tire :: crevice :**
- **a.** flower
- **b.** ice
- **c.** ice cream
- **d.** boundary
- **e.** bones

200. **utmost : least ::**
- **a.** alteration : change
- **b.** bashful : shy
- **c.** accuracy : mistake
- **d.** preferable : selection
- **e.** submerged : aerial

WORD CLUES MASTERY TEST G-19

DEFINITIONS IN CONTEXT
181. Behind the main house was a **bungalow**.
- **a.** house having two or more stories
- **b.** one-room cottage
- **c.** house with an attached garage
- **d.** house constructed of wood
- **e.** house with one story

182. The city has many lovely **residential** areas.
- **a.** having to do with business
- **b.** having to do with land
- **c.** having to do with people
- **d.** having to do with homes
- **e.** having to do with restaurants

SYNONYMS OR SIMILAR MEANINGS
183. **dwell**
- **a.** live
- **b.** remain
- **c.** vacation
- **d.** work
- **e.** build

184. **laborer**
- **a.** designer
- **b.** manufacturer
- **c.** worker
- **d.** builder
- **e.** person

ANTONYMS OR OPPOSITE MEANINGS
185. **donate**
- **a.** send
- **b.** carry
- **c.** give
- **d.** take
- **e.** help

186. **remarkable**
- **a.** usual
- **b.** rapid
- **c.** sad
- **d.** sudden
- **e.** exciting

WORDS IN CONTEXT
187. Iron is the ____ part of steel.
- **a.** residential
- **b.** remarkable
- **c.** industrious
- **d.** considerate
- **e.** basic

188. We discovered a ____ in the side of the mountain.
- **a.** structure
- **b.** laborer
- **c.** bungalow
- **d.** cavern
- **e.** bliss

ANALOGIES
189. **skin : covering :: structure :**
- **a.** skeleton
- **b.** house
- **c.** figure
- **d.** skyscraper
- **e.** blueprint

190. **industrious : lazy ::**
- **a.** visible : melancholy
- **b.** lucky : unfortunate
- **c.** acute : sharp
- **d.** independent : study
- **e.** attractive : spry

WORD CLUES MASTERY TEST **G-22**

DEFINITIONS IN CONTEXT

211. During the game we often **referred** to our programs.
 a. made a note of
 b. turned for information
 c. read carefully
 d. took out
 e. remembered

212. The **campus** looked green and beautiful in the fall sunlight.
 a. grounds of a school
 b. play area of a school
 c. field for outdoor gym
 d. entrance of a school
 e. a college building

SYNONYMS OR SIMILAR MEANINGS

213. development
 a. growth
 b. foundation
 c. change
 d. appearance
 e. composition

214. chef
 a. dean
 b. waiter
 c. president
 d. policeman
 e. cook

ANTONYMS OR OPPOSITE MEANINGS

215. freshman
 a. student
 b. youth
 c. graduate
 d. beginner
 e. team

WORDS IN CONTEXT

216. My room was on the third floor of the ____.
 a. campus
 b. anniversary
 c. development
 d. attitude
 e. dormitory

217. The college was celebrating its ____ that day.
 a. campus
 b. dormitory
 c. chef
 d. anniversary
 e. attitude

218. Tom's ____ toward college changed during the year.
 a. anniversary
 b. refer
 c. attitude
 d. campus
 e. dormitory

ANALOGIES

219. stadium : game ::
 a. track : races
 b. corpse : coffin
 c. hint : suggestion
 d. bruise : stone
 e. buoy : ocean

220. counsel : advice ::
 a. exceedingly : seemingly
 b. disobey : avoid
 c. hoist : push
 d. cautious : careless
 e. bliss : happiness

WORD CLUES MASTERY TEST **G-21**

DEFINITIONS IN CONTEXT

201. The **corpse** of a Pharaoh was prepared in a special way.
 a. soul
 b. funeral
 c. dead body
 d. mummy
 e. tomb

202. I was glad Ahmed and I were **correspondents**.
 a. persons who are close friends
 b. persons who exchange letters with each other
 c. persons who resemble each other
 d. persons who supply information
 e. persons who work with each other

SYNONYMS OR SIMILAR MEANINGS

203. burial
 a. worship
 b. ceremonial
 c. burning
 d. burying
 e. death

204. fabric
 a. bandage
 b. paper
 c. design
 d. clothing
 e. cloth

ANTONYMS OR OPPOSITE MEANINGS

205. remote
 a. backward
 b. nearby
 c. strange
 d. foreign
 e. secluded

206. remark
 a. agree
 b. say
 c. hear
 d. decide
 e. like

WORDS IN CONTEXT

207. The ____ of a Pharaoh was made of stone.
 a. coffin
 b. correspondent
 c. bazaar
 d. corpse
 e. fabric

208. There are ancient picture writings on stone that are ____ today.
 a. remark
 b. favorable
 c. industrious
 d. legible
 e. considerate

ANALOGIES

209. resolve : decide ::
 a. approximately : about
 b. consume : save
 c. occupy : fill
 d. unaware : conscious
 e. subscribe : compete

210. bazaar : stall ::
 a. shopping mall : store
 b. apologize : with regret
 c. victory : trophy
 d. extreme : utmost
 e. theater : ballet

DEFINITIONS IN CONTEXT

231. For our class assembly we selected **a drama** with a good plot.

- **a.** opera
- **b.** story
- **c.** climax
- **d.** ballet
- **e.** play

232. As we walked on stage, we were supposed to **flourish** our toy guns.

- **a.** throw away
- **b.** wave in the air
- **c.** keep out of sight
- **d.** hold down
- **e.** pick up

WORDS IN CONTEXT

233. The thought that she might fail the test ____ her.

- **a.** betrayed
- **b.** bailed
- **c.** dismayed
- **d.** composed
- **e.** flourished

234. A good ____ can be very amusing.

- **a.** counsel
- **b.** tyrant
- **c.** chef
- **d.** comedian
- **e.** alias

SYNONYMS OR SIMILAR MEANINGS

235. assassinate

- **a.** persuade
- **b.** escape
- **c.** threaten
- **d.** murder
- **e.** hide

236. compose

- **a.** assure
- **b.** calm
- **c.** train
- **d.** begin
- **e.** rot

ANTONYMS OR OPPOSITE MEANINGS

237. vague

- **a.** frightening
- **b.** familiar
- **c.** pleasant
- **d.** strange
- **e.** definite

238. dramatic

- **a.** concluding
- **b.** sad
- **c.** unexciting
- **d.** unreal
- **e.** disagreeable

ANALOGIES

239. tyrant : cruel ::

- **a.** college : freshman
- **b.** laborer : work
- **c.** correspondent : writer
- **d.** good : intention
- **e.** villain : wicked

240. professional : amateur :: remarkable :

- **a.** horrid
- **b.** ordinary
- **c.** development
- **d.** remote
- **e.** utmost

DEFINITIONS IN CONTEXT

221. The gang leader was trying to **blackmail** my friend.

- **a.** get money by threatening to tell something
- **b.** report something to the police
- **c.** try to get a share of another's belongings
- **d.** try to find out someone's secrets
- **e.** pay money to keep someone quiet

222. The gangsters planned to **kidnap** the rich banker.

- **a.** put under lock and key
- **b.** beat with their fists
- **c.** tie up with ropes
- **d.** carry off by force
- **e.** threaten with a gun

SYNONYMS OR SIMILAR MEANINGS

223. possess

- **a.** take
- **b.** have
- **c.** steal
- **d.** show
- **e.** acquire

224. betray

- **a.** hit
- **b.** punish
- **c.** reward
- **d.** deceive
- **e.** disagree

ANTONYMS OR OPPOSITE MEANINGS

225. disagreeable

- **a.** serious
- **b.** sad
- **c.** happy
- **d.** hard
- **e.** sweet

226. horrid

- **a.** terrible
- **b.** boring
- **c.** rich
- **d.** stupid
- **e.** pleasant

WORDS IN CONTEXT

227. Smith sometimes used Johnson as a(n) ____.

- **a.** blackmail
- **b.** bail
- **c.** alias
- **d.** blunder
- **e.** betrayal

228. After our arrest we all needed money for ____.

- **a.** bail
- **b.** alias
- **c.** blunder
- **d.** authority
- **e.** blackmail

ANALOGIES

229. authority : father ::

- **a.** remark : say
- **b.** legible : writing
- **c.** paper : fabric
- **d.** power : general
- **e.** announcement : notify

230. blunder : stupid mistake ::

- **a.** hoist : put down
- **b.** assemble : large room
- **c.** venture : sure thing
- **d.** bleak : very old
- **e.** satisfactory : good enough

DEFINITIONS IN CONTEXT

251. A **ballad** is written mainly for entertainment.
  - **a.** short story
  - **b.** true story
  - **c.** poem about an actual person
  - **d.** poem or song that tells a story
  - **e.** play that is easy to understand

252. This **biography** will interest readers of all ages.
  - **a.** large book on a single subject
  - **b.** list of books on a subject
  - **c.** book of travel and adventure
  - **d.** story of an imaginary person
  - **e.** written story of a person's life

SYNONYMS OR SIMILAR MEANINGS

253. **merit**
  - **a.** interest
  - **b.** ability
  - **c.** humor
  - **d.** reward
  - **e.** worth

254. **reside**
  - **a.** visit
  - **b.** dwell
  - **c.** grow
  - **d.** own
  - **e.** give

ANTONYMS OR OPPOSITE MEANINGS

255. **absurd**
  - **a.** annoying
  - **b.** foolish
  - **c.** reasonable
  - **d.** plain
  - **e.** false

256. **fad**
  - **a.** custom
  - **b.** fashion
  - **c.** requirement
  - **d.** trend
  - **e.** truth

WORDS IN CONTEXT

257. We read the _____ to get information on the size of Texas.
  - **a.** biography
  - **b.** fiction
  - **c.** ballad
  - **d.** bonus
  - **e.** encyclopedia

258. Toni was delighted to find a(n) _____ in her pay envelope.
  - **a.** ballad
  - **b.** alibi
  - **c.** merit
  - **d.** bonus
  - **e.** blunder

ANALOGIES

259. **nonfiction : biography :: fiction :**
  - **a.** book
  - **b.** pamphlet
  - **c.** novel
  - **d.** writing
  - **e.** composition

260. **painting : artist :: manuscript :**
  - **a.** publisher
  - **b.** printer
  - **c.** author
  - **d.** plot outline
  - **e.** important topic

DEFINITIONS IN CONTEXT

241. Many **tapestries** hung on one wall of the library.
  - **a.** fabrics with woven pictures
  - **b.** pictures of historical events
  - **c.** oil paintings
  - **d.** long drapes
  - **e.** old photographs

242. The statue was carved of **mahogany**.
  - **a.** burlap
  - **b.** wood
  - **c.** stone
  - **d.** decorations
  - **e.** paper

WORDS IN CONTEXT

243. Our _____ became greater as we approached the haunted house.
  - **a.** tyrant
  - **b.** anxiety
  - **c.** development
  - **d.** pillar
  - **e.** structure

244. The doorway was not _____ of a modern house.
  - **a.** ornamental
  - **b.** circular
  - **c.** typical
  - **d.** legible
  - **e.** professional

SYNONYMS OR SIMILAR MEANINGS

245. **pillar**
  - **a.** column
  - **b.** step
  - **c.** fence
  - **d.** gate
  - **e.** opening

246. **ornamental**
  - **a.** necessary
  - **b.** rare
  - **c.** decorative
  - **d.** expensive
  - **e.** ugly

ANTONYMS OR OPPOSITE MEANINGS

247. **colossal**
  - **a.** tall
  - **b.** huge
  - **c.** comfortable
  - **d.** small
  - **e.** pretty

248. **prominent**
  - **a.** popular
  - **b.** useful
  - **c.** poor
  - **d.** large
  - **e.** unknown

ANALOGIES

249. **circular : straight ::**
  - **a.** comedian : flourish
  - **b.** drama : play
  - **c.** dismay : frighten
  - **d.** vague : distinct
  - **e.** disagreeable : unpleasant

250. **anniversary : annual celebration :: era :**
  - **a.** latest trend
  - **b.** historical period
  - **c.** political event
  - **d.** olden times
  - **e.** recent war

WORD CLUES MASTERY TEST G-28

DEFINITIONS IN CONTEXT

271. The nurse was **clad** in white.
    a. completely
    b. appearing
    c. working
    d. dressed
    e. concealed

272. After the accident I realized that seeing a doctor was a **necessity**.
    a. something strongly desired
    b. something which happens often
    c. something helpful
    d. something unpleasant to experience
    e. something which cannot be done without

SYNONYMS OR SIMILAR MEANINGS

273. **nuisance**
    a. punishment
    b. disaster
    c. annoyance
    d. trouble
    e. help

274. **fearless**
    a. timid
    b. hasty
    c. strong
    d. rude
    e. brave

ANTONYMS OR OPPOSITE MEANINGS

275. **punctual**
    a. late
    b. ready
    c. right
    d. prompt
    e. wrong

276. **cordial**
    a. polite
    b. unfriendly
    c. unusual
    d. brief
    e. lively

WORDS IN CONTEXT

277. When he insulted me, I tried to make a clever ____ .
    a. chat
    b. nuisance
    c. remote
    d. venture
    e. retort

278. You should always treat a cut with a ____ .
    a. sanitary
    b. disinfectant
    c. retort
    d. necessity
    e. disposition

ANALOGIES

279. **agony : pain ::**
    a. brittle : old
    b. conceal : hide
    c. awe : wonder
    d. massive : big
    e. probably : certainly

280. **sanitary : filthy ::**
    a. memorize : forget
    b. allegiance : pledge
    c. frequent : often
    d. situated : located
    e. kind : gentle

WORD CLUES MASTERY TEST G-27

DEFINITIONS IN CONTEXT

261. The store's cashier is very **reliable**.
    a. easy to understand
    b. strong
    c. worthy of trust
    d. frightening
    e. dramatic

262. Some wild animals can be tamed with **humane** treatment.
    a. healthful
    b. human
    c. expensive
    d. kind
    e. intelligent

SYNONYMS OR SIMILAR MEANINGS

263. **acknowledge**
    a. admit
    b. believe
    c. exist
    d. compliment
    e. deny

264. **arouse**
    a. anger
    b. frighten
    c. change
    d. announce
    e. awaken

ANTONYMS OR OPPOSITE MEANINGS

265. **ferocious**
    a. noisy
    b. fierce
    c. friendly
    d. angry
    e. weak

266. **moderate**
    a. small
    b. extreme
    c. usual
    d. pleasant
    e. shy

WORDS IN CONTEXT

267. My ____ is for beef rather than lamb.
    a. awe
    b. muzzle
    c. fiction
    d. preference
    e. typical

268. We feel ____ when we stand before a great cathedral.
    a. awe
    b. ferocious
    c. blunder
    d. preference
    e. colossal

ANALOGIES

269. **dog : muzzle ::**
    a. bonus : extra
    b. fad : trend
    c. criminal : handcuffs
    d. chef : recipe
    e. painting : manuscript

270. **adapt : adjust ::**
    a. fetch : return
    b. rely : depend on
    c. attraction : approval
    d. begrudge : dislike
    e. discard : save

WORD CLUES MASTERY TEST G-30

DEFINITIONS IN CONTEXT

291. The long climb up the hill made her heart **throb**.
    a. stop beating
    b. be painful
    c. beat strongly
    d. be relaxed
    e. beat weakly

292. We tied our boat beside one of the **wharves**.
    a. loading platforms for ships
    b. large buildings for storage
    c. ships that carry cargo
    d. natural harbors for ships
    e. restaurants for sailors

SYNONYMS OR SIMILAR MEANINGS

293. **jetty**
    a. island
    b. lightship
    c. canal
    d. breakwater
    e. harbor

294. **gauge**
    a. remove
    b. record
    c. judge
    d. fasten
    e. accomplish

ANTONYMS OR OPPOSITE MEANINGS

295. **slack**
    a. careless
    b. loose
    c. dull
    d. empty
    e. tight

296. **picturesque**
    a. amusing
    b. unattractive
    c. unusual
    d. vivid
    e. colorful

WORDS IN CONTEXT

297. Without a ____, a boat would slip sideways.
    a. navigation
    b. jetty
    c. gauge
    d. keel
    e. poll

298. I was eager to learn about the ____ of a sailboat.
    a. poll
    b. navigation
    c. jetty
    d. trophy
    e. aeronautics

ANALOGIES

299. **highway : scenic ::**
    a. acquire : instruct
    b. alone : solitary
    c. ferocious : tiger
    d. overcome : desirable
    e. hospital : sanitary

300. **becalm : make calm :: preside :**
    a. make sure
    b. live in
    c. be in charge
    d. throw down
    e. give away

WORD CLUES MASTERY TEST G-29

ANALOGIES

281. **insure : make sure ::**
    a. distinguish : tell apart
    b. ajar : wide open
    c. congratulate : shake hands
    d. approval : favorable opinion
    e. remainder : take notes

282. **broadcast : speech ::**
    a. police : notify
    b. publish : book
    c. customary : unusual
    d. assistance : observation
    e. adorable : lovable

SYNONYMS OR SIMILAR MEANINGS

283. **rivalry**
    a. fighting
    b. competition
    c. campaign
    d. hatred
    e. activity

284. **poll**
    a. agreement
    b. debate
    c. dialogue
    d. question
    e. voting

ANTONYMS OR OPPOSITE MEANINGS

285. **overcome**
    a. defeated
    b. acquired
    c. surprised
    d. lost
    e. victorious

286. **opponent**
    a. supporter
    b. enemy
    c. champion
    d. senator
    e. professional

WORDS IN CONTEXT

287. The mayor's excellent ____ made him highly respected by the people.
    a. opponents
    b. qualifications
    c. polls
    d. tyrants
    e. fads

288. At the ____ moment of the battle, help arrived.
    a. sanitary
    b. fearless
    c. cordial
    d. critical
    e. punctual

DEFINITIONS IN CONTEXT

289. The newspaper story mentioned my sister's **achievements** in sports.
    a. plans for the future
    b. difficult tasks
    c. preparation for action
    d. things accomplished
    e. new ideas

290. The **publicity** was especially important to her career.
    a. public duty
    b. violent disagreement
    c. public notice
    d. extreme confusion
    e. public opinion

LEVEL G POSTTEST

1   My pony began to neigh and paw the ground. *Apparently* he heard me coming.

   Apparently means:
   a. quietly
   b. seemingly
   c. noisily
   d. heavily

2   My favorite sport is skiing. When skiing weather comes, I *begrudge* the hours I have to spend indoors.

   Begrudge means:
   a. be unhappy
   b. be happy to give
   c. be unwilling to give
   d. be unkind to

3   My father said that I should walk my bicycle when I was on the highway. One must be *cautious* when there are so many cars around.

   Cautious means:
   a. frightened
   b. quiet
   c. quick
   d. careful

4   After we had cleared away the twigs and leaves, we dug a shallow hole. Our Scout leader inspected it and said it was *suitable* for our fire.

   Suitable means:
   a. smooth
   b. clear
   c. fitting
   d. flat

5   The audience laughed a lot at our play. They seemed to be enjoying our *comedy*.

   Comedy means:
   a. serious play
   b. amusing play
   c. well-written play
   d. musical show

6   My pony does not kick and is easy to ride. I am fortunate that he has such a good *disposition*.

   Disposition means:
   a. training
   b. cleverness
   c. nature
   d. skill

7   It wasn't difficult to find the main *attractions* at the side show. One had only to look for the biggest crowds.

   Attraction means:
   a. thing that makes people laugh
   b. thing that fascinates people
   c. thing that makes noise
   d. thing that bothers people

8   The *capacity* of the hospital was two hundred beds. All of them were now filled.

   Capacity means:
   a. smallest amount that can be held
   b. largest amount that can be held
   c. amount usually held
   d. amount expected

9   I found my grandmother's collection of dried ferns in the attic. The ferns were so *brittle* that I knew they would fall to pieces if I picked them up.

   Brittle means:
   a. very old
   b. easily broken
   c. of little use
   d. in poor condition

10   You would think that a man with so much money would *donate* some of it to the poor. Instead he uses his money only to make more money.

   Donate means:
   a. sell
   b. spend
   c. give
   d. carry

11   My mother and father are celebrating their fifteenth wedding *anniversary*. They're not having a large party like the one they had last year.

   Anniversary means:
   a. a celebration
   b. something that happens only once
   c. something that happens every fifteen years
   d. the yearly return of a date

12   One of "Dirty John's" enemies *kidnaped* the gangster and kept him prisoner. His gang was helpless without its leader.

   Kidnap means:
   a. carry off by force
   b. beat with the fists
   c. leave without permission
   d. put under lock and key

13   The only buildings I had seen of that size were offices and factories. It was hard to believe that a *residential* building could be so large.

   Residential means:
   a. of or having to do with buildings
   b. located in the country
   c. belonging to a particular individual
   d. of or having to do with homes

14 A doctor, who also was *clad* in a white uniform, was talking to the nurse.

Clad means:
a. completely
b. appearing
c. dressed
d. working

15 The guide told us that the *pamphlet* would show us where the exhibits were located in the museum. We turned the pages eagerly to find out where some of our favorites were.

Pamphlet means:
a. ticket   c. map
b. booklet   d. card

16 A few patients had come to the hospital for minor operations, but the *majority* of them had come for major operations or serious illnesses.

Majority means:
a. older
b. less than half
c. more than half
d. younger

17 Since the action of the play took place in a living room, there was no need for an *elaborate* stage set. Only a few chairs and a table were needed.

Elaborate means:
a. of simple design
b. specially made
c. of many colors
d. having many details

18 The snow made it impossible for me to see the *boundary* of the field. I did not realize that I was walking on our neighbor's property.

Boundary means:
a. bottom   c. size
b. border   d. shape

19 There were many types of houses and stores in our neighborhood. We wondered what this new *structure* would look like. From what we could see, it promised to be quite unusual.

Structure means:
a. home   c. model
b. addition   d. building

20 A newspaperman must get the exact facts and use those facts with *accuracy* in his story. A newspaper cannot afford to make mistakes often.

Accuracy means:
a. skill   c. speed
b. cleverness d. correctness

21 We admired the seals and the penguins in one particularly interesting *marine* exhibit. Then we went on to the next hall where land animals were displayed.

Marine means:
a. of the forest
b. large
c. soldierly
d. of the sea

22 I thought the physical examination was a *nuisance*. It kept me from playing outside, and I did not like going to the doctor.

Nuisance means:
a. punishment
b. annoyance
c. unnecessary thing
d. harmful experience

23 We had learned much by going to the museum. To see the animals we had been studying as they would appear in real life certainly made our *excursion* most rewarding.

Excursion means:
a. bus ride
b. trip
c. walk
d. weekend

24 I had done very well in English. The book review was important. An excellent review would *assure* a top grade for me.

Assure means:
a. make unnecessary
b. make possible
c. make sure
d. make real

25 The *boulevards* in Madrid are so filled with traffic that it is dangerous to cross them. Some of the little side streets, on the other hand, are too narrow for automobiles.

Boulevard means:
a. park
b. broad street
c. parking lot
d. alley

Check your answers with the key in the front of this book. If you have 20 or more correct answers, proceed to the next level.